The Hidden God

The Hidden God

Pragmatism and Posthumanism in American Thought

Ryan White

Columbia University Press
New York

Columbia University Press
Publishers Since 1893
New York   Chichester, West Sussex
cup.columbia.edu

Library of Congress Cataloging-in-Publication Data

White, Ryan (Independent researcher)
The hidden God : pragmatism and posthumanism in American thought / Ryan White.
pages cm
Includes bibliographical references and index.
ISBN 978-0-231-17100-7 (cloth : alk. paper)
ISBN 978-0-231-53959-3 (e-book)
1. Philosophy, American.   2. Pragmatism.   3. Critical theory.
4. Humanism.   I. Title.
B851.W47 2015
191—dc23
2015003672

Columbia University Press books are printed on permanent
and durable acid-free paper.
This book is printed on paper with recycled content.
Printed in the United States of America

c 10 9 8 7 6 5 4 3 2 1

COVER AND TITLE PAGE IMAGE:
Drawing by Charles Sanders Peirce. (MS Am 1632 [1537],
Houghton Library, Harvard University)

COVER DESIGN:
Milenda Nan Ok Lee

To My Parents

For everything that is understood and sensed is nothing other than the apparition of the non-apparent, the manifestation of the hidden, the affirmation of the negated, the comprehension of the incomprehensible, the utterance of the unutterable, the access to the inaccessible, the intellection of the unintelligible, the body of the bodiless, the essence of the beyond-essence, the form of the formless, the measure of the immeasurable, the number of the unnumbered, the weight of the weightless, the materialization of the spiritual, the visibility of the invisible, the place of the placeless, the time of the timeless, the definition of the infinite, the circumscription of the uncircumscribed, and the other things which are both conceived and perceived by the intellect alone and cannot be retained within the recesses of memory and which escape the blade of the mind.

JOHN SCOTTUS ERIUGENA, *PERIPHYSEON*

PAGAN: Who is the God you worship?
CHRISTIAN: I do not know.

NICHOLAS OF CUSA, *DIALOGUE ON THE HIDDEN GOD*

Contents

Acknowledgments

I owe a great debt of gratitude to Cary Wolfe, whose mentorship and tireless patience helped to guide the idea of this book through its many iterations, from the vague glimmer of an intuition to the conceptual rigor of an argument. Without his encouragement, not to mention the example of his scholarship, this book would simply not exist. This book was also shaped along the way by a number of helpful suggestions and incisive criticisms from James Faubion, Judith Roof, Wendy Lochner, and several anonymous readers.

This project was first conceived and elaborated at Rice University, an ideal place for musement in all its forms. Behind and beneath the words of this book are many long afternoons spent idly bouncing ideas off the open skies of Texas, and I can only hope the generative spark of that initial inspiration is still somehow evident in these pages.

The Hidden God

Introduction

Observing Modernity in America

Beginnings are a special problem for modernity. To begin at the *beginning*, after all, introduces a vexing paradox: What else is the beginning but what has already happened? How to begin at all if the beginning is precisely that which is already lost? It would seem that to begin this way—to begin without *a* beginning—is to repeat again and again the question with which Ralph Waldo Emerson announces the advent of modernity in American thought: "Where do we find ourselves?" This question, appearing as it does at the very beginning, as it were, of the grief-stricken essay "Experience," initiates a vertiginous descent into a world in which, as he vividly puts it, "All things swim and glitter."[1] When we begin, it would seem that we find ourselves waking from half-remembered dreams, caught out in the interval or suspended in the passage from one secure enclosure to another. Modernity, for Emerson and for America, begins in a suspended state of confusion.

If "Experience" may be read as having something to say about beginnings, it is only because that particular essay, despite a profusion of weighty words that is notable even for Emerson, leaves the reader with the curious feeling that something *else*, something quite critical, is left aside and unsaid. The strength of this impression leads many interpreters to look past the essay itself in order to observe the lack or absence that is perceived to be at its origin: "For all of its yea-saying, there is a nagging residue in 'Experience' of the traumatic event that inspired it."[2] That residual event, the unspeakable loss of a dearly loved young child, represents a depth of trauma so comprehensive that it ceaselessly impinges on and destabilizes the foreground of "Experience," and so a text that seemingly demands the reader's full attention inexorably gives way to a suspicion that its words may possibly mean more (or less) than what they actually say; there is some persistent remainder, some excess or deficiency in its meaning that resists incorporation.

For the intellectual historian Martin Jay, this remainder can only be designated as death, the "limit of experience" that seems to circumscribe the essay: "If there is any work of mourning in Emerson's essay, it is not of the type postulated by Freud as a successful working through and reintegration of the lost object, but something more brittle and fragile, perhaps more akin to melancholic repetition than completed mourning. For there is really no end to grief, no way to complete the mourning process."[3] If we accept this description of "Experience," if we presume it expresses an unending melancholy that begins somehow outside or before itself in a *lack* and therefore confronts that lack only as something utterly and finally heterogeneous to itself, then it may be argued in turn that Emerson's disorienting encounter with grief as the sign of a lack or absence dramatizes a fundamental *dis*location into thought and therefore represents something like the beginning—call it the *un*founding—of modernity in America.

All of which suggests a simple question: When we ask where we are, how is it that we find ourselves in modernity? In his wide-ranging study of the category of "experience" in modern thought, Jay offers a familiar account: "Modernity began, it might be argued, when the world could no longer be construed as a meaningful and legible text written by God—a result, *inter alia*, of the nominalist critique of real universals in the late medieval theology, the hermeneutic challenge to singular textual authority represented by the Reformation, and the bewildering encounter with new lands during the Age of Discovery."[4] These historical developments introduced a breach or fissure, a *non*identity, into the holistic medieval cosmos: "Real presence faded from the world" and "God increasingly became a mysterious *Deus absconditus*, whose capricious and opaque will was more important than His rationality."[5] As these descriptions imply, the loss of absolute legitimacy attributed to theological descriptions of a holistic and hierarchically organized cosmos—the loss of a divine perspective from which one could observe the *whole*—could result only in fragmentation and differentiation, the "modalization of experience, its fracturing into the discrete sub-categories we have designated as epistemological, religious, aesthetic, political, and historical."[6] Modernity, this account also implies, seems to paradoxically name the absence of a category for thinking its own identity or totality, as if modernity somehow named its own dispersal or fragmentation.

Modernity discovers the condition of its ongoing differentiation in the form of an absent totality: the *Deus absconditus*, or "hidden God." As Hans Blumenberg has argued, modern philosophy's distinction between "necessity" and "contingency" ultimately derives from theological precedent: "Philosophy won its autonomy precisely on account of the renewal of the 'Gnostic' assumption that the omnipotent God and the God of salvation, the hidden God and the revealed God, are no longer conceivable by reason as identical, and hence can no longer be related to one another for the purposes of man's interest in the world."[7] As the introduction or rediscovery of differentiation and nonidentity within what had previously been holistically grounded forms of thought, the hidden God acts as the excluded but necessary condition of modernity's own possibility—the *other* side, if you will, of its proliferating self-descriptions. The theological postulate of an omnipotent God unencumbered by rationalism forces the dissolution of totalizing forms of knowledge or authority based on divine revelation: "Given the absolute and unlimited power of God to create (or destroy) whatever He pleases, with or without reason (the only ultimate reason being 'Quia voluit' [because he willed it]), the actual, finite world becomes totally contingent, no longer the embodiment of the full range and variety—the order—of what is possible."[8] This omnipotent deity, approachable only as *un*approachable through the *via negativa* of apophatic theology, represents the foundational contingency that modernity must evade in order to posit the necessity of its own claims to knowledge in the absence of divine guarantees. God, after all, always reserves the right to change his mind.

Modern philosophy, a form of thinking that posits itself as autonomous from theology, proceeds from the assumption that the omnipotent hidden God discovered at the end of the Middle Ages can be left aside in order to proceed toward a rational and scientific elucidation of the natural world. However, to begin in this way also means that the distinction between the revealed and the hidden—the very distinction that enables something like a principle of sufficient reason to be formulated in the first place—must itself be hidden or excluded in that very beginning. The hidden God initiates modernity only to be designated as radically heterogeneous to it, thus becoming in a certain sense the (excluded) epistemological condition for the achievements of modern science and rational inquiry. As Blumenberg puts it, "The radical materializing of nature is confirmed as the systematic correlate of theological absolutism. Deprived by God's hiddenness of metaphysical guarantees for the world, man constructs for himself a counterworld of elementary rationality and manipulability."[9] This ongoing "disenchantment of the world," as Max Weber famously called it, represents modernity's tendency to take only one side of its founding distinction as a meaningful ground from which to proceed in its determinations.

Nevertheless, it can hardly be denied that the hidden God, the side left behind in the beginning, has an uncanny way of popping up again at the end—a phenomenon perhaps most clearly evident in Nietzsche's declaration that the relentless pursuit of truth has led to the dissolution of truth as a value. Along similar lines, the history of modern philosophy may be described as the continual rediscovery of its own foundational contingency after the fact, an occasion that necessitates in each case a new beginning which presumes something like necessity—a secure ground or origin—on its own behalf. Ultimately, and in particular with Kant's introduction of the distinction between the phenomenal and noumenal orders, philosophy's claims to knowledge are revealed to be achievable only on the condition that it relinquish any claim to knowledge of the world *as such*. Rational thought may draw the boundary of its domain only through simultaneously positing an *other* realm that remains inaccessible to reason alone. It may even be argued that some version of this dilemma, modernity's encounter with a fundamental split or lack of identity, runs along continental lines from Kant to Nietzsche and even through to Heidegger's rendering of the "ontological difference." The upshot in each case is that rational or systematic forms of thinking fail to secure themselves in terms of identity or totality. "What is given," writes Blumenberg, "is never the maximum of what is possible."[10]

With that maxim in mind, modernity may be described as the paradoxical *non*identity of a two-sided form, the unity (as opposed to identity) of a difference. On one side is a material world described as eminently predictable, subject to reason, ironclad natural laws, and scientific determinism; on the *other* side dwells the hidden God whose incomprehensible whims are glimpsed only in modernity's procession of names for what escapes its descriptions: contingency, chaos, uncertainty, and incompleteness. The order of the possible is supplemented by another order altogether, and modernity thus finds itself in utter contingency; or rather, it *doesn't* find itself. The advance of scientific, mechanistic, causal, determinist, and rational descriptions of the world proceeds directly in the face of this contingency and so may be said to represent in each case a circumscription, bit by bit, of the omnipotent and potentially irrational sovereignty of God. In this way, contingency is progressively expunged from the realms of rational necessity, but yet remains as the ever-threatening *excluded* condition that underlies the possibility for the supposed certainty of rational determinations in the first place: the exception that proves the rules. Only by confining itself to the artificially constricted (and thus constructed) domains of reversible systems, to the *part* and not the whole, can a rationalist and scientific modernity claim its own coherence.

If these conditions are taken seriously, which is henceforth to say if *contingency* is taken seriously, then the differentiated and autonomous domains of rationality that characterize modernity are ultimately forced to account for themselves without recourse to the legitimization previously secured through theological fiat. As Jürgen Habermas has noted, "Modernity can and will no longer borrow the criteria by which it takes its orientation from the models supplied by another epoch; *it has to create its normativity out of itself.* Modernity sees itself cast back upon itself without any possibility of escape."[11] Descriptions of modernity can take place only after the fact and already *within* the various contingent and differentiated systems that constitute it. There is no possibility of what Jean-François Lyotard, in his well-known critique of modernity, calls "metanarratives," or any recourse to what Richard Rorty more straightforwardly dismisses as a "god's eye view." There is no *access* to totality or objectivity, both observational perspectives that remain either the prerogative of the hidden God or finally unattainable in his withdrawal, absence, or "death."

Modernity is left entirely to its own devices, but nevertheless retains what Blumenberg calls the pretension to a form of "total competence," an imperative to *self*-grounding in the absence of metaphysical or divine legitimacy.[12] This commitment to a theologically derived sense of totality is the true legacy, as Blumenberg sees it, of modernity's problematic understanding of itself as the progress of secularization: "Even when modern philosophy conceives itself in the sharpest possible contradiction to its theological prehistory, which it considers itself to have 'overcome,' it is bound to the frame of reference of what it renounces."[13] Despite its well-known protestations otherwise, modernity, Blumenberg contends, is inextricably beholden to what remains "outside," what is excluded, heterogeneous, or forgotten in its self-descriptions—a predicament that dooms the enterprise from the very start: "The philosophical program for the beginning of the modern age 'failed' because it was unable to analyze away its own preconditions."[14]

That point can be extended in order to argue that modernity is constituted though the unfolding of a constitutive paradox. Modernity, in other words, can be distinguished as the attempt to somehow include both itself and its necessary excluded *other* at the same time, both itself *and* its (absent) foundation or ground. In this way, modernity paradoxically reintroduces into itself the division or split that constitutes it, which is to say, modernity reproduces itself through the attempt to see what it *cannot* see, namely, its own totality. As William Rasch puts it, "The whole that is modernity is the whole that strains to see itself and thus a whole that forever divides itself with every observation into more and more 'facts.' The whole that we now deal with is a self-referential whole, thus an inescapably paradoxical one."[15] Modernity bewilders precisely because it simultaneously names its own necessity *and* contingency, the irreducibly present *and* its withdrawal, the uneasy coimplication of finitude *and* infinity. To take hold of one end only represses the other—and it is, of course, one of modernity's most prominent axioms that nothing stays repressed for very long. This is perhaps what Emerson in his ever-elusive fashion is driving at when he writes, "You are one thing, but nature is *one thing and the other thing*, in the same moment."[16] The production of an unseen *other thing* is the inescapable condition of observation. We may see the part only at the expense of remaining blind to the whole.

A lack of first or final explanatory principles—no beginnings and no endings—then leaves explanations in the embarrassing position of explaining themselves. They become bootstrapping operations confronted with a forced choice between incompleteness and incoherence. The best one can do, it seems, is split the difference. Even the quintessentially modern notion of probability only defers the problem by including the possibility of something *else* happening down the line. Or take Blumenberg's typically apt description of contingency as the "suffering of finitude in the presence of the idea of infinity."[17] For modernity, the distinction is a double bind: there is no question of perceiving infinity itself except through its worldly delimitation and likewise no possibility of taking finitude as the final measure of things.

But, inevitably, one must still begin in one way or another. Indeed, one already has. The only way to "begin," then, is to leap into the circle: if modernity is the absence of beginnings, then we cannot begin but with modernity. Therein we find ourselves confronted with a two-sided form, the unity of a distinction that cannot be resolved into identity. Along these very same lines, Niklas Luhmann's opening remarks in *Observations on Modernity* offer a model worth adopting: "This analysis does not begin with the recognition of tried laws of nature, nor with principles of reason, nor with predetermined or incontrovertible facts. It begins with a paradox that can be solved one way or another, provided one is willing to reduce infinite to finite information loads. This analysis therefore claims for itself the characteristics of its object of study: modernity."[18] In this way, Luhmann's self-inclusive analysis foregrounds its *own* contingency as a paradox solvable "one way or another." The paradox of the beginning can be unfolded—as if vacillating back and forth between this side and that—but not finally resolved in the manner of a dialectical *aufheben* or transcendental principle. This is a double bind in the cybernetic sense, one that resembles nothing so much as a particularly devious game of whack-a-mole: "Every observation (including cognition and action) is tied to the selection of a distinction, and selection necessarily means leaving something out of account."[19] To begin, in other words, it is necessary to take sides.

Luhmann begins with systems theory in its contemporary guise as the theory of self-organizing or autopoietic systems—systems based on the paradox of *self-reference*. He begins with the unity of a distinction: "a system *is* the difference between system and environment."[20] Each system, he argues, "owes its stability to itself, not to its elements; it constructs itself upon a foundation that is entirely not 'there.'"[21] Here modernity's missing origin is recast as a founding mark of distinction between a self-constructing system and an invisible and unknowable environment. The distinction is the unity, but not *identity*, of system and environment: a two-sided form representing the unity of necessity and contingency, presence and absence, part and whole. However, since the system is organized according to the system-environment difference, it is therefore constructed upon a foundation that remains inaccessible as a unity to its own operations. This means that the system, just like modernity, can only proceed from one side (the "inside") of the distinction. Thus, while it is continually confronted with the unity of the distinction between system and environment, the system persists in its organization only insofar as it chooses in each instance the "inside" or self-referential side of that distinction. As Luhmann notes, this requirement replaces the universality of the premodern whole with "the universality of selection restraints, the universality of differentiation and boundary drawing."[22]

My title makes no secret of the side that will be taken here: the hidden, negated, unthinkable, incomprehensible, and unaccounted for. But this is also, and quite paradoxically, to take the side that is *not* taken, the *other* side. In the terms of systems theory this means we will take the side of the environment against the system—a choice only possible within the system *as* paradox: the hidden unity of the distinction. This approach therefore has much in common, as will be shown, with Luhmann's suggestion that the religious system is unique in modern society because it resolves its constitutive paradoxes "through the negative value of the code, through the reflective value, and through transcendence."[23] Religion, particularly the dramatically heightened strain known as negative theology, represents a tradition of thinking that selects a *negation* of the positive values of immanence, presence, and the like in order to choose the excluded or "transcendent" side of the distinction that produces them. In other words, the unity of the distinction appears within the distinction on one side—a form that the system can only observe as a paradox and that thus must be unfolded by the system in time. At the same time, this forces the system to confront its own contingency, and it therefore represents in each instance the pragmatic possibility for a new (and equally contingent) beginning. This approach may also be described as the inclusion of the excluded, what systems theory calls a *re-entry* of the constitutive distinction into itself on one side—a reemergence or rediscovery at the end, if you will, of the paradox of contingency hidden in the beginning.

I argue in this book that a paradoxical incorporation of the negative, hidden, or excluded side of the distinction is the approach taken by the three American thinkers to be examined here: Jonathan Edwards, Ralph Waldo Emerson, and Charles Sanders Peirce. Each represents a decidedly antinomian strain of thought even from within the American philosophical tradition for which they are presumed to be central; but taken together, they offer an alternative and remarkably rigorous description of modernity in American thought that makes no recourse to positive claims of transcendence (through dialectical synthesis, transcendental subjectivity, or rationalism) or the possibility of a binding, even if transitory, immanence (achieved through empiricism, the immediacy of consciousness, or the self-assertion of a will to power). As the dual faces of modern philosophy (or the terms of its double bind), what such appeals to transcendence or immanence have in common is an unquestioned humanism—what can only be called a subject for whom immanence and transcendence ultimately represent forms of *access* to the external world, an observational position for which inside and outside become, if not identical, then at least finally adequate to each other.

It is precisely this question of access to the "outside" that modernity continually seeks to answer in the form of the humanist subject. As Jay puts it, "The nascent modern subject, withdrawn from a no longer transparently meaningful cosmos, came to rely on the fragile reed of experience, however defined, as the only bridge from interior to exterior reality."[24] More broadly, the turn to the humanist subject also represents a turn to a space in which the constitutive distinctions of modernity are resolved—a space in which modernity achieves at last its longed-for coherence and whereby contingency is transformed into necessity through the self-possession of the rational subject. For this reason, the humanist subject comes to be modernity's most potent, though by no means exclusive, means of evading contingency—the organizational lynchpin of an ideology predicated on a belief that, as Michel Foucault has described it, "the manifestation and sign of truth are to be found in evident and distinct perception."[25] This was a foundation that ensured that the project of modernity, the determination of more and more necessary "facts," could continue unabated and unthreatened by potentially chaotic remainders. The mysteries of the universe could be plumbed to their depths through the transparent observational powers afforded by science and rational philosophy—powers that ultimately derived their authority from man's unique capacity to encounter the world in itself (at least momentarily) through the self-present immediacy of consciousness and thus without the trappings of interpretive filters: "Man became that upon the basis of which all knowledge could be constituted as immediate and non-problematized evidence."[26]

Again, what is at issue here for both modern rationalism and the romanticist counterstroke is a question of *access* to the noncontingency of the "outside." For romanticism, a subjective and sensuous apprehension of consciousness performs as the portal through which the whole re-enters the part and appears in its totality—the world appears *as such* and thus leads to what Cary Wolfe, here echoing Blumenberg's point about the persistence of theological frames of reference, describes as "the various forms of idealism that have been attributed to romanticism in the all-too-familiar narratives of secularization, where Mind, Spirit, Imagination, or the equivalent comes to take the place of self-generated knowledge and its authority previously reserved for God."[27]

Peirce, for his part, would write, "Modern philosophy has never been able to quite shake off the Cartesian idea of the mind. . . . Everybody continues to think of mind in this same general way, as something within this person or that, belonging to him and correlative to the real world."[28] The Cartesian project, as Blumenberg notes, presumes to begin with the "idea of a philosophy free of presuppositions, which knows that it arises autonomously from reason" by means of the passage through methodical doubt as "the experiment that reason poses for itself under conditions of artificial difficulty in order to gain access to itself and to the beginning it proposes for itself."[29] Descartes begins at the *beginning*, with reason's self-possession in the bare present fact of consciousness (or "mind") in the subject. Ever the vociferous anti-Cartesian, Peirce takes the other side and insists in quite Emersonian fashion that philosophy can only begin in the middle of things: "We cannot," he asserts, "begin with complete doubt. We must begin with all the prejudices which we actually have when we enter upon the study of philosophy. These prejudices are not to be dispelled by a maxim, for they are things which it does not occur to us *can* be questioned."[30] Thought, in other words, has already begun; it can only find itself in utter contingency, as *unfounded*, and it is therefore faced with the pragmatic task of making decisions in the absence of objective or necessary principles.

This book presumes that forging a way past the "Cartesian idea of the mind" (in both its explicit and its implicit forms) is the central task of a pragmatism that seeks contemporary relevance, a *post*humanist pragmatism. The roots for such an alternative can be found extending from the Puritan theology of Jonathan Edwards to Emerson's relentless procession of inversions and antinomies and finally to Peirce's semiotics and "pragmaticism," a genealogy that opposes the more broadly known "antitheoretical" and humanist pragmatism that runs from William James to Richard Rorty. This study occupies what can be called the *other* side of humanism, ethnocentrism, and the immanence of feeling in order to call attention to what remains as yet unseen, unthought, and unrevealed—a kind of thinking ultimately inherited from what the famed Americanist scholar Perry Miller called the "Augustinian strain of piety" in the theology of the Puritans: "The soul of Puritan theology is the hidden God, who is not fully revealed even in His own revelation."[31] This formal condition is the link with posthumanism, for which there can be no possibility of *access* to the whole but only the self-referential *closure* of the part: only the lack, absence, or occlusion of the world that paradoxically produces its revelation.

Quasi-Transcendentalism: Romanticism, Pragmatism, and the Posthumanist Tradition in American Thought

> Man is thus metamorphosed into a thing, into many things.
> RALPH WALDO EMERSON, "THE AMERICAN SCHOLAR"

The humanist genealogy of pragmatism that acts as the opposing backdrop for this study relies on what can be generalized as an immanence that assumes its most celebrated form in Ralph Waldo Emerson's early "transcendentalist" writings, in particular a certain notorious passage from *Nature*:

> Standing on the bare ground,—my head bathed by the blithe air, and uplifted into infinite space,—all mean egotism vanishes. I become a transparent eyeball; I am nothing; I see all; the currents of the Universal Being circulate through me; I am part or particle of God. The name of the nearest friend sounds then foreign and accidental: to be brothers, to be acquaintances,—master or servant, is then a trifle and a disturbance. I am the lover of uncontained and immortal beauty. In the wilderness, I find something more dear and connate than in streets or villages. In the tranquil landscape, and especially in the distant line of the horizon, man beholds somewhat as beautiful as his own nature.[32]

It has often been remarked that these words (and more broadly Emerson's early writings through the first series of essays) laid the groundwork for a uniquely American affirmation of personal feeling as the threshold through which man meets "face to face" with nature and the universe at last achieves unity or wholeness. Here the pathway through to the totality of nature is directly through the immediacy of experience as accessed through personal consciousness, the famed "transparent eyeball" wherein the mind is no longer estranged from nature or itself and nothing, no part, is ultimately separate from the whole.

Similarly, in "The American Scholar" Emerson again writes of the possibility that consciousness may access the totality of nature. He begins by beautifully invoking nature in all its immanence: "The first in time and first in importance of the influences upon the mind is that of nature. . . . Every day, the sun; and, after sunset, night and her stars. Ever the winds blow; ever the grass grows. Every day, men and women, conversing, beholding and beholden."[33] In this early essay, the eponymous scholar takes the form of "man thinking," the one most stricken with nature's mystery: "What is nature to him? There is never a beginning, there is never an end to the inexplicable continuity of this web of God, but always circular power returning into itself."[34] Emerson resolves the paradox of immanence (no beginnings or endings) by producing a familiar romantic trope in the form of a symmetrical relationship between the infinite unboundedness of nature and its reflection in the infinite inwardness of the human mind: "He shall see, that nature is the opposite of the soul, answering to it part to part. One is seal, one is print. Its beauty is the beauty of his own mind. . . . And, in fine, the ancient precept, 'Know thyself,' and the modern precept, 'Study nature,' become at last one maxim."[35] This passage suggests something like a perfect dualism, an achievement of harmony in which every point finds its mirrored likeness in the other, part to part, and the seemingly insurmountable divide between mind and nature is overcome through the spontaneous symmetry of a magnetic attraction.

Many scholars have identified this feature of Emerson's thought with the "marriage of self and world" that is characteristic of European romanticism.[36] Russell B. Goodman's description of the genesis of that tradition is exemplary: "If our feelings, including our moral feelings, . . . help constitute the world, then the world becomes something valuable in itself, or 'ideal.' The unknowable noumenal overflow recedes or disappears, becoming part of phenomenal reality, the only reality there is. If 'human forms of feeling' reveal the phenomenal world, then at least part of the noumenal has been recovered, and part of the supernatural has been naturalized."[37] The noumenal, the Kantian name for the inaccessible *other*, is reclaimed through "human forms of feeling," a project of reclamation that may also, as Goodman goes on to argue, be connected to the emergence of American pragmatism:

> Both James and Dewey follow Emerson in focusing on the shaping power of the human mind, holding that the world we know is a malleable product of our pragmatically determined concepts. . . . Whether through their interest in feeling, in religious experience, in imagination, or in the shaping powers of the mind, the American Romantic philosophers seek to expand the narrow focus of classical empiricism while retaining the empiricist commitment to human experience for our knowledge of the world.[38]

Here, in a single sweeping gesture, emerges a continuous romantic tradition in American thought, one that connects Emerson's rapturous engagements with nature to an emphasis on the role of personal feeling in grounding a pragmatic relationship to the world in the early-twentieth-century philosophy of James and Dewey.

This narrative of American thought has a storied pedigree. From his vantage point in the mid-twentieth century, the celebrated scholar Perry Miller produced his seminal readings of the "life of the mind in America" through the adoption of a similar narrative. At the center of this story was the decline of religious authority, which led to an affirmation of the possibility for personal revelation:

> From the time of Edwards to that of Emerson, the husks of Puritanism were being discarded, but the energies of many Puritans were not yet diverted—they could not be diverted—from a passionate search of the soul and of nature, from the quest to which Calvinism had devoted them. These New Englanders—a few here and there—turned aside from the doctrines of sin and predestination, and thereupon sought with renewed fervor for the accents of the Holy Ghost in their own hearts and in woods and mountains. But now that the restraining hand of theology was withdrawn, there was nothing to prevent them, as there had been

everything to prevent Edwards, from identifying their intuitions with the voice of God, or from fusing God and nature into the one substance of the transcendental imagination. Mystics were no longer inhibited by dogma. They were free to carry on the ancient New England propensity for reeling and staggering with new opinions. They could give themselves over, unrestrainedly, to becoming transparent eyeballs and debauchees of dew."[39]

Miller's lively and beautifully rendered argument hinges on an ingenious and revolutionary reinterpretation of Jonathan Edwards. Indeed, Miller's landmark studies are notable in particular for their frequent attempts to rescue the famed author of "Sinners in the Hands of the Angry God" from the darkness of medieval religious dogma by drawing him and his God into the daylight of modern humanism. Of course, Miller would be the first to admit that Edwards was not, and could not be, any sort of humanist, but what is most intriguing about Miller's account is this intriguing tension that he finds in Edwards's theology—something often passed over in the many subsequent drawbacks of Miller's argument produced by later historicist scholars.

That tension will be fully addressed in a later chapter, but for now it is sufficient to note that Miller links Edwards to Emerson through a mutual turn to nature in the grip of a "sense of the heart," which is to say that the quest for immediacy is a quest for a self-grounding or self-validating experience of subjective feeling: "If the object—be it thing, word, abstract idea, simple idea or 'mixed mode'—is vividly realized, the mind is in a healthy relation with truth. But if the only object the mind has in view is a word, a counter for mechanical discourse, a verbal substitute, the mind is diseased and piety is bankrupt."[40] On this basis, Miller powerfully argues that the essence of American thought derives from a search for a truly personal religious experience, an outward turn to nature that is simultaneously an inward turn to the revelation of divine truth, thus in part setting the stage for Emerson's well-known clarion call in *Nature*: "Why should not we also enjoy an original relation to the universe?"[41] In keeping with this sentiment, Miller explicitly claims that Edwards turns away from any form of objective transcendentalism in favor of immanence: "In Edwards's 'sense of the heart' there is nothing transcendental; it is rather a sensuous apprehension of the total situation."[42] Drawing from these foundations, Miller quite brilliantly traces a romanticist lineage that extends from Edwards's sensuous subjectivity to Emerson's raptures—in the process creating an influential template (whether acknowledged or not) for many subsequent interpretations of American intellectual history.

However, perhaps the most sophisticated contemporary inheritor of Miller's influence, the philosopher Stanley Cavell, would seem on the face of it to be quite opposed to any such reading of Emerson. Instead, Cavell situates Emerson within the long tradition of modern philosophical skepticism, what he calls the "disappointment" resulting from Kantian philosophy's claim "to deny that you can experience the world as world, things as things; face to face, as it were, call this the life of things."[43] What is most intriguing about Cavell's embrace of skepticism is that he sees it as the necessary *other* side to the triumphant claims of romanticism. Skepticism, in other words, seems to name for Cavell the very lack that romanticism seeks to overcome as an inescapable and even necessary component of romanticism itself. As he writes,

> I continue . . . to be guided by the thought of romanticism as working out a crisis of knowledge, a crisis I have taken to be (interpretable as) as response at once to the threat of skepticism and to a disappointment with philosophy's answer to this threat, particularly as embodied in the achievement of Kant's philosophy—a disappointment most particularly with the way Kant balances the claims of knowledge of the world to be what you may call subjective and objective, or, say, the claims of knowledge to be dependent on or independent of the specific endowments—sensuous and intellectual—of the human being. And this in turn perhaps means a disappointment in the idea of taking the success of science, or what makes science possible, as an answer to the threat of skepticism, rather than a further expression of it. Romanticism's work here interprets itself, so I have suggested, as the task of bringing the world back to life.[44]

The unspoken assumption of this passage is that the world, if it is to be brought back to life, must be in some sense already dead. What Cavell calls the Kantian "settlement" (a term he characteristically imbues with rueful disenchantment) is just this trade-off between knowing the subjective contents of experience and not knowing the "thing-in-itself"—this is to be bereft, in other words, of an intimate experience with anything outside of self-knowledge: "To settle with skepticism, to assure us that we do know the existence of the world or, rather, that what we understand as knowledge is *of* the world, the price Kant asks us to pay is to cede any claim to know the thing in itself, to grant that human knowledge is not of the things as they are in themselves."[45] As Emerson famously puts it in "Experience," "I take this evanescence and lubricity of all objects, which lets them slip through our fingers then when we clutch hardest, to be the most unhandsome part of our condition."[46]

For Cavell, romanticism names the object of desire (to know things as they are in themselves and not just as they appear) but not the means of its achievement, an "unhandsome" condition which leads him to conclude that Emerson's philosophical project should not be understood as achievable, or if it is achievable then it is only achieved by a certain "onwardness" or continual abandonment of itself. As Cary Wolfe argues, Cavell paves the way for a reading of Emerson's project as

> a kind of ongoing act of radical negative capability that provides the foundation (though that is eventually not the word we would want, of course) for democratic relations with others, with those other selves I have not yet been but who also—and this is the engine of Emerson's constant polemical project—need to surpass *themselves*, in an ongoing process of democracy conceived as otherness always yet to be achieved, or *if* achieved, only achieved in the present by the other and not by me.[47]

These qualities in particular are reflected in a peculiar facet of Emerson's writing that can best be described as a persistent reversal or inversion of itself. To take just one of many possible examples, consider the claim in "History" that "all public facts are to be individualized, all private facts are to be generalized."[48] What to make of statements like this? There is an understandable tendency to attempt to resolve such statements dialectically or even to flatly declare them incoherent. Staking out a different path in Emerson's most trenchant essays, Cavell finds "the *Critique of Pure Reason* turned upon itself: notions of limitation and of condition are as determining in the essay 'Fate' as they are in Kant, but it is as if these terms are themselves subjected to transcendental deduction. . . . Emerson is, I believe, commonly felt to play fast and loose with something like contradiction in his writing; but I am speaking of a sense in which contradiction, the countering of diction, is the genesis of his writing of philosophy."[49] This passage isolates Emerson's primary philosophical gesture in what he often calls an "aversion," a countering or reversal that Cavell prefers to interpret along skeptical lines as an "acceptance of separateness" or "loss of the world" that cuts the legs out from underneath any possibility of final intimacy with the world *as such*.[50] Cavell interprets this "separateness" not as a static dualism but as something like a continual peeling apart, thus suggesting that the world is not so much *lost* as it is that which we are continually losing.

For this reason, Cavell's insightful readings of Emerson's vacillations, the maddening reversals that characterize essays such as "Experience" and "Fate," open up renewed possibilities for understanding Emerson's critical project without reducing it to the terms of romanticism, dialectics, or transcendentalism—terms that seem unable to relinquish the representationalism and humanism on which they have been traditionally founded. At the same time, while the importance of Cavell's readings cannot be overstated, his fixation on skepticism leads to some dissatisfaction because, as Wolfe puts it, "skepticism remains tied, one might argue, to the representationalism [Cavell] would otherwise seem to disown, because skepticism holds on to the desire for a representational adequation between concepts and objects even as it knows that desire to be unappeasable."[51] In other words, Cavell's skepticism seems to cling to a negative or inverted image of the world it claims as lost. Cavell can write of abandonment and aversion but the skeptical terms of his argument are fixed in advance. Skepticism remains committed to a foundational distinction between the world as such and knowledge *of* the world, but that distinction must be understood as taking place already on the side of *knowledge*—something like a foundational "disappointment" that isolates and individuates the knowing humanist subject in a decidedly Kantian (that is, transcendental) manner. As we will see, this lingering commitment to "adequation" will also undermine Sharon Cameron's moving and incisive take on "Experience" as being tasked with "representing grief" when it may be argued instead that representation is the very thing at issue in that great essay.

How to proceed between romanticism and skepticism while keeping true to Emerson's aversive spirit? How to begin with the difference *as such* without a concomitant claim of identity? For Wolfe, the Emersonian project points to an "insistence on the contingency, not transcendence of, observation."[52] In other words, in Wolfe's reading Emerson emerges as a philosopher deeply engaged with the question of the inescapably embedded (and thus always partial or limited) relationship between mind and nature: the mind is fully *within* nature, one might say encircled by it—and vice versa. To square this circle (or to *un*square it), Wolfe turns to systems theory, in particular Niklas Luhmann's ambitious description of modernity. If we wish to avoid slotting Emerson into the constricted terms of either transcendence or immanence while at the same time avoiding an equally problematic synthesis of those terms, then systems theory provides a "third" way. As Wolfe puts it, "Luhmann's work on observation will help to clarify why Emerson's relentless explorations of these problems cannot and should not resolve themselves into a dialectic."[53]

As will become clear, the argument presented here calls into question the interpretation of American pragmatism, and American intellectual history more generally, as an extension of romanticism. It does so not by rejecting romanticism wholesale but by interpreting the problems it is meant to address in a new way. As Luhmann notes, the historical movement represented by romanticism may be seen as the reemergence of the question of observational autonomy in the absence of access to the theologically designated "outside." Romanticism answers the question posed by modernity not with transcendence but with immanence: "Romanticism discovers itself as if new born in an empty space and called upon to give itself its own meaning."[54] In this way, romanticism marks the transition from "hierarchical fixed positional orders describable as nature to the primacy of the distinction between self- and hetero-reference."[55] Luhmann's characteristically technical language (what Miller might denigrate as the monstrous epitome of a "mechanical discourse") here notes that romanticism is simply performing the predicament of modernity: a derivation of meaning from "inside," as it were, without access to any authoritative or objective "outside" through the "primacy" of the very distinction between them. Unable to find itself, romanticism's search for continuity and immanence necessarily returns it again and again to difference. In much the same way as Cavell, Luhmann defines romanticism as something like a necessary failure. In this sense, it represents a particularly fraught and heightened (one might even say, with the appropriate caveats, "self-conscious" or "reflexive") unfolding of the fundamental paradox of observational autonomy that is faced by modernity.

Systems theory describes modernity through the continued unfolding of a self-referential distinction—between self and other, "inside" and "outside"—for which neither side is ultimately foundational. Dialectical forms of critique, by contrast, are traditionally grounded in an identity or absolute that unites or "synthesizes" the distinction—which is to say that the dialectic hides its *own* observational contingency, the very distinction or difference (the *non*identity) that *it* is founded on. For instance, Hegel famously conceived the role of philosophy to be the thinking of totality in the manner of an ever-widening circle: "Each of the parts of philosophy is a philosophical whole, a circle rounded and complete in itself. In each of these parts, however, the philosophical Idea is found in a particular specificality or medium. The single circle, because it is a real totality, bursts through the limits imposed by its special medium, and gives rise to a wider circle. The whole of philosophy in this way resembles a circle of circles."[56] Similarly, for American thought the problem of modernity coalesces around an image of a circle on a blank page, but with a critical difference from Hegel's totality. For Edwards, Emerson, and Peirce this image of a circle takes on a fractal recursion, something to be imagined as a drawing of circles *within* circles or a looping inward that continuously enfolds the distinction between inside and outside. Hegel would doubtlessly call this process an endless "bad infinity," but if that value judgment is discarded, it may be better understood as a continual and repeated recognition of the distinction or difference between part and whole, between the "good infinity" of the absolute totality and the "bad infinity" of recursive re-entry.

When observed in this way, the "part to part" symmetry evoked in much of Emerson's early writing comes to be disrupted by something altogether less familiar, less a depiction of intimacy and harmony than the irruption of asymmetrical otherness or disequilibrium. As already quoted, the immanence of God's creation resolves into what he describes as "always circular power returning into itself." In "The Method of Nature," the image returns to describe nature as "a work of *ecstasy*, to be represented by a circular movement."[57] Most explicitly, "Circles" adopts what is seemingly a Hegelian framework at first, but in the end it seems to recursively include even its own beginning, an image in which there is no final circle: "The eye is the first circle; the horizon which it forms is the second; and throughout nature this primary figure is repeated without end. . . . There is no end in nature, but every end is a beginning."[58]

These visions suggest nothing so much as a Möbius strip: a form that turns inside out and outside in, as if nature contains the mind and the mind

contains nature. Turning inward diffuses the self into the great impersonal expanse of nature, and turning outward to nature inevitably brings
to bear an encounter only with one's own face. These ideas—double gestures that take at the very same moment they give—are not uncommon
in Emerson's writings, and in fact his text is replete with paradoxes that
destabilize the balanced symmetry or "part to part" harmony of mind
and nature, leading to what Wolfe describes as the "insistent strangeness,
the unremittingly heretical quality, of his writing, in which a signature
feature is to take precisely the turn of thought or phrase that seems to
undermine at a stroke the entire argument just made, a seemingly relentless drive to pursue thought where it may lead, even into paradox and
conceptual meltdown."[59] Straightforward versions of romanticism or
skepticism cannot cope with this "insistent strangeness"—a method of
writing, it would seem, that disrupts the complacency of consistent interpretations by making them continually fall over into their contrary. As
Wolfe convincingly argues, what is needed instead is a "posthumanist"
approach, a theoretical paradigm that can cope with a constant decen-
tering or displacement of the identity implied in the humanist subject
without replacing it.

   Though it is still in many respects a highly contested term, "posthumanism" as a rigorous theoretical orientation may be traced back
to Michel Foucault's decoupling of the "humanist thematic" from the
Enlightenment ideal of "permanent critique."[60] Humanism, he writes,
"can be opposed by the principle of a critique and a permanent creation
of ourselves in our autonomy: that is, a principle that is at the heart of
the historical consciousness that the Enlightenment has of itself. From
this standpoint, I am inclined to see Enlightenment and humanism in a
state of tension rather than identity."[61] Foucault here initiates a transition
away from descriptions of the humanist capacity for self-critical reflection or objectivity—observational positions above, apart, or otherwise
exempt from modernity's scientifically ordered cosmos and "rationally
administered" society—and one toward *post*humanist accounts of observational contingency. Foucault's critical point is that the humanist gesture solves the problem of modernity's contingency by exempting itself
from its own critique: the observer him- or herself remains unobserved
in the observation.

   Posthumanism, by contrast, places contingency front and center by
considering observation as always embedded within complex networks

of communication, technology, language, and prosthesis. Systems theory, particularly Luhmann's articulation and expansion of it to encompass social systems that operate in what he calls the "medium" of meaning, provides a rigorous theoretical framework for observing radical contingency and represents in many respects the culmination of the genealogy that is the subject of this book. One major contention will be that there is but a short line to draw from Peirce's revolutionary investigations into logic and semiotics to the formation of cybernetics and "first-order" systems theory in America in the decades after World War II—a story with a cast of characters that includes the likes of Norbert Weiner, John von Neumann, Warren McCulloch, Gregory Bateson, and W. Ross Ashby.[62] What is known as the "second-order" turn in systems theory begins with George Spencer-Brown's embrace of self-reference in the formal calculus of his *Laws of Form* and then continues to Heinz von Foerster's extension of that calculus for investigations into systems capable of self-observation as well as to Luhmann's sociological description of modernity.

The gambit of the present study can be stated in the following premise: systems theory raises the possibility of observing a countertradition in American thought that is very different from humanist or representationalist models, a tradition for which the theological and philosophical writings of Edwards, Emerson, and Peirce play a central role. This tradition performs a questioning of the foundational immanence of feeling or consciousness by stressing *contingency* and *self-reference*. The humanist presumption of *access* to the outside is replaced by a more fundamental *closure* that (re)produces the possibility for any relationship with the "world" in the first place. The outside does not become available in a romantic immanence or self-grounding that unites self and world, nor can we rest content in a skeptical posture that presumes "separateness" since that posture still constructs its *own* identity. We have to begin in contingency, in the paradox of difference *as such*. That paradox is—and this is the sense in which systems theory departs decisively from Hegelian or Marxist traditions in critical theory—the generative condition of system organization and not merely a "limit" to be overcome.

A second and equally important claim to be made is that this posthumanist tradition does not, of course, emerge out of thin air but in fact draws upon a form of thinking that is front and center in most accounts of American intellectual history, the very tradition that Miller claimed was progressively abandoned and excluded throughout the eighteenth and nineteenth centuries. In fact, as Wolfe notes, "The closest thing we could find to Emerson's work in the theological tradition would be not Quakerism or Unitarianism but the line of medieval theology that works its way from Saint Augustine through John Scottus Eriugena to the fifteenth-century theologian Nicholas Cusanus."[63] As later chapters will show, one need not look very far to find the American provenance of this Augustinian heritage in the Calvinism of the early Puritans. At the other end of this argument stands the semiotics of Charles S. Peirce. It is no small irony that while Peirce's anticipations of systems theory and cybernetics have already been widely noted in those disciplines,[64] his status in narratives of American thought is far more troubled. That topic will be addressed in greater detail in chapter 2 of this book.

For now we can state that the chaotic "hidden God" of the Puritans and the supremely ordered abstractions of Peircean semiotics are the twin poles of a posthumanist tradition in American thought. This tradition brings to the fore questions deflected by romantic or secular philosophies of the subject: How does the world observe itself? How does the observation *of* nature take place *in* nature? How can the world be in my head and yet my head be in the world? As the British mathematician George Spencer-Brown puts it, "It seems hard to find an acceptable answer to the question of how or why the world conceives a desire, and discovers an ability, to see itself, and appears to suffer the process."[65] While the mainstream of modern philosophy was often occupied with the occlusion or overcoming (one way or another) of such problems through the postulate of an objective observer that is excluded from what is observed, medieval theology addressed them head on. The concept of God, that is, points to what remains hidden or excluded in our worldly distinctions. As Luhmann notes, "A God who experiences everything and is accessible through communication but who does not belong to society is a singular exception that exactly copies the recursive totality of the societal system itself, a duplication that makes it possible to experience the world in a religious way."[66] Only God retains the ability to observe the latent or unobserved *other* side of every distinction (only God sees *both* sides at the same time), but this idea in turn holds the observer accountable for what he or she *cannot* see. In this way, the hidden God is an exemplary case of *re-entry*: the original distinction (revealed/hidden) reappears within the distinction on the "revealed" side, a circumstance that "exactly copies the recursive totality of the societal system itself" (or the unity of what is revealed and what is hidden) but that does not, critically, provide a secure ground from which to proceed because it does not itself "belong" to society—it provides only a rendering of contingency *within* the system and to which the system must respond with a further distinction. For the self-referential paradox of a "recursive totality" to be unfolded, in other words, a side must still be taken.

For many readers, the critical interventions of systems theory will recall a more familiar form of critique: the deconstruction of Jacques Derrida. Indeed, Luhmann identifies deconstruction as an exemplary form of what systems theory calls "second-order" observation.[67] In particular, Derrida provides a key thematic concept for this study in the form of "transcendental questioning," a mode of critique that is particularly evident in Rudolph Gasché's insistence on the importance of the "quasi-transcendental" for deconstruction. As Derrida puts it in *Deconstruction and Pragmatism,*

> Something that I learned from the great figures in the history of philosophy, from Husserl in particular, is the necessity of posing transcendental questions in order not to be held within the fragility of an incompetent empiricist discourse, and thus it is in order to avoid empiricism, positivism and psychologism that it is endlessly necessary to renew transcendental questioning. But such questioning must be renewed in taking account of the possibility of fiction, of accidentality and contingency, thereby ensuring that this new form of transcendental questioning only mimics the phantom of classical transcendental seriousness without renouncing that which, within this phantom, constitutes an essential heritage.[68]

The question that follows is just what exactly such "quasi-transcendental" questioning might in practice look like: "Do I speak of this 'quasi' in an ironical, comic, or parodic manner, or is it a question of something else? I believe both. There is irony and there is something else."[69] That something *else*, which remains hidden and as yet unrevealed (which is to say that it remains to be determined), refers to what Derrida characterizes in *Positions* as "an undecidable resource that sets the system in motion."[70] In that text he goes on to state that undecidables represent

> unities of simulacrum, "false" verbal properties (nominal or semantic) that can no longer be included within philosophical (binary) opposition, but which, however, inhabit philosophical opposition, resisting and disorganizing it, *without ever* constituting a third term, without ever

leaving room for a solution in the form of speculative dialectics. . . . In fact, I attempt to bring the critical operation to bear against the unceasing reappropriation of this work of the simulacrum by a dialectics of the Hegelian type . . . for Hegelian idealism consists precisely of a *reléve* of the binary oppositions of classical idealism, a resolution of contradiction into a third term that comes in order to *aufheben*, to deny while raising up, while idealizing, while sublimating into an anamnesic interiority (*Errinnerung*), while *interning* difference in a self-presence.[71]

Rather than raise a binary opposition into synthesis, the undecidable persists in its slippery oscillations, taking definitive form, the form of a decision, only if its condition of possibility is at the same time the condition of its impossibility:

The undecidable is not merely the oscillation or the tension between two decisions. Undecidable—this is the experience of that which, though foreign and heterogeneous to the order of the calculable and the rule, must nonetheless . . . deliver itself over to the impossible decision while taking account of law and rules. A decision that would not go through the test and ordeal of the undecidable would not be a free decision; it would only be the programmable application or the continuous unfolding of a calculable process.[72]

That which is irreducible to the calculations of a discernable program forces an act of reduction to be rendered within the program (what Luhmann might designate as the distinction between finite and infinite information loads). Along these lines, the quasi-transcendental is a form of questioning that erases itself, kicks its own legs out from underneath itself, as a way to broach or traverse the undecidable as a "resource" of meaning. Transcendental questioning, conceived in this way, is the same as deconstruction itself: "This deconstruction does not *apply* itself to such a text, however. It never applies itself to anything from the outside. It is in some way the operation or rather the very experience that this text, it seems to me, first does itself, by itself, on itself."[73] Much like the observational necessity of self-reference, the quasi-transcendental is a self-transcending gesture from *within*, fully within, a particular text. It is for this reason that I will have occasion to speak, tongue planted halfway in cheek, of "quasi-transcendentalism."

However, in the final analysis it is systems theory that offers the conceptual rigor needed to engage with contingency in a way that can foreground its *own* contingency and thus make as clear as possible what Luhmann might call its "theoretical architecture." This is done so that what is at stake in theoretical decisions—both what is gained and what is lost—may be presented with as much transparency as possible. By supposing that self-reference simultaneously entails *other*-reference, systems theory is able to draw a line around its own constricted domain and indicate in this way its own limitedness and thus what lies outside of the boundaries of the theory:

> There is an external world—which results from the fact that cognition, as a self-operated operation, can be carried out at all—but we have no direct contact with it. Cognition could not reach the external world without cognition. In other words, cognition is a self-referential process. Knowledge can know only itself, although it can—as if out of the corner of its eye—determine that this is possible only if there is more than mere cognition. Cognition deals with an external world that remains unknown and, as a result, has to come to see that it cannot see what it cannot see.[74]

In this way, self-reference leads to the conclusion that, as Luhmann colorfully puts it, "the epistemologist him/herself becomes a rat in the labyrinth and has to reflect on the position from which he/she observes the other rats."[75] The principal innovation of systems theory is that it is a theory which can foreground its own contingency, a self-limiting gesture that makes even its own adoption and deployment yet another situation that calls for a pragmatic decision to be made "one way or another." One can only observe by making a distinction (a term closely related, we will see, to concepts such as decision and determination), by adopting an observational position that necessarily hides something else.

One-sidedness is inevitable, but systems theory intervenes by insisting on the paradoxical *unity* of the distinction that constitutes an observation, a "second-order" observation *of* observation that is itself based on a first-order distinction. This does not means that second-order observation obtains a privileged or transcendental position that is unavailable to first-order observation but merely that the second-order observation observes the unity of the distinction put in play by first-order observation. This means that any second-order observation can, in principle, be observed by another second-order observation—and that it too is constituted through a blind spot, the unity of a distinction that it cannot see. As Luhmann notes,

> We have become more and more accustomed since the nineteenth century to working with distinctions without questioning the unity of the distinction itself. The narrator presents the narration, be it of a novel or of a world history, in which he is no longer present and, as evidenced in the case of Hegel, no longer able to be present. Likewise, the physicist has no place in the "univers automate" of classical physics. He is not physically present, neither as observer nor as actor. . . . Rationality itself can also be made a component of a distinction, whose other side must then be something irrational, for example, pleasure, fantasy, or imagination. But does this irrational then perhaps serve to protect a deficient concept of rationality?[76]

He goes on to note that this "onesidedness of attributions of rationality, and the renunciation of the question of what the unity of the particular distinction might be, illustrate the inability of modern society to reflect on its own unity."[77] Luhmann's theory is developed in order to address this problem, and he argues that modernity's disavowal of theology means that theoretical architecture of this sort could not have developed previously: "No traditional epistemology . . . could dare go this far—obviously because the position from which it would have had to deal with distinctness was occupied by theology. . . . The partner for radical constructivism is therefore not traditional epistemology, but traditional theology."[78] To find precedents for systems theory, one has to look elsewhere than modern philosophy, and I will argue that in the religious inheritance of the American Puritans one readily finds an emphasis on the "hidden God" as the excluded unity of the distinction: the unseen, occluded, and radically *un*available that runs from Edwards to Emerson and Peirce. Systems theory provides the tools for a description of such trends in American thought because it is systems theory that provides the theoretical grounds for a second-order observation that can draw our attention to something *else*, the unseen, "the indistinct which once was called *God*, and today, if one distinguishes system and environment, is called *world*, or, if one distinguishes object and cognition, *reality*."[79] Systems theory's call for second-order observation is a call to observe the hidden unity behind our distinctions, the "indistinct" that subsequently represents the necessity for a new (one-sided) pragmatic distinction, selection, decision, or determination.

This book will often circle back to the primal scene of an asymmetrical and self-referential distinction, an act that indicates one thing only to lose sight of the other—an act that is in some sense always exceeding (and succeeding) itself. In America this idea begins with the Calvinist distinction between the transcendent sovereignty of God and a fallen material creation. There can be no greater demonstration of an "asymmetrical" relationship or one that more dramatically demonstrates the religious imperative to choose the "negative" (reflective, transcendent) value in that relationship. On this point, my argument follows from Hans Blumenberg's contention that Karl Löwith's well-known description of modernity in terms of secularization should be redescribed "not as the *transposition* of authentically theological contents into secularized alienation from their origin but rather as the *reoccupation* of answer positions that had become vacant and whose corresponding questions could not be eliminated."[80] Contents may change but the form has a striking resilience:

> The only reason why "secularization" could ever have become so plausible as a mode of explanation of historical processes is that supposedly secularized ideas can in fact mostly be traced back to an identity in the historical process. Of course this identity, according to the thesis advocated here, is not one of contents but one of functions. It is in fact possible for totally heterogeneous contents to take on identical functions in specific positions in the system of man's interpretation of the world and of himself. In our history this system has been decisively determined by Christian theology, and specifically, above all, in the direction of its expansion. Theology created new "positions" in the framework of the statements about the world and man that are possible and are expected, "positions" that cannot simply be "set aside" again or left unoccupied in the interest of theoretical economy.[81]

Modernity, that is, continually repeats or reinscribes its essential problematic: the paradox of self-reference and the consequent re-entry of the distinction into itself. To go a step beyond Blumenberg—and as theorists such as Luhmann and Derrida would be the first to point out—it is the issue of "theoretical economy" that now comes to the forefront, precisely because its possibility remains out of reach for reasons of form that go to the heart of *any* theoretical apparatus. Here we may take some inspiration from Perry Miller's comment that if the "history of ideas" is to be "anything more than a mail-order catalog" we must demand of ourselves "not only a fluency in the concepts themselves but an ability to get underneath them."[82] However, it cannot be a question of delving into some subterranean reality but only of a commitment to contingency and the formal requirement of self-reference—a condition that applies (it too often goes without saying) to this study as well: "The observer must recognize himself as a system-within-an-environment while he carries out observations operatively and then links them recursively. The narrator appears in what he narrates. He is observable as an observer. He constitutes himself in his own field and therefore necessarily in the mode of contingency, that is, with a side-glance toward other potentialities."[83] We begin, and end, with the autological inclusion of the excluded middle.

Luhmann's central distinction takes place between a system and an environment of infinitely greater complexity than the system itself. The system, in other words, functions only by reducing the complexity of its environment. The distinction is a boundary, a circle that marks a line between "inside" and "outside." But this is not the whole story. Since the initial distinction indicates only *one side* (it is asymmetrical), the system cannot operate (cannot produce further distinctions) unless the initial distinction (system/environment) is copied within the system. The circle reappears within the circle. This is what Gotthard Günther calls the distinction between an "inner" and "outer" environment and what Luhmann (following George Spencer-Brown) calls *re-entry*. The mark of distinction "re-enters" the system as a paradox and enacts a determinative oscillation between its binary terms.

Every distinction, every re-entry, connects to further distinctions: "The mark is repulsed and attracted by the paradox of the re-entry, as it were, and the world becomes ordered in this interplay of repulsion and attraction. Beginning and end are the same, and not the same; and in between (or: in the meantime) the world achieves its organized complexity."[84] This interplay describes the sense in which what is experienced as the present, the given, and the immediate is only produced through hiding something *else*. Every end is a beginning, and every private virtue, every circle, and every sign refer through the paradox of self-referential closure, just out of the corner of its eye, to the infinitely open.

— 1 —
The Double Consciousness

American Thought and the Theory of Theory

One key, one solution to the mysteries of human condition, one solution to the old knots of fate, freedom, and foreknowledge, exists, the propounding, namely, of the double consciousness. A man must ride alternately on the horses of his private and public nature, as the equestrians in the circus throw themselves nimbly from horse to horse, or plant one foot on the back of one, and the other foot on the back of the other. So when a man is the victim of his fate . . . he is to rally on his relation to the Universe, which his ruin benefits. Leaving the daemon who suffers, he is to take sides with the Deity who secures universal benefit by his pain.

RALPH WALDO EMERSON, "FATE"

"Do your own thing" is a useful metaphor to play with when the things are doing you.

ANTHONY WILDEN, *SYSTEM AND STRUCTURE*

The essays of Ralph Waldo Emerson have a rather easy way with paradox. It is not uncommon to encounter an assertion delivered with his customary boldness only to find the contrary asserted shortly thereafter, sometimes even within the same sentence. Consider, for instance, "Nominalist and Realist," which categorically declares, "No sentence will hold the whole truth, and the only way in which we can be just is by giving ourselves the lie. . . . Things are, and are not, at the same time."[1] If we take these words as something like a thesis statement (an arbitrary designation, it must be admitted, for a writer whose essays appear at times to consist entirely of a procession of thesis statements), then what is perhaps most striking about it is the way it seems to have an antagonistic relationship to its own meaning, one not unlike the involutions of a paradox that assumes its own truth while simultaneously asserting its own falsity—as if these words were an incantation that, once uttered, allows the speaker to vanish in a puff of smoke.

On an intuitive level, it is hard for all but the most literal-minded to deny that there is indeed a meaning to Emerson's words, even a readily understandable one, but it is equally hard to deny that the meaning cannot consist in what is explicitly said. Taken alone, the words do not admit of coherence, and so their ultimate effect is to force a shift of perspective from the *content* of the statement, what one might take to be its signified object or meaning, to its *form*: the statement draws attention to itself *as a statement*, as if it were a painting that somehow included its own frame. Opposing and contradictory values are asserted together as a unity, a paradoxical assertion that at the same time may be said to effectively draw a boundary around itself. This boundary indicates the possibility of selecting a third value—neither one side nor the other—on the *other* side of the boundary. There is a dim vision of totality here, a sense of the whole, but only in the manner of an inversion or self-limitation of the part, a perspective in which the whole is not so much visible but, if you will, visible as *in*visible. The paradox invites, or even demands, its own negation.

Emerson's *Essays: Second Series* (1844), to which "Nominalist and Realist" belongs, is often claimed to constitute a break with the collection of essays published just three years before. In the earlier essays, Emerson is apt to reconcile the vexing discontinuities of his rhetoric through an affirmation of a cosmic continuity or balance that enfolds even the most intractable of oppositions. In "Compensation," for instance, the central dilemma of the essay is undone by positing the supreme individuality of the soul as the point of access to the whole, the fixed hub around which the flux of experience swirls: "The soul is not a compensation, but a life. The soul *is*. Under all this running sea of circumstance, whose waters ebb and flow with perfect balance, lies the aboriginal abyss of real Being. Essence, or God, is not a relation, or a part, but the whole. Being is the vast affirmative, excluding negation, self-balanced, and swallowing up all relations, parts and times within."[2] Strangely (a strangeness that is by no means unusual in Emerson's essays) it seems that here the individual soul is said to produce something like its own dissolution. As Branka Arsić puts it, these moments speak to "a stepping out of oneself . . . intense becomings or elevation."[3] In such passages, Emerson describes an experience in which the universal or whole ("not a relation, or a part") becomes available through an experience of particularity, as if the utmost experience of the personal is at the same time to be subsumed or suffused in the great *impersonal*. This is a vision, for Arsić, of "self-renewal" in which "all is luminous, healed of demonological divides."[4]

Along similar lines, if we accept such readings of Emerson, it would seem plausible to claim that he belongs to the tradition of American romanticism, but that designation in turn fails to note the degree of extremity to which Emerson pushes romanticist frameworks, almost as if forcing them to collapse in on themselves. Indeed, as Sharon Cameron astutely notes, while "the goal of the essays *is* generality," at the same time "the point of the essays' climactic figures is the representation of an encounter whose truth is somehow tied to its stylistic or rhetorical singularity."[5] The utmost general or impersonal, "the aboriginal abyss of real Being," is then revealed only through an experience of the utmost specificity and singularity. If, as Cameron argues, the essays are intended to dramatize "that moment when the personal is annihilated by the influx of the impersonal,"[6] then it would also seem that "the impersonal calls into question the very idea of a self as stable or predictable entity, for the moods which define our perceptions, beliefs, thoughts are in effect only contingent on circumstance."[7] Here Cameron finds an enduring tension in Emerson's project. By pursuing a form of romantic individualism to its breaking point, the author of "Self-Reliance" unwittingly undermines the very distinction that makes the notion of a "self" coherent in the first place:

Consequently, what deprives Emerson's voice of authority is that his statements are *insufficiently* personal, except in the passages I have discussed, and there only by inference. That is, their authority is neither functional *nor* personal. The *content* of Emerson's impersonal implies a heroic *context*: an encounter, as well as an acknowledgement of the real or, in the language of "Character," the *"know[ing of] its face."* But the heroic implies a *person's* contact with the real. . . . Emerson, strangely, *doesn't* know this. He invents a mode of discourse dissociated from the institutionally religious. He produces a discourse that has access to the real prior to the mediating symbol or rite whose necessity it obviates. The legitimacy of that discourse therefore depends on the visibility of the person speaking. It depends on the fact that an epiphanic encounter occurs to someone *in particular* who, by virtue of that particularity, is in a position to describe it. But except in the essay's climactic moments—moments that, as I've argued, are typified by their idiosyncrasy—Emerson then erodes the representation of any self-articulated distinction which would make his discourse legible and meaningful.[8]

I quote this passage at length because it artfully brings to the table a paradox that threatens the entirety of Emerson's philosophical project. If the soul is the point of access to Being, then insofar as it operates in that capacity it is no longer *my* soul. Or put differently, if I may encounter God only by essentially vacating myself, this circumstance in turn suggests that it is an encounter that can only happen to no one, to no actual person. In Emerson's essays, it seems that the individual's capacity for "epiphanic encounters" is then predicated upon and at the same time undercut by a more fundamental *incapacity* to actually experience them *as* an individual.

Cameron thus finds in the heart of Emerson's discourse a paradox that undermines its own stated meaning. While this argument is exceptionally perceptive, it nevertheless construes such paradoxes as debilitating to meaning rather than, as I intend to argue, generative of meaning in the first place. We can turn the matter on its head: the paradox can instead be construed as the boundary that encloses and thus makes possible Emerson's project—not its failure (or not *only* its failure) but the source of its distinctive power. This is not an affirmation of continuity underlying discontinuity, but an affirmation *of* discontinuity—an affirmation, as it happens, that is possible only as paradox, one might even say the affirmation of a negation. In the magisterial "Fate," Emerson even admits as much: "This is true, and that other is true. But our geometry cannot span these extreme points, and reconcile them. What to do? By obeying each thought frankly, by harping, or, if you will, pounding on each string, we learn at last its power."[9]

"Fate" signals that Emerson takes discontinuity and paradox as the very condition of speaking, a partiality that in some sense negates or unsays *itself*, or at least its claim to generality: "The riddle of the age has for each a private solution."[10] One may take this statement on its own as the affirmation of a familiar form of American individualism, but within the contextual or formal qualities of "Fate" such statements have an undeniably circular way about them. This is to say that even within a body of work notable for its audacious (even Whitman-esque) embrace of self-contradiction, "Fate" stands apart—if only for the sense in which it appears to directly address Emerson's fascination with a certain conflicted doubling in consciousness. Or as he puts it, "Man is not order of nature, sack and sack, belly and members, link in a chain, nor any ignominious baggage, but a stupendous antagonism, a dragging together of the poles of the Universe."[11] "Fate," it seems, ties a knot that cannot be cut but only pulled tighter.

It is no wonder: "We are incompetent to solve the times."[12] Indeed, the essay has a beguiling way of performing its own incompetence through a persistent self-negation, as if chasing its own tail in perpetuity. The reader is left not enlightened but bewildered. "Let us build altars to the Beautiful Necessity," we are told in the stirring and still mystifying final pages, "that Law rules throughout existence, a Law which is not intelligent but intelligence,—not personal nor impersonal,—it disdains words and passes understanding."[13] This is a law that "holds nature and souls in perfect solution, and compels every atom to serve a universal end."[14] But even the most general end still affirms the particular: "If we must accept Fate, we are not less compelled to affirm liberty, the significance of the individual, the grandeur of duty, the power of character."[15] What to make of these endless involutions?

Emerson's embrace of discontinuity *as such* puts his reader in a predicament that brings to mind a Zen parable that the pioneering systems theorist Gregory Bateson was fond of using to illustrate his theory of communication, particularly its relevance for discerning the logical structure of schizophrenia. In Bateson's version of the parable, the master says to his pupil, "If you say this stick is real, I will strike you with it. If you say this stick is not real, I will strike you with it. If you don't say anything, I will strike you with it." The pupil, much like the hapless reader of "Fate," finds himself trapped in a double bind, damned (and inevitably bruised) no matter what course of action he selects from those made available to him: "We feel that the schizophrenic finds himself continually in the same situation as the pupil, but he achieves something like disorientation rather than enlightenment. The Zen pupil might reach up and take the stick away from the master—who might accept this response, but the schizophrenic has no such choice since with him there is no not caring about the relationship."[16]

The crux of this predicament is that the schizophrenic is not capable of what Bateson calls "metacommunication" because he remains captive to the terms of the relationship as defined by the master. He cannot, as it were, shift the communicational framework in order to communicate within the terms of a different type of relationship—one in which, for instance, the ontological status of the stick isn't at issue but the scope of the master's authority. As the communication theorist Anthony Wilden puts it,

> So long as the Zen master is defined as the subject-who-is-supposed-to know by the pact between master and pupil, the pupil is in a double bind. That is, he can neither obey nor disobey the master. But if he perceives the real nature of the situation, he has only to metacommunicate about it in order to be released from the double bind. He can communicate with the master at a higher level of communication: he can grab the stick and take it away, or he can hit the master with it.[17]

As is well known, Bateson derived the notion of metacommunication from Russell and Whitehead's Theory of Logical Types as presented in *Principia Mathematica*. As Bateson observes, "The central thesis of this theory is that there is a discontinuity between a class and its members. The class cannot be a member of itself nor can one of the members *be* the class, since the term used for the class is of a *different level of abstraction*—a different Logical Type—from terms used for members."[18] Bateson goes on to note that the Theory of Logical Types was initially intended as a sort of prohibition on the paradoxes that result from applying the same logical terms across classes—as if shifting levels indiscriminately were the source of the problems that arise from paradoxes. But he also makes the rather surprising point that the Theory of Logical Types can claim to restrict only what falls within its *own* domain. This means that a prohibition against confusing logical types can really hold only within the discursive demands of formal logic: "Although in formal logic there is an attempt to maintain this discontinuity between a class and its members, we argue that in the psychology of real communications this discontinuity is continually and inevitably breached."[19] In other words, while the discontinuity between logical types remains a requirement in order to communicate logically, this is itself a circular or self-referential presumption of logic's own mode of communication. Indeed, Bateson argues that a failure to breach the discontinuity between types in "the psychology of real communication" leads to the familiar pathologies of schizophrenia. By drawing from these insights, and additionally along the lines set by Cameron, it now becomes possible to see how Emerson violates the continuity of his own discourse by selecting at the *same time* two mutually opposing values.

This description of metacommunication cannot help but ring a few familiar bells in the minds of those who are concerned with critical theory. To ask about the possibility (or lack thereof) of shifting to a "different level of abstraction" is to ask about the possibility of critical theory in the first place. After all, is not seizing the stick from the hands of the master the whole objective? Gillian Rose, for instance, affirms in *Hegel Contra Sociology* that the practice of critical theory holds out the possibility of broaching the distinction (the double bind) between the finite and the infinite: "The limitation of 'justified' knowledge of the finite prevents us from recognizing, criticizing, and hence from changing the social and political relations which determine us. If the infinite is unknowable, we are powerless. For our concept of the infinite is our concept of ourselves and our possibilities."[20] The infinite, in Rose's formulation, already *contains* the distinction between finite and infinite within itself and therefore the resolution of contradiction always takes place on the "side," as it were, of the infinite as the final or ultimate level of metacommunication.

To be sure, Rose is careful not to determine the *actual* characteristics of the infinite, but merely insists on its possibility as a function of consciousness resolving contradictions until the terms "become adequate to each other."[21] As she puts it, "Once it is shown that the criterion of what is to count as finite and infinite has been created by consciousness itself, then a notion is implied which does not divide consciousness or reality into finite and infinite."[22] Here Rose supposes that consciousness can continually frame the distinction between finite and infinite as a unity from the side of infinity: "a notion of the absolute which *includes* the finite."[23] Consciousness itself thus has access to a "relative identity" between finite and infinite that operates as an "identity or unity which re-cognizes the difference or negativity of the finite, not as the opposite of the infinite but part of it."[24]

"We are limited," claims Rose, "but can become aware of the determinations of the limit."[25] In a similar manner, any assertion of discontinuity is at the same time asserted to contradict itself and therefore negate itself (the "negation of negation") or else erase the framework that makes it meaningful—thus making available a reflective critical position that can observe the limits, even if *only* the limits, of the determined domains of ideology. To offer a more recent and quite prominent example, consider the following from Slavoj Žižek:

> That is to say, the hegemonic ideological field imposes on us a plane of (ideological) visibility with its own "principal contradiction" . . . and the first thing we must do is reject (subtract from) this opposition, recognize it as a false opposition destined to obfuscate the true line of division. Lacan's formula for this redoubling is 1 + 1 + a: the "official" antagonism (the Two) is always supplements by an "indivisible remainder" which indicates its foreclosed dimension. In other words, the true antagonism is always reflexive, it is the antagonism between the "official" antagonism and that which is foreclosed by it (this is why, in Lacan's mathematics, 1 + 1 = 3).[26]

As with Rose, it is already quite clear from this passage that Žižek's brand of dialectics via Lacanian psychoanalysis commits him (rhetorically at least) to a "true line of division" from which something like a totalizing or absolute form of communication becomes available, a plane of ideology that remains momentarily exempt from its own critique while providing a space from which one can speak authentically of a distinction between "true" and "false" antagonisms. This gesture may also be characterized as a seizure of the space of the excluded middle as the unity of the distinction. In an earlier text, Žižek refers to this "psychoanalytic act" as the moment when "it *is* possible to touch the Real through the Symbolic . . . the act as a gesture which, by definition, touches the dimension of some impossible Real," which then "redefines the very contours of what is possible (an act accomplishes what, within the given symbolic universe, appears to be 'impossible,' yet it changes its conditions so that it creates retroactively the conditions of its own possibility)."[27] In this way, "the subject gains the space of free action."[28] This is a means of "opting for the *impossible*, fully assuming the place of the exception."[29] The supplemental exception, in other words, always proves the symbolic rule.

Arguably deriving in large measure from Emerson's *Nature* and the first collection of essays, similar gestures are not uncommon in American thought. In an early essay, John Dewey claims that pragmatism "has given to the subject, to the individual mind, a practical rather than an epistemological function. The individual mind is important because only the individual mind is the organ of modifications and institutions, the vehicle of experimental creation."[30] Dewey additionally describes the capacity for individual reflection in this tradition as the capacity for "an indirect response" that involves "a prospective control of the conditions of the environment."[31] What is most notable about this description is that it ties reflection to *control*—in particular, the possibility of achieving a more productive relationship to the environment. Dewey's sense of the concept of reflection as construed by the American philosophical tradition can then be said to involve something like both detachment *and* selective reengagement, a gesture that keeps the environment at arm's length while at the same time allowing for what he calls a "taking account" and arrangement of "more effective and more profitable" relationships.[32] Yet again, the presumed identity of consciousness undergirds and makes possible the observation of mind and environment together as a unity, however fleeting.

And that, in sum, is the whole problem—and exactly the type of gesture that I want to argue is entirely foreclosed by "Fate," an essay in which a seemingly endless procession of "principal contradictions" are stubbornly and repeatedly *asserted*. "Person makes event," Emerson claims, "and event person."[33] Where is the true line of division here? How to achieve "more profitable" relationships with an environment that at the same time fully determines the "individual mind," which is said to be the means of those changes in the first place? Where is the space of free action? It is as if each side is somehow included in *and* excluded from the other. Emerson seems to utterly deny the possibility of an "authentic" intervention into the "symbolic field" that issues "from the standpoint of this inherent impossibility"[34]—something that Žižek describes in the manner of a heroic assumption of the impossible within the possible (or seizing the stick). In "Fate," however, the distinction between possible and impossible is somehow retained—as if Emerson is concerned to *evade* unity. It is thus not a Žižekian assumption of the place of the excluded but a confrontation with the excluded *as* excluded.

These are surely difficult notions, and they suggest that if we want to achieve a better understanding of "Fate" we will need a different theoretical approach. Here we can agree with Cary Wolfe's axiomatic claim that "everything we know (scientifically, theoretically) and say (linguistically or in other forms of semiotic notation) . . . takes place within some contingent, radically nonnatural (that is, constructed and technical) schema of knowledge."[35] Wolfe's jettisoning of the possibility of "natural," necessary, or absolute forms of communication asserts a radical *discontinuity*—a discontinuity, moreover, that in turn applies to *itself* and that therefore cannot stand as a "true line of division." Wolfe's point is a "second-order" or circular one: metacommunication is always already communication, and this makes the more general point that communication is always contingent upon a "principal contradiction," a radical discontinuity to which it remains bound as the possibility for communicating at all.

It is for this reason, as Wilden points out, that the third condition given by the master ("if you don't say anything at all, I shall hit you") is so important: it marks the boundary within which the double bind holds sway and prevents simultaneity or equivalence. The difference between the stick being "real" or "not real" is significant only if one accepts that distinction as meaningful (that is, for a "first-order" observer) and therefore remains unable to see the potential of a "second-order" (and paradoxical) *unity* of real and not-real. The third condition as given by the master makes explicit what is usually only implicit: you have to choose sides. In this way, it works as a kind of hint for the pupil by including the third possibility in the inverted or negative manner of a prohibition much like the one asserted by the Theory of Logical Types: don't cross levels! However, the "second-order" approach pursued here deviates from a dialectical understanding of metacommunication because even if one takes the stick away and thus chooses *neither* side (Žižek's "impossible" act) this communication is *still* based on a double bind (and thus an excluded "third") of its own. In a manner of speaking, the excluded middle is *already* excluded even in a supposedly "authentic" act. As Wilden puts it, "The transcendence itself generates paradox at the metacommunicative level . . . the paradox of paradox."[36] The move to transcendence, seeing the double bind as a unity, only reproduces the paradox. Because of this, communication cannot shift vertically to a higher level of abstraction, but only, as it were, laterally. After all, the master can always hit you back.

Things are, and are not. We might even adopt the following premise: "Truth is a character which attaches to an abstract proposition, such as a person might utter. It essentially depends upon that proposition's not professing to be exactly true."[37] One can imagine that these words, coming from the American pragmatist philosopher Charles Sanders Peirce, might receive Emerson's approval due to his own stated preference for submitting to "the inconvenience of suspense and imperfect opinion."[38] In fact, the theoretical framework outlined thus far makes it possible to observe a commonality of form between two otherwise quite different thinkers. If we accept Dewey's declaration that the difference between Peirce and his fellow pragmatist William James boils down to the fact that "Peirce wrote as a logician and James as a humanist,"[39] then that dichotomy raises the difficult question of just where Emerson falls along that continuum. In turn, answering that question will lead to the conclusion that it is Peirce—and not the arguably humanist form of pragmatism that runs from James to Dewey to Richard Rorty—who carries on the investigations into the possibility for observing the paradoxical unity (not *identity*) of communicational forms that is initiated by Emerson.

This gambit also situates Peirce and Emerson within the purview of systems theory, a heritage that stretches from Norbert Weiner's cybernetics to Bateson and then to the "second-order" turn characterized by the likes of Anthony Wilden, Heinz von Foerster, and Niklas Luhmann. Finally, and most decisively for my purposes, Cary Wolfe's recent groundbreaking work on Emerson ties him directly to the formalization of "second-order observation" that he finds in Luhmann's work—a theoretical turn of the screw that Wolfe characterizes as the decisive gesture of posthumanist theory. As Wolfe puts it, "Enlightenment rationality is not, as it were, rational enough, because it stops short of applying its own protocols and commitments to *itself*."[40] This self-implication or self-inclusion is the extra step, the "second-order" move, the "post-" in posthumanism—and I hope to show that it is precisely this gesture that makes it possible to better see what is at stake in a theory of the "double consciousness" that can evade the implicit supposition of a humanist identity achieved in the immanence of consciousness.

Amusingly, Wilden claims, "I have never met or heard of anyone who understood Peirce's theory of signs."[41] Fortunately, that daunting task lies well beyond our scope here, yet Wilden's comment is symptomatic of the great difficulty of gaining a clear understanding of Peirce, a difficulty for which responsibility is not without some warrant often laid at the feet of Peirce himself. Nevertheless, it is precisely this issue of intelligibility that is tackled in Peirce's thought—and we cannot fail to recall that his first major statement (and the inspiration for the pragmatism of James) was the essay "How to Make Our Ideas Clear." In retrospect, that title marks an inauspicious start to the academic career that Peirce pursued unsuccessfully throughout his life, but it also happens to draw our attention to what is at stake in the rather perplexing semiotic category of Thirdness, an idea that Peirce considered to be his most important innovation. This is a famously (and, I will argue, necessarily) difficult concept. Peirce claims that Thirdness is "subject to the Principle of Contradiction" but nevertheless "throws off the yoke of the Principle of Excluded Third."[42] After recovering from the inevitable confusion that this statement provokes, one may begin to discern a meaning in the unusual precision of that distinction: Thirdness includes the excluded third but does not allow it to be a stable value (or an identity) in its own right. The "third" is in this case somehow both included *and* excluded. One cannot determine Thirdness *itself* as meaningful because it effectively names the shift or transition to another system of meaning that then excludes a third of its own. That is, Thirdness itself cannot be meaningful because it names the possibility for meaning to occur in the first place.

Why introduce a third principle (neither subject nor object, mind nor matter) into the universe that cannot assume its *own* identity? Moreover, how can one even begin to understand a concept as *neither* identity nor difference, but instead as the difference between them—the difference *of* difference? This is not a doubling as "both/and" or "either/or" but as "neither/nor." For this reason, Thirdness offers a unique opportunity to theorize the twisting inversions of "Fate" while also representing in many respects the continuation of Emerson's critical project, a "second-order" project and thus a turn to *form* that represents, if you will, "the theory of theory." And in conclusion, it is in fact systems theory, a tradition with a distinctly American heritage of its own, which makes it possible to tie these projects together with unprecedented clarity.[43]

As Wilden asserts, "Without the benefit of cybernetic and communication theory, [Peirce's] 'law of mind,' for example, is easily dismissed as idealist anthropomorphism."[44] Wilden alludes to the essay "The Law of Mind" (1892), one of the more ambitious descriptions of Thirdness that Peirce would offer for a more or less popular audience. The title, somewhat oxymoronic given the traditional associations for both terms, signals the intent of the essay. Intending to address the nature of consciousness, he begins with a discussion of a boundary line: "Suppose a surface to be part red and part blue; so that every point on it is either red or blue, and, of course, no part can be both red and blue. What, then, is the color of the boundary line between the red and the blue?"[45] He answers that "the boundary is half red and half blue." Here one is understandably tempted to cry "paradox!" and point out that the boundary would seem to signify the containment of *itself*—a boundary, as it were, inside the original boundary, a re-entry or an enfolding of itself.

Quite interestingly, Peirce goes on to connect this idea to a theory of consciousness: "In like manner, we find it necessary to hold that consciousness essentially occupies time, and what is present to the mind at any ordinary instant, is what is present during a moment in which that instant occurs. Thus, the present is half past and half to come."[46] This analogy proposes that consciousness involves the encounter with a two-sided form, something he would characterize eleven years later in the Harvard lectures from 1903 as "a double consciousness at once of an *ego* and a *non-ego*."[47] Earlier in the same lecture, he claims, "Perception really does represent two objects to us, an *ego* and a *non-ego* . . . a past self that turns out to be nothing but a self and . . . a self that is to be faithful to the Truth in future."[48] There is, all at once, a supposedly immediate *content* of perception accompanied and undercut by its shadow, a "not" or an other that Peirce often prefers to characterize as an indeterminate "future." In between, as noted, is a boundary line that somehow contains *itself*, a difference that in turn contains difference, and so on.

This is a recursive process in which elements act on one another in the manner of "this then that," which resembles the oscillating values of imaginary numbers. This is a duality within a singular phenomenon. As Peirce writes, "If two singulars A and B react upon one another, the action of A upon B and the action of B upon A are absolutely the same element of the phenomenon. Nevertheless, ordinary language makes the distinction of *agent* and *patient*. . . . That is, a formal distinction is drawn between the action of A on B and the action of B on A although they are really the same fact."[49] This suggests that Thirdness *cannot* be observed except as a general process or law that continually transcends its own actual instantiation. For instance, a statement like Emerson's declaration that "person makes event, and event person" becomes a description of *process*—it goes beyond, or perhaps within, itself. A acts on B and B acts on A, but only recursively or alternately, creating a rudimentary sense of irreversible time: "One of the most marked features about the law of mind is that it makes time to have a definite direction of flow from past to future."[50]

Thirdness as such is indeterminate and infinitely complex, and therefore any particular observation of it must involve a reduction or simplification that it then cannot help but exceed. Put differently, the observation of Thirdness *as* complexity compels what can be only a limited or partial determination of it:

> It is certainly hard to believe, until one is forced to the belief, that a conception so obtrusively complex as Thirdness is should be an irreducible unanalyzable conception. What, one naturally exclaims, does this man think to convince us that a conception is complex and simple, at the same time! I might answer this by drawing a distinction. It is complex in the sense that different features may be discriminated in it, but the peculiar idea of *complexity* that it contains, although it has complexity as its object, is an unanalyzable idea.[51]

Floyd Merrell, one of Peirce's most important contemporary interpreters, offers a particularly apt description of this process: "What is *overdetermined* (the field of all possibilities), cannot but become, after account has been rendered regarding that which was actualized from the possible, *undetermined*, and hence there will always be something left unknown."[52] In the terms of this essay, Thirdness as the "double consciousness" implies the *unity* of values in a binary system, and thus from the point of view of the system it constitutes a paradoxical observation of the *unobservable* (irreducible and unanalyzable), which, as the condition of being observable, must inevitably be broken down again into (now different) binary terms. The indeterminate cannot appear as such, but only within and conditioned by the determinate.

By way of catching our breath, what Peirce is attempting to do can be clarified by comparing it to the work of the systems theorist Gotthard Günther, a kindred spirit who had the benefit of writing six decades later and therefore with the likes of Gödel, Heisenberg, and Bohr in his rearview mirror. Günther attempted to introduce "transjunctional operations" (as opposed to conjunction or disjunction) into logical analysis as a kind of "third" term. More broadly, Günther wanted to describe in exclusively logical terms the phenomenon of subjectivity or reflection. For Günther, this means that in logical terms reflection represents a value that rejects both values of a binary system: "Where there is a choice of values offered by 'p' and 'q' the *very choice is rejected*. . . . Any value that does not accept the proffered choice is a rejection value: it transcends the objective (two-valued) system in which it occurs."[53] This offers, according to Günther, a logical description of reflection: "Where there is a choice of two alternative values both are rejected. It is impossible for us to connect any other formal logical meaning with terms like 'subject,' 'subjectivity' or 'consciousness' but rejection of an alternative that is total as the (exclusive) disjunction between true and false."[54]

But as Günther is careful to point out, the selection of a transjunctional value is still the selection of a value because "one value is not sufficient to define a system."[55] As he puts it, "We stated that if a system is rejected the value which acts as rejector places itself outside of it. By doing so, it establishes a boundary or a logically closed surface for the rejected system. In other words: it makes a distinction between the system and something else, that is, an environment."[56] The rejection of the distinction is itself produced through a distinction—a "second-order" distinction. By way of conclusion, Günther formulates something like his own version of the double consciousness: "Any content of thought is, as such, strictly objective; it consequently obeys the laws of two-valued logic. It follows that for the content the classic alternative of two mutually exclusive values has to be accepted. On the other hand, the form of a thought, relative to its content, is always subjective. It therefore rejects the alternative."[57] Günther's point is that, in terms of *content*, we are bound to the system, but when we engage in a second-order reflection on *form*, we may draw the boundary of a new system, but, as always, one that is itself bound to the internal logic of its own binary values. As Niklas Luhmann puts it,

> [Günther] comes very close to Derrida's attempt to transcend the limitations of a metaphysical frame that allows for only two states: being and non-being. It comes close to a rejection of logocentrism. But it does not imply a rejection of logics or of formalism. Günther is not satisfied with the fuzziness of verbal acoustics and paradoxical formulations and tries, whether successfully or not, to find logical structures of higher complexity, capable of fixing new levels for the integration of ontology (for more than one subject) and logics (with more than two values).[58]

In other words, this approach does not retreat from the limitations of form for the sake of content, but suggests instead that content only happens, in every single case, *by* form.

Günther's distinction between system and environment brings us to the most sophisticated contemporary articulation of the double consciousness. This is Luhmann's theory of social systems, which builds from the formal calculus of George Spencer-Brown and the cybernetics of observing systems as studied by Heinz von Foerster in order to propose a radically self-referential theory of communication. Luhmann's theory of communication is built entirely on difference without a concomitant concept for identity. There is neither a final structural framework that contains all differences nor any possibility for representational adequation between terms. But as Luhmann notes, this insistence on difference as such necessarily entails "third" terms:

> In constructing a theory formulated in terms of differences . . . we notice we are always dealing with a triad of elements. Why three elements? In most instances, we are dealing with two sides: good and bad, big and small, the universal and the particular, and so on, and like to exclude any possible third side. Now, however, we are suddenly dealing with a tripartite distinction. How are we to conceive of this? Perhaps one way is to assign to the third factor the task of seeing the other two as a duality, as a distinction, which it then unites.[59]

This unity, according to Luhmann, is itself founded on *dis*continuity, on difference. In particular, it is through his concept of the medium of "meaning" that Luhmann is able to construct a theory of communication founded on the difference of self-referential closure and not on the "identity" presumed in communicational theories of transmission. The question is, as he puts, "How is it possible to observe frames?"[60] In other words, how do we observe the unity of two-sided forms without the humanist presumptions of the identity of consciousness?

> If we want to observe paradoxical communications as deframing and reframing, deconstructing and reconstructing operations, we need a concept of meaning that does not prevent or restrict the range of such operations. "Meaning" cannot . . . be understood in relation to the subjective aspiration of individuals and what seems meaningful to them and for them. Such definitions of meaning exclude unmarked possibilities and are valid only within their methodological or subjective frames. They are, that is, deframable (deconstructable) meanings and do not fulfill

the requirements of a medium that gives access to *both* sides of *any* frame. . . . To avoid such limitations, we need a concept of meaning that is . . . coextensive with the world. Meaning in this sense will have no outside, no antonym, no negative form.[61]

Here we find that meaning, much like Thirdness, is in fact *in*accessible for any actual or individual determination because any such determination necessarily coproduces an "outside" that represents its environment. Thus, while meaning is "coextensive" with the world, this should not be confused with a presentation of the world as such. Instead, "every meaning reformulates the *compulsion to select* implied in all complexity. . . . Meaning is consequently—in form, not in content—the rendering of complexity, indeed a form of rendering that, wherever it attaches, permits access at a given point but that simultaneously indentifies every such access as a selection and, if one may say so, holds it responsible."[62]

Again, we are confronted with the "compulsion" to distinguish between form and content. There is in fact no other way to understand "meaning" in Luhmann's theory, since he not only describes it as having "no outside" but also at the same time suggests that it is itself a two-sided form, a "distinction between actuality and potentiality (or between the real as momentarily given and as possibility)."[63] If we judge from this discontinuity, it would seem that meaning, exactly like Thirdness, is a concept *without* identity: the paradoxical assertion of discontinuity *as such*. Meaning is subject to the principle of contradiction (one is forced to choose sides), but it is also free of the principle of the excluded third (one can move laterally, as it were, and draw a different distinction that treats the first as a unity). Meaning is paradoxically the simultaneous presentation *and* foreclosure of possibility. Meaning is not intended, not communicated, and not the object of a directed consciousness. As Emerson might say, "It is of the maker, not of what is made. All things are touched and changed by it. This uses, and is not used."[64] To use a phrase with a touch of Zen about it, meaning is not meaningful.

How else to understand this but as the "stupendous antagonism," the "law of mind," the "double consciousness"? Luhmann's central claim that communication is subject to self-referential closure, which simply means that all distinctions must take place on *one side* of a two-sided form, brings him in remarkable proximity to Emerson and Peirce. Luhmann's innovation is to assert that the distinction between finite and infinite takes place, quite paradoxically, on the side of the finite. This is in fact the critical gesture of systems theory, which encloses itself as a means to relativize itself—or at least to indicate that possibility. It draws a boundary around itself in the manner of a self-referential paradox ("this statement is false"), or the difference it makes, in order to refer to the radical complexity of the "world" as its *other*. As he puts it, "The closure of the self-referential order is synonymous here with the *infinite openness of the world*."[65] As usual, this is accomplished only through a rejection value: "The world remains invisible even when, and precisely when, it is laced with forms."[66] Taken together, these statements imply that the world is only visible as *in*visible.

To understand the concept of form in this way involves a radical transformation of the concept of observation: to observe means to draw a distinction. Observation is always the observation of difference, a two-sided form without identity. I submit that this idea owes a great deal to pragmatism and in particular to Peirce's insistence that concepts have meaning *only* insofar as they lead to determinate conduct—a designation that always leaves "open" the possibility that different determinations can be made. As Luhmann puts it, "A difference theoretical reconstruction of the concept of form shifts the emphasis from the (ordered) content of form to the difference it makes. It extends and places on the 'other side' of form the realm of what used to be considered chance and thereby subsumes under the concept of form any difference that marks a unity."[67] Form represents the severance of a distinction that is self-referential or asymmetrical, a distinction that indicates *one side* at the expense of the other, since "indicating both sides at once dissolves the distinction."[68] Form is difference, and the difference of that difference, and so on. Distinctions are therefore not static but continually subject to re-entry on one side: "Forms must be articulated *asymmetrically*, since only one of their sides (the internal side) but not the other (the external side) is needed for further operations. . . . Forms are generated by a *rupture of symmetry*."[69] Forms, in this way, are continually forced to include their own exclusions. We are again and again returned to difference, to discontinuity, to the double consciousness.

It is for this reason that the "second-order" cyberneticist Heinz von Foerster is fond of rather Emersonian pronouncements: "In fact, you can turn anything you hear upside down."[70] Likewise, "Every statement has a finite range."[71] Any statement or assertion always includes within itself the possibility of its own negation or rejection—it includes what it *excludes*. Emerson writes, "There is an intrinsic defect in the organ. Language overstates. Statements of the infinite are usually felt to be unjust to the finite, and blasphemous."[72] Peirce presents a somewhat similar claim in his own more limited way: "Truth is that concordance of an abstract statement with the ideal limit towards which endless investigation would tend to bring scientific belief, which concordance the abstract statement may possess by virtue of the confession of its inaccuracy and one-sidedness, and this confession is an essential ingredient of truth."[73] Peirce asserts that truth is not "part and parcel" of Being but essentially *apart* from it, false to it, and this is the very possibility of truth in the first place. As Floyd Merrell puts it, "Everything is both affirmative and negative, pregnant with its contrary. The universe incessantly engages in ongoing agonistics."[74]

These are assertions of the double consciousness. And when they are placed in this context, it is no great leap to suggest that Emerson's body of work ("Fate" and the later essays in particular) represents a major intervention on behalf of articulating what the biologist Francisco J. Varela has called a "post-hegelian paradigm" in systems theory, for which "dualities are adequately represented by imbrication of levels, where one term of the pair emerges from the other. . . . The basic form of these dualities is asymmetry: both terms extend across levels."[75] This is also the reason why Wolfe has so perceptively drawn Emerson into the orbit of systems theory—because it is only systems theory that avoids slotting Emerson (and therefore Peirce) into the familiar one-sided frameworks of idealism, realism, dialectics, and romanticism.

We are left with a sense of being in two places at once, like some exotic subobservable particle that exists only where you *don't* look. "Fate slides into freedom, and freedom into fate," muses Emerson.[76] Likewise, in "Design and Chance," a kind of scientifically inclined younger sibling to "Fate," Peirce claims, "Chance is indeterminacy, is freedom. But the action of freedom issues in the strictest of law."[77] That is to say, Peirce finds these contrary terms to be mutually *in*clusive: "The hypothesis of absolute chance is part and parcel of the hypothesis that everything is explicable, not absolutely, rigidly without the smallest inexactitude or sporadic exception, for that is a self-contradictory supposition but yet explicable in a general way. Explicability has no determinate & absolute limit."[78] Again, in the *form* of this statement, we find two contrary terms welded together. "Explicability" and "absolute chance" are two sides of the same coin, one always within the terms of the other—which is to say that the very *condition* of explicability involves the simultaneous asser-tion of a kernel of absolute chance that cannot be explicated and there-fore asserts the possibility of explicability in the first place. Chance as such is continually displaced to the *other* side but never done away with entirely. It is as if every gesture of inclusion paradoxically moves far-ther *inward*, leaving untouched a more fundamental exclusion, a process revealed in Louis H. Kauffman's description of the recursions of Peirce's semiotics: "There comes through the possibility of seeing anything at all the possibility of seeing a separate part. And so does the part become divided from the whole while still enfolded within it."[79] The distinction between part and whole takes place within the part.

In "Nominalist and Realist," Emerson writes, " 'Your turn now, my turn next,' is the rule of the game."[80] Or in "Intellect": "We are stung by desire for new thought; but when we receive a new thought, it is only the old thought with a new face, and though we make it our own, we instantly crave another; we are not really enriched."[81] It is new, and it is old. Again and again, we are thrown into a process constituted by the negation of the particular or individual for the sake of a greater general-ity. As Wolfe puts it, Emerson's project "directs us not to an originary fixed self-substance but toward a *power* and a *process*: not toward the past but toward the future, or rather toward futurity itself, conceived as a horizon, where, paradoxically, the only 'self' to recover is a self that one has not yet been, for the self *only* exists in its becoming."[82] Indeed, how else to take Peirce's declaration that "a person is not absolutely an indi-vidual. His thoughts are what he is 'saying to himself,' that is, saying to that other self that is just coming into life in the flow of time"?[83] This in turn echoes Emerson, who writes, "This one fact the world hates, that the soul becomes."[84] This is a leaving of the *ego* for the sake of the *nonego*, a dispersal of the present self for the sake of the future. The individual is subject to a certain *becoming* other, a *post*humanism. We find that even our selves are contingent—given over to the *other*, indeterminacy, futurity, or onwardness. We take sides against ourselves.

In a quite extraordinary essay titled "Evolutionary Love," Peirce mov-ingly ties these themes to an argument that love, quite like Luhmann's articulation of meaning, cannot abide its negative form: "Love cannot have a contrary, but must embrace what is most opposed to it."[85] On a somewhat similar note, Jacques Derrida writes, "If you love only those who love you and to the extent that they love you, if you hold so strictly to this symmetry, mutuality, and reciprocity, then you give nothing, no love. . . . In order to deserve or expect an infinitely higher salary, one that goes beyond the perception of what is due, you have to give without taking account and love those who don't love you."[86] This is, I think, the meaning of Emerson's vision of the universal benefit secured by private pain. It is also perhaps the gesture, a choosing of the *nonego*, that is contained within Peirce's astonishing moral: "Sacrifice your own perfection to the perfectionment of your neighbor."[87]

Do we not find here a call for taking on the burden of your own division to contribute to another's unity? Love is (the word insistently suggests itself) *asymmetrical*. It can be given but not received: "For self-love is no love."[88] And von Foerster: "Whatever happens to you happens to me. And whatever happens to me happens to you. And in so doing, someone gives you their life, and you give them yours."[89] And Peirce, once more: "Growth comes only from love, from—I will not say self-*sacrifice*, but from the ardent impulse to fulfil another's highest impulse."[90] And Emerson: "That which is so beautiful and attractive as these relations must be succeeded and supplanted only by what is more beautiful, and so on for ever."[91] And so on.

love → growth
(unity)

— 2 —

Inside-Out

Pragmatism and the Meaning of America

The actual universe is a thing wide open, but rationalism makes systems, and systems must be closed.

WILLIAM JAMES, *PRAGMATISM*

Philosophical thought in America is often distinguished from its European counterpart through what Cornel West has called pragmatism's "evasion of epistemology-centered philosophy," which is characteristic of pragmatism. West contends that pragmatism breaks with modern philosophy's pursuit of objective and ahistorical standards of truth and value—standards that might presume to describe the American essence prior to its existence—in order to insist instead on the historicist, situational, and contextual limits of thought in relation to experience and practice, an interpretation of "philosophy as a form of cultural criticism in which the meaning of America is put forward by intellectuals in response to distinct social and cultural crises."[1] "In this sense," he continues, "American pragmatism is less a philosophical tradition putting forward solutions to perennial problems in the Western philosophical conversation initiated by Plato and more a continuous cultural commentary or set of interpretations that attempt to explain America to itself at a particular historical moment."[2]

The idea that pragmatism can potentially articulate "the meaning of America" has special resonance for a nation with what is perhaps a unique need to account for itself. In this context, pragmatism represents the means of defining the parameters of the American community without reliance on tradition or authority—categories considered foreign to what is unique about the American experience. America, that is, has no recourse to standards of value or meaning outside of itself, and so America, much like modernity as a whole, finds itself left to its own devices. "What is American in philosophy," writes the similarly minded

John J. Stuhr, "is the use of the method of experience, not the endless cataloging of it independent of the context of its use, not the tedious formalization of its results into sacred categories. What is American is the emphasis on the continuity of belief and action *in experience*, not the mere assertion of this unity and continuity in theory alone."[3]

There is much to admire in this argument for the uniqueness and significance of American thought; it ably captures what is most compelling about the pragmatic tradition for which Charles S. Peirce's early essays—particularly "How to Make Our Ideas Clear" and "The Fixation of Belief"—laid the seeds. The ideas planted in those essays would decades later come to full bloom in the early-twentieth-century thought of William James and John Dewey, but even at this early stage Peirce's role in pragmatism was already dwindling. In the end, he was to be excluded almost entirely by the time Richard Rorty's galvanizing appropriation of pragmatism appeared after the "linguistic turn" of twentieth-century philosophy. In fact, as Rorty claims, "Peirce himself remained the most Kantian of thinkers—the most convinced that philosophy gave us an all-embracing ahistorical context in which every other species of discourse could be assigned its proper place and rank."[4] Such statements cast Peirce as representing the opposite of what is presumed to be the uniquely American contribution to philosophy. Indeed, as H. O. Mounce writes, "The development of Pragmatism from Peirce to Rorty exhibits a movement between two sets of ideas which are directly opposed to each other. The former may be taken as a paradigm of Realism; the latter of Anti-Realism. The two have nothing in common except that they are called by the same name."[5]

What is already clear in these understandings of the pragmatic tradition is that Peirce is the odd man out—a circumstance that uncannily echoes his exclusion from the educational establishment of his day, the extremes of isolation and poverty that he endured, and the near-total silence that greeted the immense intellectual output of his later years.[6] Despite the fact that West proclaims a "deep respect" for Peirce (a feeling, it must be said, that is quite evident in his sympathetic and perceptive readings of Peirce in *The American Evasion of Philosophy*) and even though he finds room, however slight, for Peirce at the table of contextual and historicist thought, the founder of pragmatism is demoted to something like a secondary status for his "preoccupation with logic."[7] Anyone familiar with Peirce's tireless advocacy for the primacy of logic in his work can easily imagine an undoubtedly indignant response to finding his pioneering logical experiments dismissively labeled a "preoccupation." However, what is at stake in these designations is something far more critical for pragmatism than a simple disinclination toward logic: the exclusion of Peirce from the pragmatic tradition reveals something important about how, as Tom Cohen has persuasively argued, the "neopragmatism" disseminated by West and Rorty performs a "misreading of its own pedigree,"[8] an evasion of "the very materiality (of language, of the sign) that *it* has implied from the start."[9] Moreover, if we accept West's claim that pragmatism is to be the means by which thought and criticism seek to "explain America to itself," then this pointed exclusion—of Peirce, of logic, of *theory*—also has something to tell us about America.

Cohen's critique of neopragmatism runs parallel to Peirce's well-known divergence from the earlier form of pragmatism disseminated by James, and together they begin to outline a very different kind of pragmatism, one that prefigures Cary Wolfe's call to "pursue pragmatism *on the site of theory*, one whose price is not the politically disabling repression of theory that has proved so tempting for pragmatism when its commitment to contingency becomes inconvenient."[10] As Wolfe argues, what is at issue here is the contingency of theoretical descriptions, a contingency that must in turn apply even to pragmatism itself. Pragmatism can no longer claim for itself, implicitly or explicitly, the necessity it has denied to theory. The distinction between pragmatism and theory is then called into question even at the very moment it is drawn. The thesis advocated here departs from Mounce's well-founded argument for "the two pragmatisms" by insisting instead on a form of pragmatism that can observe the excluded middle between them.

On one side of this divide is found James and Rorty, while Peirce presumably remains on pragmatism's *other* side—the side of theory. Peirce is therefore to be excluded from pragmatism's construction of an interiority in the form of either James's "pure experience" or what Rorty designates as the "ethnocentric" basis of communal values. The philosophies of James and Rorty (the paragons of Mounce's "antirealist" tradition) both attempt the occupation of something like a secure or immune "inside" from which to launch a critique of the "outside" impositions of theory, a gesture that Cohen describes as "a fairly mystified attempt to return to a space of the subject or self that pragmatism was implicitly designed to empty or exceed."[11]

As is well known, James attributed (perhaps too generously) the discovery of pragmatism to his old friend from Harvard. He recounts in *Pragmatism* that the idea "was first introduced into philosophy by Mr. Charles Peirce in 1878. In an article titled 'How to Make Our Ideas Clear,' in the 'Popular Science Monthly' for January of that year Mr. Peirce, after pointing out that our beliefs are really rules for action, said that, to develop a thought's meaning, we need only determine what conduct it is fitted to produce: that conduct is for us its sole significance."[12] James isolates Peirce's contribution in the claim that the meaning of any belief, idea, or theoretical concept is to be solely determined by the concrete effects or actions to which it leads. Meaning is no longer secured from above—from an objective, a priori, or transcendental position—but produced instead through the interaction of thinking and doing. Meaning is taken down from its transcendental perch and put to work *in* the world, and theory is thus no longer a self-sufficient description of objective truth but a tool or instrument designed to obtain particular ends.

Although presumably grateful for the tribute, Peirce took the opportunity to radically distinguish his philosophy from what was being offered to far greater acclaim by James. Christened by James but disowned and abandoned by its supposed father, pragmatism finds itself from the very beginning to be the product of a division within and against itself. It was a word, as Louis Menand notes, that no one wanted to claim:

> It is a minor peculiarity . . . that none of the principle figures who became indentified with pragmatism much liked the name. James used it only because it was the term he remembered Peirce coining back in their Metaphysical Club days; he would have preferred "humanism." . . . Peirce himself, who had never used the word in print until James's lecture, saw the chance he had been given to repackage his views with a label publicized by a celebrity; but he soon realized that the resemblance between his own thought and what James and Dewey were doing was not deep.[13]

In response, Peirce eventually coined "pragmaticism"—a term he claimed was "ugly enough to be safe from kidnappers."[14] There can be no doubt that posterity has proved him right in this assessment, but the word retains some fascination for imposing a certain ungainliness on its parent term, as if foregrounding its own artificiality or constructedness: pragmat(ic) ism. With some imaginative license, we may even claim that this word is for proper pragmatism something of an unwanted half-sibling. In keeping with Peirce's admitted incapacity for what he called "natural expression," it fails to roll off the tongue, imposing a kind of stutter or intrusive foreignness. The very act of speaking it suggests—even at the very beginning—that pragmatism's emphasis on the personal, contextual, and historical is disrupted from within by a kind of hiccup, a changing of tracks or reversal that inaugurates the reign of the impersonal, abstract, foreign, prosthetic, mechanical, technological, or theoretical. In this way, "pragmaticism" points to nothing less than the re-entry from within of pragmatism's excluded *other*—the contingency not just of theory, but of its own emergence.

Pragmaticism does not reject pragmatism but turns it in the other direction, to something *else* sometimes conceived as the horizon of an unlimited and indefinite community. Peirce argues that any determinate "inside" must continually renegotiate its borders with the continuity of an "outside" reality that remains unknown and irreducible. Against the rigid distinctions (inside and outside, antirealism and realism, experience and theory) constructed by pragmatism's inward turn, Peirce insists that reality is continuous, and further argues that any designation or determination of that continuity, any *part* of it, essentially involves a break with it: "It seems necessary to say that a continuum, where it *is* continuous and unbroken, contains no definite parts; that its parts are created in the act of defining them and the precise definition of them breaks the continuity."[15] Indeed, his reliance on the concept of continuity leads Peirce to write, "The truth is that pragmaticism is closely allied to the Hegelian absolute idealism, from which, however, it is sundered by its vigorous denial that the third category . . . suffices to make the world, or is even so much as self-sufficient."[16] We cannot grasp the world in passive intellectual reflection but must instead progressively determine it—and so the self-sufficient inside of pure continuity is automatically turned outside into the contingency of action and decision.

As Robin Robertson notes, this also means that reality, as continuous, is radically heterogeneous to any particular determination of it: "The continuum is an inexhaustible source of numbers but does not, itself, consist of points or numbers!"[17] And furthermore, as Matthew E. Moore points out, to determine a point on a continuous line does not produce autonomous individualities but instead produces parts that are "not points but continuous lines infinitely short."[18] In other words, breaking continuity produces parts that are both continuous (in themselves) *and* discontinuous with the larger whole, and in this way every determination leaves itself open to, and even necessitates, further determinations. As Moore explains, "Because reality is continuous, our theories and explanations can never be more than approximately correct, and can never attain such a pitch of precision and completeness that nothing remains to be explained."[19] Reality, in this sense, represents the *unity* of a determinate inside and an indeterminate outside.

Ultimately, this means that the distinction or boundary that separates inside from outside—the sorting mechanism for who or what belongs and who or what does not—becomes perpetually indefinite. In this respect, Peirce's thought has much in common with Ranulph Glanville and Francisco Varela's theoretical descriptions of the contingent nature of boundaries in a continuous field. In an essay inspired by the Beatles, "Your Inside Is Out and Your Outside Is In," Glanville and Varela write, "The edges dissolve BECAUSE the forms are themselves continuous— they re-enter and loop around themselves."[20] In other words, the boundaries between determinate forms are both distinct *and* continuous, closed *and* open. The act of *intension* (marking "inside") coinvolves *extension* (marking "outside"). The distinction, as the excluded middle between inside and outside, repeats or "re-enters" itself: "So the assertion of ultimate extension and intension requires the continuity of re-entry. And so, 'Your Inside is Out, and Your Outside is In,' for there are, for selves, no in and out sides, in the selves themselves, while for external observers the appearance of in and out sides necessitates the continuity of re-entry just because the act of distinguishing always implies just-one-more distinction. . . . Thus is the continuity of all things and no thing necessitated."[21] This difficult passage suggests that once a distinction between inside and outside is introduced a necessity for "re-entry," for "just-one-more distinction," is also introduced. Therefore, the difference between inside and outside becomes contingent, pragmatically motivated by the external observer (that is, the one observing/making the distinction: the "second-order" observer). In the same way, the inward turn of pragmatism's distinction between itself and theory is inevitably brought to loop around on itself in order to become pragmat(ic)ism: the inside is continually turned outside.

In order to flesh out this (rather abstract) argument—and then to deploy it in the service of a definition of community that runs counter to Rorty's idea of solidarity—it is first necessary to place the divergence between Peirce and James in context. In particular, Peirce's seemingly metaphysical conception of "reality" must be squared with adjectives like "indefinite" and "unlimited." The question on the table is rather simple: does Peirce's thought issue from an objective a priori that pragmatism would categorically deny? Though it is true that Peirce enthusiastically claimed the mantle of "realism," it is difficult to square a straightforward understanding of that term as an "all-embracing ahistorical context" with the fact that Peirce, as John Patrick Diggins notes, "often vacillated between idealism and realism, between the belief that objects are internal to the mind and that they exist independent of consciousness."[22] Peirce's indecision, implicitly a suggestion that the difference between realism and idealism is a matter of who is doing the observing, cuts right to the heart of the matter. His vacillations show that the birth of pragmatism in America was in fact the establishment of a split or breach with *itself*, which thus reintroduced a difference or distinction *within* pragmatism that changes not only our understanding of American intellectual history but also the meaning of the American community.

Face to Face: Immanence in American Thought

The assertion of a space apart from the formalisms of philosophy, what James calls "pure experience," is often claimed to be the quintessential gesture of American thought reaching at least as far back as Ralph Waldo Emerson. This form of thinking seeks to unite the characteristic divisions of modernity (mind and body, subject and object, self and other) through a more fundamental continuity in experience—a gesture principally accomplished by distinguishing the immediacy of actual experience from the formal abstractions of theory that pretend to describe it. Along these lines, James conceived pragmatism as a means of access to the *non*theoretical. As Martin Jay puts it, "Against the alienation of experience into the seemingly objective instruments of measurement that had characterized the scientific revolution . . . James wanted to reassert the primacy of the perceptual, embodied world."[23]

For many scholars, this reassertion of a "perceptual, embodied world" places James within a familiar tradition of American thought, a narrative that claims that James, along with forebears such as Ralph Waldo

Emerson and Jonathan Edwards, represents an ongoing rebellion against the religious inheritance of Calvinism and its picture of a material world principally characterized by what Calvin termed (with memorable bluntness) "total depravity." At the same time, however, pragmatism's critique of rationalism is indebted to that very same tradition. As John Patrick Diggins reminds us, "This issue, now called the 'logocentric fallacy,' may be as old as philosophy itself, and certainly as old as American history, which began, intellectually at least, with Calvinists warning us that all pretence to the sufficiency of reason amounts to the sin of pride."[24] Calvin's God, possessed of absolute omnipotence beyond even natural law, prefigures James's understanding of the excess or flux of nature in the manner of an absolute chaos irreducible to rationalistic description. The critical difference is that James would dissolve Calvinist dualisms in what he called a "pantheistic field of vision."[25] This means that if pragmatism is an inheritor of Calvinism, then it is so only in the sense that Calvinism set the terms that pragmatism would reverse; pragmatism overturns the content or truth-value assigned by Calvinist doctrine but keeps the same structuring logic. To better understand this gesture, one must look more closely at the Puritan theology against which James was rebelling. In this context, it can be argued that pragmatism's insistence on the contingency of theory (the contingency of science, rationalism, and "objective instruments of measurement") is predicated on a rejection of its *own* contingency, a fact reflected most starkly in James's reversal of Calvinist providentialism. This is a matter, to put it precisely, of human control versus divine will.

The Calvinist picture of the universe places nature to one side and God to the other, in essence vacating nature of any possible value. Truth, such as it is in this scheme, is always on the *other* or transcendent side of a distinction. Interestingly, James does not reject this scheme so much as reverse its truth-value, turning instead to what he calls "sensational immediacy," an immanent movement *inside* that "redeems the nature of reality from essential foreignness."[26] As Diggins notes, "If James was rescuing philosophy from science, he was also liberating modern religion from its Protestant heritage in Calvinist determinism."[27] For instance, in the early chapters of *A Pluralistic Universe* James rejects the "dualism and lack of intimacy"[28] of Christian Theism for a "vision of God as the indwelling divine rather than the external creator, and of human life as part and parcel of that deep reality."[29] How, we may ask, did American thought arrive at this point? How did what was the most *outside* become that which is closest and most intimate?

By way of answering that question, we may turn to Perry Miller's classic essay "The Marrow of Puritan Divinity" (1935). There Miller places his finger upon a tension in Puritan theology that, in the twists and turns of its unfolding, expressed one of the central intellectual problems of the eighteenth and nineteenth centuries. In sum, that tension stemmed from Calvin's intractable demand that his followers "contemplate, with steady, unblinking resolution, the absolute, incomprehensible, and transcendent sovereignty of God."[30] Faced as they were with the practical necessity of survival in an unfamiliar wilderness as well as the creation and maintenance of a religious community that could serve as a shining example to all of European Christendom, the early American Puritans found that squaring these demands was an impossibly tall order. As Miller tells it, the Puritans found themselves confronting a common intellectual dilemma of the seventeenth century: how to reconcile a material world utterly devoid of grace with an affirmation of human agency? To what extent is the universe knowable, and how may we know it "without reducing the Divinity to a mechanism, without depriving Him of unpredictability, absolute power, fearfulness, and mystery"?[31] How is intimacy with either God or nature possible on these conditions? In practice, they could only attempt to artificially constrain divine sovereignty through a covenant that provided a stable and knowable world, thus "bringing God to time and reason."[32]

This terms of this dilemma derived from what Herschel Baker has called the "anthropocentric" premises of seventeenth-century theologies: "In the main stream of Christian humanism man's prestige was immense; in the theology which Calvin had revived primarily to combat such optimism man's degradation was made the pivotal fact of history. The seventeenth century, inheriting both views, spent its best efforts, as we shall see, in trying to resolve the antinomy."[33] With Thomas Aquinas representing one pole and Calvin the other, Baker argues that both take as their point of departure an essential humanism, or just as essentially its negative mirror image:

> By emphasizing one rather than another of its components St. Thomas could construct his massive theology of reason, Calvin his of will—but both the Angelic Doctor and the Tyrant of Geneva were securely within

the limits of the Christian epic. Their views of man were radically different, yet both derived from the central tradition of western thought. They appeared to be primarily concerned with the nature of God, and to adjust all the facts of the physical, spiritual, and moral universe to God; yet at the hidden center of both their systems was man—essentially good or essentially bad—and the whole universe took its meaning with reference to him, his nature, and his needs. Their systems were of course theistic, but the main lines of those systems radiated from an anthropocentric hub.[34]

The Puritans found themselves torn in two directions: "They wished to preserve untainted the sovereignty of God, yet they were reluctant to leave man and nature in the hopeless iniquity described by the early Reformers."[35] They could not depend for security on an intuitive rational consciousness—nor could they, as Calvin may have wished, cast themselves entirely upon the whims of Divine providence.

In a succession of beautifully written and still incisive works, Miller investigated this dilemma and the series of compromises it entailed, sketching a vivid picture of the Puritan as a hopelessly conflicted figure, one marked through the very foundation of his or her being with a breach: an emerging modern subject that nonetheless turns upon the supposed rational certainty that subjecthood guarantees as suspect at best and as impious blasphemy at worst. Moreover, charged with the contradictory aims of modern rational humanism *and* providentialist Calvinism, the Puritan was in a unique position to observe the contingency of the reductionist basis of modern science. This was the *other* side of scientific determinism as represented in the form of God's absolute sovereignty. As Baker notes,

> Though among the most zealous devotees of the doctrine of providence, the Puritans were not unsympathetic to science or to a Baconian scrutiny of natural processes. None the less, they insisted that providence be acknowledged as the surest sign of God's sovereignty, for unless they could keep inviolate the heart of God's sovereignty and mystery from the claims of rationalism and natural philosophy, they would gut their theology and forfeit their title as Puritans. They never honestly met the philosophical difficulties of their Augustinian-Baconian position; but men who could believe simultaneously in predestination and Ramean logic

would certainly have no trouble in assuming that, though God ordinarily permits nature to act by second causes, He can at any moment disrupt them for His own inscrutable purposes.[36]

Likewise, Miller describes the covenant of the American Puritans as an ingenious attempt to overcome the difficulties that Baker describes, though it is one marked inexorably by a "fundamental distrust."[37] The Puritan finds himself attempting to describe and delineate the laws of Nature, to find what he may rely upon, while simultaneously pledging his faith to a fearsomely powerful and unknowable God who reserves the right to change those laws as He sees fit: "Most of the issues that were so hotly contested among seventeenth-century theologians were connected with attempts to resolve this discrepancy between the God of everyday providence and the God who dispensed His grace according to no rule but His own pleasure."[38] No easy task, and one only exasperated by the absolute demands made on either end. For, as Miller again and again points out, "It is of the essence of this theology that God, the force, the power, the life of the universe, remains to men hidden, unknowable, unpredictable. He is the ultimate secret, the awful mystery. God's nature 'is capable properly of no definition,' so that all that one can say is that 'God is an incomprehensible, first, and absolute Being.' He cannot be approached directly; man cannot stand face to face with Him."[39] This essence, Calvin's radical challenge to the prevailing religious order and the driving force of the Reformation by Miller's estimation, does not provide an alternative to the political and social structures of the day so much as it utterly annihilates them in order to pave the way to an unadulterated experience of grace. Delivered over to God, the Puritan returns to find a fallen material world stripped of all intrinsic value.

Nature, in this scheme, unexpectedly finds resonance with the mechanical systems of cause and effect described by modern science, leading Baker to argue that Calvinism's austere distinction between God and creation can be seen as running parallel to Cartesian dualism: "Obsessed with the impious claim of man's natural faculties for achieving a life of rational well-being, Calvin made the whole realm of nature the sink of corruption, alien from the realm of grace. Theologically, he fractured the medieval synthesis as sharply as Descartes would fracture it philosophically."[40] By vacating the material world of all spiritual value, Calvinism ironically enabled a dualism that would seek to delineate the world as a predictable mechanical system and thus, little by little, constrain God's ability to surprise us. This was in fact the unavoidable outcome of the attempt to preserve God's absolute sovereignty in the face of the technological and scientific progress of modernity, and so God was in effect further and further removed from the domain of material creation. While modern philosophy would take this ball and run with it into the end zone of certainty guaranteed by the rational subject, the Puritan found him- or herself unable to do the same without a little (or a lot of) guilt about the matter. As Joan Richardson has observed, "A persistently disturbing element of this environment . . . was/is the incommensurability of nature, its unavailability to the categories of description embedded in the language of the settlers. Nature literally amazed them."[41]

Needless to say, the encroachment of an unapproachable natural world above and beyond language was a critical threat to the task of building an exemplary community in the wilderness of North America. The Puritans found themselves wrestling with the unadulterated sovereignty of the Calvinist God, a potentially chaotic force uncannily represented in physical terms by a severe and unforgiving wilderness awaiting Christian civilization and populated by natives who in their seemingly inscrutable motives alternately represented God's wrath and Satan's temptations. Nature, likewise, is both beyond any possible description and yet also the passive object of scientific scrutiny. How, then, to reconcile these extremes? As Miller writes, "Calvinism could no longer remain the relatively simple dogmatism of its founder. It needed amplification, it required concise explication, syllogistic proof, intellectual as well as spiritual focus. It needed, in short, the one thing which, at bottom, it could not admit—a rationale."[42]

Miller shows that the Puritans sought to reconcile the irreconcilable through a divine covenant. God would of his own free will abide by certain rules: "For all ordinary purposes He has transformed Himself in the covenant into a God vastly different from the inscrutable Divinity of pure Calvinism. He has become a God chained—by His own consent, it is true, but nevertheless a God restricted and circumscribed—a God who can be counted upon, a God who can be lived with. Man can always know where God is and what He intends."[43] Thus assured, the practical project of the "shining city on the hill" could continue unthreatened by the very same irresistible force that propelled it into being: "To describe this theology as 'rationalism' would be very much to overstate the case. . . . But in this way of thought appears an entering wedge of what must be called, if not rationalism, then reasonableness."[44]

One need not dwell long upon this bargain to determine something untenable in it. Inevitably, there is a missing piece in the foundation, an incompleteness or hole through which the irrational can always sneak back in—something lurking on the *outside*, waiting for its chance to upset the applecart of rational system building:

> The Puritan, as long as he remained a Puritan, could never banish entirely from his mind the sense of something mysterious and terrible, of something that leaped when least expected, something that upset all regularizations and defied all logic, something behind appearances that could not be tamed and brought to heel by men. The covenant thought kept this divine liberty at several removes, placed it on a theoretical plane, robbed it of much of its terror, but it could not do away with it entirely.[45]

This threat, this fundamental distrust, represents the crux of Miller's argument, which is not so much about the Puritan's repression of the real force of Calvinism as about their *inability* to do precisely that. An open environment continually threatened the security of closed systems, a dilemma that seemingly runs parallel to modern philosophy's attempts to secure an equation of the universe only to have it unbalanced by unexpected remainders. However, despite this similarity, the Puritan mind is not fully synonymous with the modern mind that attempts in Cartesian fashion to place a grid over all experience, to make the real into the ideal forms and figures of geometry. Instead, the Puritan recognizes that the remainder, that which passes just out of sight of the formal strictures of his descriptions, represents the very force and meaning of his entire project.

For these reasons the Puritan could hardly rely on the foundational claims of the emerging modern subject, a figure that was, as Leigh Eric Schmidt notes, already an inherently anxious construct: "The construction of an autonomous modern subject, at once certain of an authentic voice and ever afraid of falling to pieces, turned the noises of an eruptive divine world into dangerous signs of inward multiplicity."[46] This anxiety was, of course, also inherited by James, but his solution was not the relentless self-policing of the Puritans documented by Miller and others. Instead, James turned inward to embrace the potentially dangerous exuberance and "inward multiplicity" of feeling as a means of preserving and purifying an interior space apart from foreign impositions. While the Puritan could be said to face a formidable double bind between the impossibility of a self-grounding "inside" and an unknowable and uncontainable "outside," James insists that one be grounded in the other.

For pragmatism, the inviolable distinction between the Creator and creation re-enters into itself on the side of creation and transforms into a distinction between scientific determinism (the material world as machine) and its human observer. In this fashion, the world assumes the characteristic determinisms of science, but the extraneous element transforms from God's sovereignty into man's through the control mechanisms afforded by science. Thought transitions from being a mediation between man and God to being instead a tool at man's disposal—in turn producing man as the *user* of tools. James describes this transition in decidedly theological terms: "The trail of the human serpent is thus over everything. Truth independent; truth that we *find* merely; truth no longer malleable to human need; truth incorrigible, in a word; such truth exists indeed superabundantly . . . but then it means only the dead heart of the living tree."[47] Truth is not transcendent or "outside" but produced only through a living engagement with nature. Faced with modernity's vision of the universe as an immense and impersonal machine, James stakes a claim for the primacy of human personality.

The impersonal God of the Puritans is thereby emphatically rejected: "The place of the divine in the world," writes James, "must be more organic and intimate."[48] In common understandings of American thought, this claim has roots that reach as far back as Jonathan Edwards. Most prominently, in his "From Edwards to Emerson" (1940), Miller presents Edwards as the harbinger of a distinctly American mystical tradition that endeavors to experience God, as it were, face to face: "What is persistent, from the covenant theology (and from the heretics against the covenant) to Edwards and to Emerson, is the Puritan's effort to confront, face to face, the image of a blinding divinity in the physical universe, and to look upon that universe without the intermediacy of ritual, of ceremony, of the Mass and the confessional."[49] Miller's notion of the search for a "face to face" encounter that extends from Edwards to Emerson forms the backbone of a particularly influential understanding of American thought, a humanist genealogy that culminates in the pragmatism of James as well as the neopragmatist revival initiated by Richard Rorty.

In a preface to "From Edwards to Emerson," written in 1956 for the publication of his important collection *Errand into the Wilderness*, Miller immediately blunts any easy comparisons between his subjects: "There can be no doubt that Jonathan Edwards would have abhorred from the bottom of his soul every proposition Ralph Waldo Emerson blandly put forth in the manifesto of 1836, *Nature*."[50] Indeed, it would seem on the face of it difficult to see any link from Edwards to Emerson at all:

> Could he have lived long enough to witness the appearance in New England of "transcendentalism," he would have beheld in it the logical and predictable collapse of the "liberal" theology which, in New England, became institutionalized as Unitarianism. If Edwards ever laughed, then he would have laughed—along with the other theologians of his party, few of whom were given to laughter—over the discomfiture of the Unitarians upon discovering a heresy in *their* midst, but I suspect he would have seen even more vividly than did the Princeton pundits the threat which the gentle Emerson raised against everything Edwards stood for. In that strictly historical regard, then, there is no organic evolution of ideas from Edwards to Emerson.[51]

No *organic* evolution then, but Miller's argument depends not so much on the content of their philosophies as on their formal gestures. No identity of doctrinal belief or continuity of content but a turn or orientation, a step outside into nature that initiates an ineluctable progression inward:

> The real difference between Edwards and Emerson, if they can thus be viewed as variants within their culture, lies not in the fact that Edwards was a Calvinist while Emerson rejected all systematic theologies, but in the quite other fact that Edwards went to nature, in all passionate love, convinced that man could receive from it impressions which he must then try to interpret, whereas Emerson went to Nature, no less in love with it, convinced that in man there is a spontaneous correlation with the received impressions.[52]

Miller goes on to say that one might

> define Emerson as an Edwards in whom the concept of original sin has evaporated. . . . Edwards sought the "images or shadows of divine things"

in nature, but could not trust his discoveries because he knew man to be cut off from full communion with the created order because of his inherent depravity. But Emerson, having decided that man is unfallen, . . . announced that there is no inherent separation between the mind and the thing, that in reality they leap to embrace each other.[53]

If we leave aside for now the implicit suggestion of a continuity between Emerson's early thought and his later thought (of which, if nothing else, one cannot claim the absence of an "inherent separation"), it seems that Miller's claim may be easily extended: Edwards inaugurates a turn toward nature in search of a trace of the divine, a turn that becomes for Emerson, once the foreign imposition of original sin is abandoned and the mediating form of a shadow is no longer needed, a direct experience of the divine *in* nature. Finally, James places paramount value on a direct and personal intimacy with experience, an insistence on an immanence or immediacy that remains irreducible to the descriptive claims of conceptual thought. In this lineage, Edwards's search for the divine beyond nature becomes the discovery of immanence *in* nature, a space that resists the foreign impositions of science and philosophy and proclaims the inward sovereignty of a "sense of the heart." Ultimately, man claims possession of the open environment by turning away from inhuman or impersonal abstractions, and so that which is fundamentally *outside* is taken *inside*, domesticated and appropriated as the interior space of a turn away from the inhuman and impersonal tide of scientific and materialist determinism.

This is a satisfying narrative principally because it presumes a fundamental identity concerning the progress of secularization in American thought in the centuries after Edwards, a familiar journey away from medieval superstition or authority and toward modern humanism. For instance, Joan Richardson's exceptional study *A Natural History of Pragmatism* may be considered as an ideal recent example of this narrative. Richardson defines the pragmatic tradition as "the realization of thinking as a life form, subject to the same processes of growth and change as all other life forms."[54] Much as in Miller's "face to face" encounters, this organic form of thinking depends on what Richardson calls an experience of the "aesthetic" involving recourse to "expressions of the feelings earlier embodied in purely religious forms, prayers, and rituals."[55] Richardson conceives pragmatism as thought in relation to its environment, and her choice of subjects is distinguished in particular by what she says of Edwards, whose "faithful recording in linguistic forms mimetic of the conditions under which his perceptions developed provides invaluable documentation of a mind coming to know itself in a new relation to an environment."[56]

What is most compelling about Richardson's argument for the continuity of the tradition first identified by Miller is the suggestion that it undergoes a change from a religiously mediated experience to a secular and aesthetic one, a transformation (and here one cannot fail to note a tinge of romanticism) that she explicitly characterizes as "naturalization." As she puts it, "While the figures who are my subjects understood the role of the American writer to be a religious one, it was with a sense of religion naturalized and at the same time returned to its purest etymological meaning as 'binding together'—in this case, binding perception to the order of things."[57] Richardson shows the progress of a certain idea of religious experience, from outer and literal to inner, private, and subjective—an astute and powerful narrative that descends in many respects from James's pioneering studies of religious experience. Consider *The Varieties of Religious Experience*, where James argues for a distinction between received religious belief and that which issues from personal experience. Speaking of a nonreflective religious type, he writes,

> His religion has been made for him by others, communicated to him by tradition, determined to fixed forms by imitation, and retained by habit. It would profit us little to study this second-hand religious life. We must make search rather for the original experiences which were the pattern-setters to all this mass of suggested feeling and imitated conduct. These experiences we can only find in individuals for whom religion exists not as a dull habit, but as an acute fever rather.[58]

This sense of religion as fever derives from what he calls "moments of sentimental and mystical experience . . . that carry an enormous sense of inner authority and illumination with them when they come."[59]

Similarly, Richardson finds in formerly religious forms of experience the means of uniting modernity's divisions, a form of "grace understood as fact informed by feeling."[60] In such heightened moments—recurrences

of secularized, romanticized, and organic transformations of feeling—
she observes a life-form negotiating its environment:

> In America the combined threat of nature and the fragility of the body
> politic provided the *occasion* whereby propositions implicit in the Lock-
> ean theory of language became what Whitehead calls *lures for feeling*:
> in this setting, for feeling the anomie attendant on the breakdown of the
> old order of things. . . . As Whitehead observes, it is the translation of
> the welter of emotional experience in the face of "stubborn fact" . . .
> into a private, self-conscious form that marks the aesthetic. In the case
> of the American experience, the imported theological framework inap-
> propriately structures this aesthetic translation.[61]

Here the emotional or aesthetic experience is irreducible to conceptual
thought, or as she writes (quoting Emerson), "Words failed in 'this new
yet unapproachable America.' "[62] For Richardson, it is this confrontation
with the irreducible that produces the relational type of thinking that
would come to be expressed in pragmatism.

Richardson seeks in her subjects a secular representation of the "face to
face" encounter: "The solutions these writers found to fill the anguished
space, the expanding void opened by the gradual disappearance of God,
were, in the most primary sense, aesthetic."[63] In this respect, the aesthetic
also performs the role of a resource or *capacity of access* possessed by the
human subject. The experiences evoked by Richardson, and indeed evoked
by the texts she perceptively writes about, are the presentation of a binding
wholeness that represents the limits of conceptual thought—a limit taken
within and appropriated, or indeed *represented*, in the texts she examines.
The outside, however briefly, is fully observable, the difference is healed,
and unity is presumed as a "binding together"—and this would seem to
be the product of a capacity to experience and then express the primacy
of aesthetic experience or feeling in contrast to the foreign abstractions of
philosophy or even language itself. An identity between thought and feeling is then expressed in the fleeting momentary experience of the aesthetic.

It is also possible to see in this narrative a turning that rejects the foreignness and monstrosities of conceptual thought in the service of a construction of an identical inner self, a carving out of a space of interiority
and freedom that may remain inviolable to the threat of determinism

so vividly invoked by James. Here what is distinctly human risks being overwhelmed by the rising waters of determinism, shrunken to nothingness in the infinite expanse of the ocean, only to respond through the embrace of humanism as a kind of purification achieved in the distinction between thought and feeling. Most tellingly, Richardson excludes none other than Charles S. Peirce from her study of pragmatism because his texts do not appear to express the capacity for feeling: "Peirce has not been chosen . . . because, while he certainly did describe throughout his writing the effects of Darwin's theory on the process of thinking, on the refashioning of logic, on perceptual categories, his concern was not that his texts themselves serve as the corrective lenses through which this new universe of chance could be perceived."[64] This is a revealing omission. Peirce does not express an adaptive relationship to an environment *in* his writing. In fact, as we will see in some detail, Peirce quite pointedly excludes the expression of that relationship.

To step back briefly into a broader context, the evolution of humanism from Edwards to Emerson and then James may be seen to run parallel to a similar story on the European continent. In a pair of illuminating studies, Michael Allen Gillespie traces the fate of the "nominalist God" that so terrorized premodern intellectuals: "This idea of God came to predominance in the fourteenth century and shattered the medieval synthesis of philosophy and theology, catapulting man into a new way of thinking and being, a *via moderna* essentially at odds with the *via antiqua*. This new way was in turn the foundation for modernity as the realm of human self-assertion."[65] Modernity, in Gillespie's reading, is achieved through the construction of a fortress of selfhood that acts as a defense against divine whims:

It is the story of the way in which the late medieval conception of an omnipotent God inspired and informed a new conception of man and nature that gave precedence to will over reason and freedom over necessity and order. . . . Scholasticism rested on the assumption that God and the cosmos are essentially rational. Nominalism argued that it contradicts God's divinity to assume that he is subordinate to nature or reason. The intention of this critique was to reaffirm the importance of scripture, but its effect was to sever reason and revelation. It thus liberated natural science from the constraints of religion and opened the door for empiricism, but it also established an omnipotent divine will unrestrained by any rational notion of the good. The nominalist revolution thus fostered a growing doubt about the ground of science and morality in a cosmos ruled by a willful, transrational God. The rise of natural science is consequently concomitant with the rise of universal doubt. To secure himself and his science, man must build ramparts against divine caprice or malevolence. The first to raise such ramparts was Descartes.[66]

According to Gillespie, Descartes, because he identified thinking with willing, initiated "the secularization of the idea of divine omnipotence"[67] and thereby opened up a space of human freedom: "Man is thus free only within the circle of his self thinking. Outside this bastion of reason, the chaos set loose by the possibility of a malicious God still reigns."[68]

Back in America, a parallel development passes from Edwards to the Emerson of "Self-Reliance" and then culminates with James, in particular his immensely influential essay of 1896, "The Will to Believe." There James makes a foundational claim that underlies much of his later philosophy: "There is but one indefectibly certain truth, and that is the truth that pyrrhonistic scepticism itself leaves standing—the truth that the present phenomenon of consciousness exists."[69] The theme of that important essay concerns man's place in an impersonal cosmos. James insists on the necessity of feeling as the excluded condition of scientific and philosophical thought and ends with a moral: "We ought . . . delicately and profoundly to respect one another's mental freedom."[70] Each man, he contends, retains the absolute freedom of his own inner kingdom.

The Control of Control

The scope of the practical control of nature newly put into our hand by scientific ways of thinking vastly exceeds the scope of the old control grounded on common sense. Its rate of increase accelerates so that no one can trace the limit; one may even fear that the *being* of man may be crushed by his own powers, that his fixed nature as an organism may not prove adequate to stand the strain of the ever increasingly tremendous functions, almost divine creative functions, which his intellect will more and more enable him to wield. He may drown in his wealth like a child in a bath-tub, who has turned on the water and who can not turn it off.

WILLIAM JAMES, *PRAGMATISM*

This section argues that the pragmatic turn away from theory is accomplished *through* theory, a thorough "instrumentalization" of thought that carves out an internal space of freedom apart from materialism or determinism—what I will call a designated space of control. In what follows, the particular sense of the term "control" is borrowed from James Beniger's groundbreaking study *The Control Revolution*. Scant justice can be done to the full scope of his important book here, but Beniger's principal point is relatively straightforward: "The Industrial Revolution and the harnessing of inanimate sources of energy to material processes more generally led inevitably to an increased need for control."[71] Moreover, control technologies operate through channeling flows of energy or information into determinate frameworks. As he writes, "Control can be increased not only by increasing the capability to process information but also by decreasing the amount of information to be processed."[72] Control, in other words, is accomplished through the *reduction* of information—and this is the only basis on which further action can be taken.

The necessity for a reduction of information, as well as the consequent recognition of the selected information's contingency (the fact that *other* or different reductions or determinations can also be accomplished), is in fact the critical insight of pragmatism. As Isabelle Stengers has argued, pragmatism represents "a thinking that accepts as a constraint the exclusion of every idea that implies, among its consequences, a transmutation of *our* reasons into *Reason*."[73] Pragmatism, in this sense, represents a control *of* control. Put differently, if the profusion of theoretical or philosophical perspectives within modernity represents exemplary forms of control, then pragmatism points to the fact that such theoretical or conceptual framings operate by means of one-sided or asymmetrical distinctions—sorting mechanisms that generate information only at the expense of leaving something *else* out. In this way, pragmatism points to what theory cannot see (notably, as Stengers points out, its own multiplicity and contingency) and so holds theory accountable for what escapes its descriptions. As James put it, "The whole system of experiences as they are immediately given presents itself as a quasi-chaos through which one can pass out of an initial term in many directions and yet end in the same terminus, moving from next to next by a great many alternative paths."[74]

That fascinating passage demonstrates at once the great insight into control that James offers while also pointing to the core of the problem with it. The "immediately given" or "quasi-chaos," or what James refers to later in the same essay as "a simple *that*, as yet undifferentiated into thing and thought,"[75] presents a certain wholeness or totality to consciousness. This simple *that* remains always prior to its articulation—something Peirce described early on as the semiotic category of "Firstness":

> The First must therefore be present and immediate, so as not to be second to a representation. It must be initiative, original, spontaneous, and free; otherwise it is second to a determining cause. It is also something vivid and conscious; so only it avoids being the object of some sensation. It precedes all synthesis and all differentiation: it has no unity and no parts. It cannot be articulately thought: assert it, and it has already lost its characteristic innocence; for assertion always implies a denial of something else. Stop to think of it, and it has flown![76]

It is perhaps true that James would find much to agree with in this passage, and it may be said that the great connecting thread between James and Peirce remains this emphasis on a certain continuity in experience, but James's thought nevertheless moves in the opposite direction through a possession and control of what Peirce claims cannot be caught. If Peirce, as the passage already implies, develops a logic and a semiotics to describe the progressive and partial *determination* of the undetermined ("assertion always implies a denial of something else"), then James seeks to climb back up that same ladder for the sake of making different and better determinations—the assertion of a simple *that* without a consequent denial. If Peirce's understanding of determination is asymmetric or irreversible, then James asserts the symmetry of a reversible system. For James, we are fundamentally at home in the quasi-chaos—or more precisely, it is at home *in* us. It is the true substance and reality of our conscious lives, that which we always return to, and through this continual return, it operates as a space from which human agency and control can be exerted. The ultimate problem with this, simply put, is not pragmatism's critique of theory, but the fact that pragmatism presumes for itself the wholeness or unity it denies to theory.

In "A World of Pure Experience," James takes pains to distinguish his "radical empiricism" from traditional empiricism by stressing that "radical empiricism . . . is fair to both the unity and the disconnection" in our experience.[77] He continues, "The holding fast to this relation means taking it at its face value, neither less nor more; and to take it at its face value means first of all to take it just as we feel it, and not to confuse ourselves with abstract talk *about* it."[78] What is described here as "disconnection" or "relation" represents what contemporary thought prefers to call "difference"—but what James is really driving at is in fact an underlying *continuity*: the continuity of discontinuity (to use a formulation with Hegelian overtones that would undoubtedly have horrified him) that adheres in actual experience. Pure experience takes the relation *as it is*, at "face value," "neither less nor more." As James writes in the same essay, "There is no other *nature*, no other whatness than this absence of break and this sense of continuity in that most intimate of all conjunctive relations, the passing of one experience into another when they belong to the same self."[79] Here something like a personal and continuous *self* emerges in order to ground the claim that "pure experience" is an experience of continuity. This inner self claims access to nature; it is the nub around which—and within which—the quasi-chaos swirls.

It is from the possession of this inward space of continuity that pragmatism stages its critique of modernity and rationalism, a space that James in particular is apt to give the name of "nature." Here what is most personal or "inside" is united with what is most "outside." In the famous lecture of 1906 that bore the title of the new American philosophy of pragmatism, James declares that his thinking calls on "the open air and possibilities of nature, as against dogma, artificiality, and the pretence of finality in truth."[80] Later, in *A Pluralistic Universe*, he writes that nature is "a name for excess; every point in her opens out and runs into the more."[81] Such claims place James within a familiar tradition in American thought, what he called—using a phrase that cannot help but anticipate Miller's "From Edwards to Emerson"—an "attitude of orientation"[82] as opposed to a set of static doctrines. This orientation is informed, in particular, by Emerson's notion in *Nature* of an "original relationship to the universe" in opposition to the inhuman and unnatural abstractions of European metaphysics. Ideas are not isolated representations of abstract truth; they are in contact with a natural world—an excess, a flux, or an overflowing that surges past the confinements of conceptual thought. Philosophy thus runs up against its limits through contact with nature understood as a vast openness in contrast to the closed systems of the purely rational. Nature is the space of abandonment, a path of flight from the prisons constructed by the strictures of language.

Nature, it is already clear, occupies a privileged and at the same time highly fraught position in pragmatist thought: it is both the outward plentitude, the unlimited external condition of thought, *and* the immediate inner life of sensation. James addresses this duality directly as "the paradox that what is evidently one reality should be in two places at once, both in outer space and in a person's mind."[83] The solution is again the notion of pure experience:

> The puzzle of how the one identical room can be in two places is at bottom just the puzzle of how one identical point can be on two lines. It can, if it be situated at their intersection; and similarly, if the "pure experience" of the room were a place of intersection of two processes, which connected it with different groups of associates respectively, it could be counted twice over, as belonging to either group, and spoken of loosely as existing in two places, although it would remain all the time a numerically single thing.[84]

In this respect, the pure experience at the heart of pragmatism represents something like a point of contact between nominally opposed categories. Nature offers to the personal self the space of an inward *turn*, a liminal space or "intersection" that provides at the same time a capacity for disengagement that frees us from the grip of impersonal absolutes.

Turning to nature turns inward to the resources of personal feeling—or more precisely it is an act of *turning* because in the completion of a turn one merely faces in a new form the totalizing grasp of a theoretical or conceptual apparatus. "Turn your face toward sensation," James urges, "that flesh-bound thing which rationalism has always loaded with abuse."[85] Our thoughts may be inherently belated, but the thought of pragmatism makes it possible to pass through the potentially disruptive interface between thinking and feeling, a hinge in the very forming of our theoretical concepts. In this respect, as Giles Gunn notes, pragmatism is "beyond ideology and transcendence alike not because it can escape their superventions but only because it can resist their simplifications."[86] The power of this resistance, what might be termed the source of its capacity for control, resides in this turn toward the immediacy of feeling or sensation—a realm that defies the defacement of its expression in formal thought or language.

Pragmatism thus turns away from what James calls the "foreignness and monstrosity" of concepts and absolutes:[87] "Take any *real* bit, suppress its environment and then magnify it to monstrosity, and you get identically the type of structure of the absolute."[88] With such concepts, one finds that "in the deeper sense of giving *insight* they have no theoretic value, for they quite fail to connect us with the inner life of the flux, or with the causes that govern its direction. Instead of being interpreters of reality, concepts negate the inwardness of reality altogether."[89] Again, this emphasis on "insight," together with the use of "inner" and "inwardness," demonstrates a movement *inside*, an insistence on the continuity of what is intimate, immanent, and immediate. For James, as Frank Lentricchia argues, "Immediate experience is the single generative ground of knowing and being, the last and only Garden of modern man, the Eden from which he, in his radical autonomy, can be expelled only by himself, by an exercise of the simultaneously redemptive and self-damning transmutational powers of his own mind, by his desire to create a world apart from the one immediately, blessedly given."[90] The inner life of feeling is forever being spoiled.

James's idea of the pragmatic method is a turn away from theory and toward the continuity of pure experience, a retreat back to a space of sovereign control: "A pragmatist turns his back resolutely and once for all upon a lot of inveterate habits dear to professional philosophers. He turns away from abstraction and insufficiency, from verbal solutions, from bad *a priori* reasons, from fixed principles, closed systems, and pretended absolutes and origins. He turns towards concreteness and adequacy, towards facts, towards action and towards power."[91] As Gunn notes, James wants "consciousness to explore what yet remained ineffable and undecidable but still irrepressible on its own borders. James spoke of this as the 're-instatement of the vague to its proper place in our mental life.' What he meant by 'the vague' was that whole mysterious shadow world of feeling, intuition, implication, conjunction, disjunction, and change that undergirds cognition and motivates action."[92] The upshot of this "re-instatement" is, as James notes explicitly, a kind of humanism: "In our cognitive as well as in our active life we are creative. We *add*, both to the subject and to the predicate part of reality. The world stands really malleable, waiting to receive its final touches at our hands. Like the kingdom of heaven, it suffers human violence willingly. Man *engenders* truths upon it."[93] This engendering of truth is, as noted at the outset of this section, accomplished through control as the very determination or reduction of the plenum accessed in pure experience.

If it is accepted that the "awareness of the dualism between nature and spirit that enhances the means of control while diminishing a conception of moral ends might be regarded as one definition of the modernist sensibility,"[94] then pragmatism doubles down on this sensibility by affirming the control *of* control. In this respect, pragmatism represents a dual-minded reaction to the rising tide of scientific determinism in the nineteenth century, what Max Weber famously described as "the disenchantment of the world." Consequent upon the discoveries of Newton, Darwin, and Clausius was the realization of the world as a faceless, even monstrous, mechanical system—a world, it seemed increasingly likely, that must do without the guiding hand of divine providence. Taking control in God's place were impersonal mechanisms like natural law, evolution, and entropy. An anxious question arose in response to these developments: where does all this leave the self-determined "being" of man?

In his important study of American religious experience as the manifestation of counter-Enlightenment tendencies, Leigh Eric Schmidt describes modernity as the "devocalization" of the world: a privileging of sight (the objective and impersonal observational stance of science) at the expense of the passive or receptive qualities of hearing (one might call this knowledge of the *unseen*) that ultimately results in modernity's abandonment of the "primacy of the living voice over the dead letter."[95] Working within and against this tradition, James describes modernity as the depersonalization of the world, and Jacques Barzun goes so far as to argue that James was "the man who showed that 'personality' is an elemental force among others in the cosmos."[96] James campaigned against what he called the "systematic denial on science's part of personality as a condition of events" and its belief that "in its own essential and innermost nature our world is a strictly impersonal world."[97] He was "preoccupied with self-knowledge, introspection, and personal consciousness."[98] Indeed, the great majority of James's psychological and philosophical output is concerned with the inability of modern scientific and rational thought to fully represent the flux of private conscious experience, and his thought capitalizes on this failure in order to preserve and protect an inner space of feeling apart from impersonal mechanisms of control.

As James often points out, science offers a means of increased control over the natural world that is purchased at the expense of individual human agency—that is, science offers humanity a means of control while at the same time threatening to control in turn. Seen in this way, the "instrumentalization" of thought accomplished by pragmatism simultaneously represents both the apotheosis of and a powerful reaction against the emergence of control technologies in the late nineteenth century. In this context, James's descriptions of the intellectual landscape of his day are compelling principally for their underlying anxiety, a sense that as such controls extend ever further they may engulf even man himself. As Lentricchia has ingeniously argued, James's model of selfhood valiantly turns the market-based logic of private property against itself in order to "preserve a human space of freedom, however interiorized, from the vicissitudes and coercions of the marketplace."[99] Along these same lines, James is often at his most lyrical when describing a world *without* human freedom, as in "The Will to Believe":

When one turns to the magnificent edifice of the physical sciences, and sees how it was reared; what thousands of disinterested moral lives of men lie buried in its mere foundations; what patience and postponement, what choking down of preference, what submission to the icy laws of outer fact are wrought into its very stones and mortar; how absolutely impersonal it stands in its vast augustness—then how besotted and contemptible seems every little sentimentalist who comes blowing his voluntary smoke-wreaths, and pretending to decide things from out of his private dream![100]

These "icy laws of outer fact" are in fact the corollary to pragmatism's turn to feeling, even its precondition. The primacy of feeling implies and depends on an emphasis on thought as an instrument or tool, the sense in which, as James puts it, *"theories thus become instruments, not answers to enigmas, in which we can rest."*[101] But an instrument requires in turn a *user*. A double gesture thus prevails: the pragmatic instrumentalization of thought in turn preserves an interior space of personal feeling that is occupied through a purification or purging of the impersonal, foreign, and monstrous mechanisms of theoretical control—the control *of* control.

It is at precisely this point that there begins a divergence, a threshold at which pragmatism seems to fall over and reverse itself. Despite writing its founding documents, Peirce rejected pragmatism as understood by James. If Jamesian pragmatism consists in a turning away from thinking to feeling, Peirce turns in the opposite direction, toward concepts and abstractions, toward the general and away from the particular and individual. His thought dramatizes something like a *becoming technological* of the immediate flux, a movement also expressed by what David Wills describes as prosthesis: "a displacement of original plenitude into the kinetics of working parts."[102] If James seeks the reinstatement of the vague, Peirce seeks its ever-greater determination. As if opposing James even in the forbidding technicality of his language, Peirce writes, "Pragmatism is the principle that every theoretical judgment expressible in a sentence in the indicative mood is a confused form of thought whose only meaning, if it has any, lies in its tendency to enforce a corresponding practical maxim expressible as a conditional sentence with its apodosis in the imperative mood."[103] This movement from the indicative to the imperative, from statements about being (vague, indefinite) to statements about doing (definite, actual), shows how Peirce's thought is concerned with a movement from the indeterminate to the determinate. The plane of immanence evoked by James as a space apart from the technological or mechanical workings of the world is in Peirce's writing broken up and differentiated into the gears and levers of a semiotic system. There is thus no access to an inviolable space of interiority, but only its continual exposure to difference—even, ultimately, a difference from itself. The following and final section of this chapter will contrast Peirce's inside-out form of pragmatism with what Tom Cohen calls the "interiority" presumed by Richard Rorty's neopragmatic inheritance of James. In conclusion, it will be shown that if James and Peirce are both pragmatists, then they face in opposite directions.

Pragmatism After Humanism: Reality, Solidarity, and the Unlimited Community

Without this *non-contemporaneity with itself of the living present*, without that which secretly unhinges it, without this responsibility and this respect for justice concerning those who *are not there*, of those who are no longer or who are not yet *present and living*, what sense would there be to ask the question "where?" "where tomorrow?" "whither?"

JACQUES DERRIDA, *SPECTERS OF MARX*

Charles Sanders Peirce had an inveterate habit for confounding state-ments that is perhaps surpassed only by Ralph Waldo Emerson. One of the more perplexing, remarkably enough, happens to be common to both. In a letter to William James—while taking issue, as usual, with James's individualistic psychologism—Peirce wrote that "thought . . . is more without us than within. It is we that are in it, rather than it in any of us."[104] Emerson's version, from "Fate," is nearly identical: "It is not in us, but we are in it."[105] Indeed, Peirce seemed to have little patience for notions of interiority at all. Early on he would write,

> There is no element whatever of man's consciousness which has not something corresponding to it in the word; and the reason is obvious. It is that the word or sign which man uses *is* the man himself. For, as the fact that every thought is a sign, taken in conjunction with the fact that life is a train of thought, proves that man is a sign; so, that every thought is an *external* sign, proves that man is an external sign. This is to say, the man and the external sign are identical. . . . Thus my language is the sum total of myself; for the man is the thought.[106]

If pragmatism distinguishes itself from theory through a distinction between inside and outside, then in this passage it would seem that Peirce undermines or reverses that distinction. The pragmatic inside (here "man's consciousness") is turned inside-out to endure the exposure of the boundary or excluded middle that constitutes it. The inside *becomes* outside: "Man is an external sign."

Theoretically speaking, these assertions initiate a movement from an internal to an external observational perspective, something systems theory describes as a shift from "first-order" observation to a "second-order" observation *of* observation. As Niklas Luhmann puts it, a sec-ond-order observer "can observe another observer (who can be one and the same) with regard to what he sees and what he cannot see. . . . We do not see what functions within the context of distinction as the one side or the other, but rather the exempted third."[107] The movement from inside to outside, then, is a transition from first-order observation (an observer "who only sees what he sees and does not see what he does not see") to second-order observation (an observer who can see that "the observer himself is always the exempted third party"). In effect, second-order observation reintroduces the unity of the distinction (the excluded middle between inside and outside) within the distinction and demands the selection of one side or the other. This, I will argue, is a quintessentially pragmatic gesture because it foregrounds the necessity of a decision in the absence of transcendental criteria—a necessity that applies even to pragmatism itself.

Peirce's second-order pragmatism can be seen more clearly when placed in contrast to Richard Rorty's "neopragmatism"—so named because it abandons the explicit individualism of James for communal "solidarity." There is an important distinction to be drawn between Rorty's valorous embrace of the full consequences of critical thought's embeddedness in the myriad determinative contexts from which it emerges and Peirce's perhaps quixotic quest to provide a formal logical proof for his "pragmaticism." As already noted, Rorty argues that Peirce remained committed to transcendence, a leaping out of the world that violates what could be called the Rortyan maxim: "It is impossible to attempt to step outside our skins—the traditions, linguistic and other, with which we do our thinking and self-criticism—and compare ourselves with something absolute."[108] However, if we take this point about the inaccessibility of the "outside" seriously (and we should), then there still remains an extra step: not simply a turn away from theory but a return or looping back to theory, a negotiation of the foundational contingency of both inside *and* outside.

Rorty abandons the search for external truths by foregrounding the forging of values that constitutes communal solidarity. Such communities are the end of the line, enforcing a commitment to "ethnocentrism"—which simply means there is no access to the "outside" of a particular community's beliefs, no standard of evaluation beyond communal preferences, which are themselves the result of the various preconditions ("linguistic and other") of our thinking. As he puts it, "If one reinterprets objectivity as intersubjectivity, or as solidarity, . . . then one will drop the question of how to get in touch with 'mind-independent and language-independent reality.' One will replace it with questions like 'What are the limits of our community?'"[109] Not only does this passage already begin to demonstrate how Rorty domesticates the "outside" (here termed "objectivity") within the "inside" ("solidarity"), it also raises a pointed question about "limits." Solidarity, it is clear, tasks itself with the drawing of limits through the erasure or expulsion of that which is designated as alien or other. Solidarity *is* exclusion, a definite boundary that determines who or what gains membership to the communal "us" from which values are derived—something Rorty makes abundantly clear in his comprehensive dismissals of thought he deems beyond the pale of the Western democratic liberalism, which can be considered the final framework for his own thought.

Rorty's philosophy is most instructive when it is seen as a demonstration of the circularity that inevitably results from thinking through the consequences of antifoundationalism. In this way, he demonstrates a valiant commitment to designate value not from outside but from entirely within, a commitment that leads to a frank acceptance of "ethnocentrism" as the only nonmetaphysical way forward. Clearly, Rorty cannot claim to have an objective or foundational argument for adopting this approach that isn't self-refuting, and so his thought often confronts moments of decision in which the circular tension he finds himself in becomes most evident. When faced with an either-or but deprived of objective or transcendental criteria for choosing one side or the other, the neopragmatist can be found straddling a decisional abyss in the manner of Buridan's ass: hungry and thirsty in equal measure. Near the end of *Consequences of Pragmatism* there is a moment that crystallizes this dilemma with laudable candor:

> Pragmatists follow Hegel in saying that "philosophy is its time grasped in thought." Anti-pragmatists follow Plato in striving for an escape from conversation to something atemporal which lies in the background of all possible conversations. I do not think one can decide between Hegel and Plato save by meditating on the past efforts of the philosophical tradition to escape from time and history. One can see these efforts as worthwhile, getting better, worth continuing. Or one can see them as doomed and perverse. I do not know what would count as a noncircular metaphysical or epistemological or semantical argument for seeing them in either way. So I think that the decision has to be made simply by reading the history of philosophy and drawing a moral. . . . Nothing that I have said, therefore, is an argument in favor of pragmatism.[110]

Here Rorty finds himself in the pragmatic situation par excellence. He makes the case for a decision in the absence of any objective or metaphysical criterion for that decision. He chooses nonetheless—a gesture that would seem to be nothing less than an act of will—and finds the grounds for that decision within the cultural values and beliefs of the community to which he already belongs. Having chosen, he rightly sacrifices the ability to justify his choice in terms of an objective or metaphysical reality. As he puts it elsewhere, "The pragmatist cannot justify these habits without circularity, but then neither can the realist."[111] In these situations, Rorty finds the wherewithal to make a decision through a retreat back to the resources of the historical, cultural, and situational circumstances he already finds himself in, thus performing a turn away from the universalist and objective pretentions of "theory" in order to push epistemological or ontological questions out of view as irrelevant.

But for this very reason, this turn away from theory, Tom Cohen argues that neopragmatism's evasion of philosophy can also be shown to represent an evasion of its *own* tradition, a circumstance that eventually leads Cohen to ask "whether what [neopragmatism] ends up evading is not, in a sense, America itself."[112] Interestingly, Cohen also adopts the term "the *thing*" as that which is evaded by neopragmatism, something that might just as well be identified by what Theodor Adorno calls the "preponderance of the object" or "thingness" that is evaded in the affirmation of the bourgeois subject's freedom.[113] Something like a sense of impersonality is at stake here, a sense in which the clear boundaries of the individual or communal solidarity are threatened, as if made indistinct or unstable. As Cohen shows, Rorty's recovery of pragmatism operates through the deployment of a stark division between *us* and *them*: "Here it is the American way that forms a certain *us* (the human), while the binarized other—alien, unhuman, theoretical—forms a *them*."[114] Thus when neopragmatism turns "against theory" and toward principles that are "pragmatic, situationist, individualist, historical, interventionist,"[115] it also turns away from the *thing* and from *them*. Is this not the rejection or exclusion that occurs in the affirmation of solidarity? And does this not also mean that if, as Cohen argues, neopragmatism evades *America*, then it may be argued in turn that Rorty's embrace of solidarity is in fact accomplished only through a rejection or refusal of *community*?

All of this suggests that the problem with neopragmatism, in short, is that it is a theory that cannot account for itself *as* a theory; it pretends to transcend its *thingness*, its *own* instrumentality, in order to find itself within a space of interiority (a maneuver that in its formal respects repeats the Jamesian reliance on "pure experience" as an inner space immune from the "outside"), in order to validate a basis of decision and control ex post facto. If, as Rorty insists, the pragmatist is "a partisan of solidarity, [and] his account of the value of cooperative human inquiry has only an ethical base, not an epistemological or metaphysical one,"[116] then there is a kind of purity at stake in this gesture, a repossession of voice or self-presence that rejects the imposed abstractions of theory as totalitarian and inhuman, as *them*:

> Is it clear just how classically this ideology of neo-pragmatism is constructed: locate an outside . . . and reject it as alien, though what is being ejected, the pragma or evil "thing," materiality as such, in fact lies behind one's own (American) pragmatism (in Poe, in Emerson, in Peirce, and so on); then refashion what is called "our" pragmatism itself as that which, having ejected the alien or unhuman figures, can be restituted as a legitimized morality of the integral human subject and a seamless model for action to boot.[117]

For these reasons, Rorty's rejection of philosophy isn't just an epistemological error but an act with political consequences. The neopragmatist presumption of solidarity as the basis for decision, which is to say, as something that is *already* achieved, seeks to transform questions of ontology and epistemology into questions of ethics and politics. As Rorty puts it, "For now one is debating what purposes are worth bothering to fulfill, which are more worthwhile than others, rather than which purposes the nature of humanity or of reality obliges us to have. For antiessentialists, all possible purposes compete with one another on equal terms, since none are more 'essentially human' than others."[118] All well and good, but as Cary Wolfe remarks about this passage: "Here, precisely at this juncture, the radically pluralist imperative of Rorty's pragmatist commitment to contingency begins to break down—or more specifically, begins to be recontained by a more familiar, more complacent and uncritical sort of pluralism."[119] That sort of pluralism being, of course, a familiar form of Western liberal humanism.

In this vein, Rorty adroitly frames his project as an attempt to "peel apart Enlightenment liberalism from Enlightenment rationalism."[120] However, this abandonment of "Enlightenment rationalism" unfortunately ends up throwing out any possibility of *critique* along with the familiar Rortyan bugbears of objectivity or necessity. Indeed, as scholars such as Reinhart Koselleck have argued, the Enlightenment was already a site of tension between such ideals and a more radical notion of critique.[121] Koselleck perceives that this tradition of critique has the troublesome habit of concealing its own contingent political motivations by donning the garb of necessary or absolute forms of morality: "The political decision becomes the determinant of a moral process. This, too, intensified the crisis morally but shrouded its political aspect. Providing a veil for this concealment became the historical function of the bourgeois philosophy of history."[122] In other words, the moral basis of critique claims to issue from an absolute position over and above the politically and historically contingent circumstances of its expression, an observational position outside of society revealed in the subject's claim to absolute morality. Similarly, Rorty's explicitly one-sided approach—his attempt to "peel apart" rationalist claims about objective necessity from the contingent decision-making processes of liberalism—reverses the truth-value of the "bourgeois philosophy of history" while remaining within its structuring logic. In effect, he claims that there is *nothing but* contingency, a claim that hides its *own* contingency. Necessity sneaks in the back door, and in this way neopragmatism presumes to evade any possibility of critique—the possibility of an external or second-order observer—altogether.

To fall back on solidarity as the basis for decision is itself a "political" (and thus contingent) decision that must exclude something, or someone, else. Solidarity constructs a self-present or immanent sociality by papering over the contingent decision that sustains it, a contingency that exposes itself most directly through a valorization of liberal political values at the expense of real social inequality. As Wolfe puts it,

> When Rorty claims that "we" should encourage the "end of ideology," that "anti-ideological liberalism is, in my view, the most valuable tradition of American intellectual life," Rorty is staging a claim that is itself ideological through and through. . . . What Rorty does not recognize, in other words, is that there is a fundamental contradiction between his putative desire to extend liberal advantages to an even larger community, and the fact that those advantages are possible for some only because they are purchased at the expense of others.[123]

Here Wolfe locates a blind spot in Rorty's political and ethical vision that bears directly on his reading of Peirce's supposed containment of contingency within realism. John Patrick Diggins puts the matter in similar terms: "In following the pragmatic tradition and treating knowledge as what comes to be validated by conventional methods of validation (and interpretation), Rorty overlooks the poststructuralist point that what comes to be accepted is at the expense of what has been excluded."[124] Rorty's neopragmatism excludes but cannot recognize *that* it excludes, let alone *what* it excludes, and its refusal of something like "theory" in the service of protecting or immunizing a self-grounding interiority means that it cannot simultaneously recognize (or refuses to recognize) its *own* contingency.

In the face of these circular dilemmas both Cohen and Wolfe find a return to epistemological questions to be vital. But, as also noted by both, one cannot simply reverse course without falling into the exact same dilemmas. Turning back to theory would represent an evasion of the very specificity and individuality that pragmatism wants to privilege. How to keep both "inside" *and* "outside," the very difference itself, without grounding one in the other? For his part, Cohen turns to a machine-like repetition:

> The renowned but often banally translated "Man is the measure . . ." could more interestingly be tracked, perhaps, if we did not assume "Man" as the given narcissistic subject, but reflected "him" back into the parameters of "measure" itself. Such a text might no longer be called simply relativist *or* humanist, since it also constitutes a defacement of "man." "Measure" could now be rendered by a series, not of letters but of marks, knocks, or bars that are almost possible to render graphically (/ / / /). Precisely such a bar series can become the emblem not only of repetition and narrative, but of castration, materiality, anteriority, allegory, exteriority, semiotic "death," listing, the machinal, and the generative point of linguistic consciousness as such.[125]

Following from this point, my contention is that if we turn back to the origins of American pragmatism in search of this graphic and machinal repetition, then we must turn back to Peirce: to his Existential Graphs, his semiotics, and even his realism. This is not, however, a metaphysical realism that proposes that the mind can represent the world as it is in itself within the space of a transcendental consciousness, but instead an insistence upon the *thing*, the materiality as such that appears only on the other side of a constitutive difference. This is the real as pure alterity, as something *else*. *Them* re-entering into *us*:

> It seems to me that we are driven to this, that logicality inexorably requires that our interests should *not* be limited. They must not stop at our own fate, but must embrace the whole community. This community, again, must not be limited, but must extend to all races of beings with whom we can come into immediate or mediate intellectual relation. It must reach, however vaguely, beyond this geological epoch, beyond all bounds. He who would not sacrifice his own soul to save the whole world is, as it seems to me, illogical in all his inferences, collectively. Logic is rooted in the social principle.[126]

Here Peirce suggests that the very nature of "logic" is itself a force that leads outside of itself to the *other*, to reality as an indefinite and unlimited community.

Peirce includes the excluded middle between pragmatism and theory by understanding the individual as necessarily excluded from any general system of meaning. This exclusion is the generative condition of semiosis and the source of its infinite deferrals. One may draw a circle around an inside but only through the simultaneous (and then repeated, continuous) reference to an outside—and so the inside itself becomes contingent and elusive, only available through the repetition of its constitutive difference (inside/outside) in the form of a "re-entry" of that distinction into itself. This is how Peirce's "pragmaticism" dramatizes the intrusion of materiality, the very overtaking of the voice or self by the machine of meaning.

At this point, a brief digression into Peirce's semiotics may be instructive because his notions of both reality and community conform to his more general notion of a sign. A sign, as what Peirce calls "Thirdness" or a "general," is a potential representative of continuity because it is not "actual" unless it is determined as such: "[Thirdness] is an essential ingredient of reality, yet does not by itself constitute reality, since this category . . . can have no concrete being without action."[127] But at the same time, the reality of what is determined by the sign is withheld from any specific determination marked by the sign: "The object of a Sign, then, is necessarily unexpressed in the sign, taken by itself."[128] In this way, signs can be conceived as boundaries that mark a distinction between inside (determined) and outside (undetermined). The object is thus always prior to the distinction, and the interpretant (or determination) is always after it: "The object and the interpretant are thus merely the two correlates of the sign; the one being antecedent, the other consequent of the sign."[129] The sign is the excluded middle: before the interpretant and after the object. The object of the sign never appears as *itself*, but only as a determination that is always limited or partial.

Signs designate a partial determination of an indeterminate and continuous reality, the unity of a distinction between a determinate *actuality* and an indeterminate realm of *possibility*: the excluded middle between what has been determined and what remains to be determined. As Floyd Merrell argues, this makes the final meaning of a sign elusive:

> Consequently, the concept of meaning eludes one at the very moment it seems to be within one's grasp. Yet, signs and their meanings are inseparable, for signs would not be signs in the full-blown sense if devoid of meaning. So to the question "Where is meaning?" the answer is "Not in the confines of the skull, in the sign itself, in the thing to which it presumably refers, or somewhere in the imaginary—though illusory—conduit, that invisible conduit tube between sign emitter and sign receiver." Meaning is nowhere and at the same time it is everywhere; it is in the interrelations of the sign interaction incessantly being played out on the stage of *semiosis*. Meaning is largely an informal, virtually unspecifiable and untheorizable, commodity.[130]

Signs are the simultaneous presentation of both actuality *and* possibility. Every actual determination automatically refers at the same time to infinitely further potential determinations: "In short the idea of a general involves the idea of possible variations which no multitude of existent things could exhaust but would leave between any two not merely *many* possibilities, but possibilities absolutely beyond all multitude."[131] The meaning or truth-value of a sign is consequently asymmetrical, what Peirce calls "one-sided," and this asymmetry instigates a reversal or vacillation that resembles the stabilizing mechanisms of negative feedback loops. Similarly, Peirce's "vacillations" regarding realism versus idealism are not simply inconsistencies but the result of seeing any belief or description as a necessarily limited or partial sign and therefore subject to further, infinitely further, determinations. Signs are always potentially more or less than what they actually "are." Because of this, the sign relation may also be characterized by a phrase from Ranulph Glanville and Francisco Varela that is itself a kind of Möbius strip: "The inside of one is the outside of the other, and vice versa."[132] A sign, after all, only leads to another sign, and to determine one by means of another is to turn it "inside-out."

In an important late essay, Peirce declares, "My pragmatism . . . [has] nothing to do with qualities of feeling," and argues that "concepts . . . essentially carry some implication concerning the general behavior either of some conscious being or of some inanimate object, and so convey more, not merely than any feeling, but more, too, than any existential fact, namely, the '*would-acts*' of habitual behavior; and no agglomeration of actual happenings can ever completely fill up the meaning of a 'would be.'"[133] This language is characteristically difficult, showing all by itself the intrusion of a foreign or inhuman *other*. Here both individual feeling and discrete facts are overtaken by the generalizing machinery of a semiosis that does not designate what *is*, but only designates its distribution into parts that remain incomplete: an indeterminate *would be*. This "more than," which is never exhausted, represents something like a quasi-transcendentalism—not a grasping of the outside itself, but the repetition or re-entry of a circular boundary that loops back around to difference and contingency. The inside marked by this boundary is forever elusive, deferred through series of bars, marks, or circles that represent the sense in which the situational, specific, or individual is *already* produced by the general, foreign, or mechanical. It is as if our own limbs do not belong to us—as if consciousness itself, seemingly the inviolate space of interiority, was from the beginning a prosthesis or technological apparatus. Pragmatism finds itself outside of itself: pragmat(ic)ism.

Likewise, Peirce's sense of reality is intimately tied to his early notion of community: "The very origin of the conception of reality shows that this conception essentially involves the notion of a COMMUNITY, without definite limits, and capable of an indefinite increase of knowledge."[134] If Rorty tames contingency within a familiar liberal humanism, creating the "inside" of a homogenous *us* in the process, then his thought cannot observe the *non*identity of the social space it professes to describe; it remains blind to its own exclusions. In his later thought, Peirce avoids this fate only by refusing to claim reality for any specific individual, sociality, or discourse:

> That is *real* which has such and such characters, whether anybody thinks it to have those characters or not. . . . Thought, controlled by a rational experimental logic, tends to the fixation of certain opinions, equally destined, the nature of which will be the same in the end, however the perversity of thought of whole generations may cause the postponement of the ultimate fixation. If this be so, as every man of us virtually assumes that it is, in regard to each matter the truth of which he seriously discusses, then, according to the adopted definition of "real," the state of things which will be believed in that ultimate opinion is real.[135]

Peirce carefully stresses that the character of the real is that which has particular qualities independent of any particular mind. As Susan Haack writes, "Is truth, in Peirce's conception, mind-independent? Yes and no. Yes: what is true does not depend on what you, or I, anyone *thinks* is true. No: there could be no truth in principle unknowable by us."[136] There is no particular human mind in which the world can appear as it is in itself, nor is there a world as it is in itself since the real is not independent of the "ultimate opinion" that, after all, cannot be the opinion of any particular person or group of people (a group being just as "individual" as a single person). When Rorty approvingly cites a comment of Michael Williams that "we have no idea what it would be for a theory to be ideally complete and comprehensive . . . or of what it would be for inquiry to have an end,"[137] one may respond that this inability or incapacity to imagine the end of inquiry is precisely the point. Reality, in other words, cannot be thought as a singular idea, mind, or solidarity because it is a concept without identity—it holds our beliefs accountable to the perspective of those who are *not there.*

At this point, the distinction between *us* and *them* again comes to the foreground because reality evades being in the possession of either. Reality is not in the possession of any particular individual or group, since "individualism and falsity are one and the same."[138] Nor is reality a noumenal object that cannot be known, since Peirce clearly identifies it with the "ultimate opinion." Reality represents a "more than," an Emersonian "onwardness," a reference to the future found in the present's lack of identity: "The rational meaning of every proposition lies in the future."[139] The alterity or indeterminacy represented by *them* continually re-enters into *us* and beckons forth a new determination.

At first blush it would seem that Peirce's unlimited community expresses what Adorno calls the "central antinomy of bourgeois society": namely, "To preserve itself, to remain the same, to 'be,' that society too must expand, progress, advance its frontiers, not respect any limit, not remain the same. . . . It eliminates all heterogeneous being."[140] On the one hand, Peirce's sense of community does indeed profess the totalizing and hegemonic bourgeois value of unlimited inclusion. It is in just this sense that Rorty's attention to "limits" and the necessity of exclusion is a signal virtue of his thought. But on the other hand, Peirce's idea of community, I want to argue, ultimately evades the totalization implied in Adorno's critique because the concept of community does not operate as an identity in Peirce's thought—it is not what Adorno calls a determinate concept but is itself a sign. Community represents the excluded middle between inside and outside, the paradoxical unity of that distinction, and in this way it does not prop up the hegemonic order implied in a notion of solidarity but holds it accountable to its exclusions. Community is the nonidentity of solidarity. Peirce doesn't hide this antinomy, he places it front and center—and in just this sense he seems to anticipate what Adorno calls "a doubled mode of conduct: an inner one, the immanent process which is the properly dialectical one, and a free, unbound one like a stepping out of dialectics. . . . Both attitudes of consciousness are linked by criticizing one another, not by compromising."[141] Inside *and* outside, not in synthesis but a contradiction implied in every conceptual determination: "To be known, the inwardness to which cognition clings in expression always needs its own outwardness as well."[142]

Communities cannot, therefore, definitively answer Rorty's question of "limits" because they are never singular or identical even to themselves; they can never achieve the identity implied in solidarity because they are founded on a difference from, a lack or exclusion of, reality. Community then paradoxically names itself as precisely that which *isn't* yet achieved, what remains excluded by solidarity. What is included is only included on the condition of what is excluded, and so community is joined to solidarity as the name for its *other* or external side. Community may then be defined as the excluded middle between solidarity and community, between inside and outside. Community is then split in two and opposed to itself as that which is left behind or outside the drawing of its own boundaries. It cannot be determined except through a process of inclusion/exclusion that in each and every case returns it to that very same contingent decision: inside or out? To put a rather fine point on it, the question of community *is* the pragmatic necessity of that decision as well as the necessity of its repetition.

Recently, Roberto Esposito has espoused a similar idea of community: "Community isn't joined to an addition but to a subtraction of subjectivity, by which I mean that its members are no longer identical with themselves but are constitutively exposed to a propensity that forces them to open their own individual boundaries in order to appear as what is 'outside' themselves."[143] Is this not in some large measure what Peirce means when he defines man as an *external* sign: that even the very thoughts that would seem to constitute a "self" are in some sense produced through a process of externalization or exposure? Isn't this also what Peirce means when he suggests that the individual can only be defined as a *negation*: "The individual man, since his separate existence is manifested only by ignorance and error, so far as he is anything apart from his fellow, and from what he and they are to be, is only a negation."[144] The individual is negated for the sake of futurity, the yet to be determined, the "more than" that is the essence of community.

Esposito writes, "Community appears to be definable only on the basis of the lack that characterizes it. It is *nothing other* than what history has negated, the nonhistoric backdrop from which history originates in the form of a necessary betrayal."[145] I want to suggest that what Esposito here calls "history" is the same as what Rorty means by "solidarity"— and so community represents for Esposito a radically contingent "nonhistoric backdrop," a *historicity* opposed to historicism, that solidarity must negate or exclude in order to secure its borders. And yet community is *also* the "more than" that arrives only with the future. Community is the excluded middle, both before *and* after: that which is negated at the beginning and therefore what returns or re-enters at the end only to be negated yet again (and again). The unlimited and indefinite community can be formed (is yet to be formed) only from a common *lack* or negation, a lack that leaves it open to the re-entry of the indeterminate and therefore the necessity of continually redrawing its boundaries. Community, in a word, is a *non*identity that forces a pragmatic decision, and the closure ("solidarity") entailed in that decision in turn loops back around to contingency, to openness, an "unlimited" and "indefinite" community that forces yet another actualizing decision.

It is on this terrain, this reversal in which *it* is not in us but *we are in it*, that Peirce's semiotics intersects with Jacques Derrida's figure of the "event-machine." That figure represents a joining together of the event (singular, individual, nonrepeatable) to the machine (general, inhuman, iterative): "The new figure of an event-machine would no longer be even a figure. It would not resemble, it would resemble nothing, not even what we call, in a still familiar way, a monster. But it would therefore be, by virtue of this very novelty, an event, the only and the first possible event, because im-possible. That is why I ventured to say that this thinking could belong only to the future—and even that it makes the future possible."[146] Impossible because thinking the event and machine *at once* requires seeing two sides of a distinction at the same time, a paradox that can only inaugurate what Merrell calls the "uncertain, vacillating scandal of meaning."[147] We are captive to an oscillation that kicks us from one side to the other, onward into the future. Perhaps the event-machine also takes on the character of the "messianic" as described in *Specters of Marx*: an expectation of arrival, not the arrival per se but the expectation of arrival built into the present, the "irreducibility of affirmation."[148]

Peirce's own attempt to corral this monstrous and messianic event-machine is represented in his semiotics—an unsightly slouching beast if there ever was one. His vision of reality and community can be reconciled to a vision of America as a nonidentity, as *them*, as those not (yet) present—a vision of an indeterminate future produced through the paradoxical thought of an event-machine: "To think *both* the machine *and* the performative event together remains a monstrosity to come, an *impossible* event. Therefore the only possible event. But it would be an event that, this time, would no longer happen without the machine. Rather it would happen by the machine."[149] Here we find ourselves pondering America as a sign, an (im)possible event hosting the irruption from within itself of a parasitical foreign *other*. As Esposito puts it, "The community is both impossible and necessary. Necessary and impossible. Not only is it given as a defect (it is never fully realized) but community is defective, in the specific sense that what is held in common is precisely *that* defect, *that* default, *that* debt, or also our mortal finitude."[150] Esposito's reversal of "necessary" and "impossible" in this passage reveals that community is never quite either, but always somewhere in between *as* that very difference or distinction, that excluded middle. Peirce's realism (which represents yes *and* no) names that difference as the (un)founding of community.

We find ourselves again at a beginning: an identification of the *thing*, of materiality as such, the machine of semiosis, or an encroaching foreign *them*, with America. Far from Rorty's vision of ethnocentric solidarity couched in the familiar terms of Western liberal democracy, Peirce allows us to envision America without limits: "Individual action is a means and not our end. Individual pleasure is not our end; we are all putting our shoulders to the wheel for an end that none of us can catch more than a glimpse at—that which the generations are working out."[151] I cannot help but imagine that Rorty must have found this imagery alarming. It is a vision of America as some machine or monstrous inhuman *thing* that repeatedly and endlessly negates the situational and individual for something more than either.

We find America as a hope or futurity or—with Emerson's "Experience" this time—an expectation: "Bear with these distractions, with this coetaneous growth of the parts: they will one day be *members*, and obey one will. On that one will, on that secret cause, they nail our attention and hope. Life is hereby melted into an expectation or a religion. . . . And what a future it opens! I feel a new heart beating with the love of the new beauty. I am ready to die out of nature, and be born again into this new yet unapproachable America I have found in the West."[152] Peirce cannot match Emerson's gift of expression, but his vision of community remains equally compelling:

> This infinite hope which we all have . . . is something so august and momentous, that all reasoning in reference to it is a trifling impertinence. . . . So this sentiment is rigidly demanded by logic. If its object were any determinate fact, any private interest, it might conflict with the results of knowledge and so with itself; but when its object is of a nature as wide as the community can turn out to be, it is always a hypothesis uncontradicted by facts and justified by its indispensableness for making any action rational.[153]

We are turned inside-out in America: it is not in us, we are in it.

— 3 —
On True Virtue

Jonathan Edwards and the Ethics of Self-Reference

Self-reference is the infinite in finite guise.

LOUIS H. KAUFFMAN, "SELF-REFERENCE
AND RECURSIVE FORMS"

Beginning with the classic texts of Perry Miller and including even the most sophisticated contemporary accounts, the Puritan theology of Jonathan Edwards (1703–1758) is often found at its heart to resemble modern humanism. Miller's seminal biography of Edwards casts his thought as a quest for immanent communion with the divine: "Edwards went to nature and experience, not in search of the possible, but of the given, of that which cannot be controverted, of that to which reason has access only through perception and pain, that of which logic is the servant and from which dialectic receives its premises."[1] Miller describes this search as expressing a desire for "face to face" encounters with the unaccountable God of Calvinism, a desire that links Edwards to Ralph Waldo Emerson and thus the entire tradition of American humanism that culminates in the psychological empiricism of William James. However, this narrative, while certainly compelling, betrays a central tenant of Edwards's Calvinism. Miller's own words mark the difference: "God's nature 'is capable properly of no definition,' so that all that one can say is that 'God is an incomprehensible, first, and absolute Being.' He cannot be approached directly; man cannot stand face to face with Him."[2]

Of course, Miller was well aware of this inconsistency, as it forms the backbone of many of his most trenchant insights. As he writes, "Most of the issues that were so hotly contested among seventeenth-century theologians were connected with attempts to resolve this discrepancy between the God of everyday providence and the God who dispensed His grace according to no rule but His own pleasure."[3] It is this paradox, what might be said to be a simultaneous presentation of immanence and transcendence that is characteristic of modernity, to which Edwards's theology is addressed. But it is at precisely this point—a liminal space between the grasping after "face to face" encounters and "the absolute, incomprehensible, and transcendent sovereignty of God"[4]—that a different account of Edwards's theology can emerge that forgoes the humanism that inevitably attends its unfolding.

My argument relies in part on Michael Clark's assertion that the Puritan "never could accept the material world as a basis for their epistemology; such a premise would subordinate the rational soul to the senses and, more important, would deny the transcendent authority that the Puritans granted to the basic tenets of their theology."[5] This is a key point. As Clark goes on to argue, "The most fundamental principle of Puritan semiology was the absolute discontinuity between two of the three 'forms' constituting any fully significant sign."[6] This "absolute discontinuity"—a formulation that resembles what Miller called a "fundamental distrust"[7] or the "discrepancy" noted above—represented "neither a dualistic oscillation between this world and the next nor a continuous hierarchy connecting the two. Rather, it was much closer to a dialectic, a gesture toward synthesis built out of the dramatic conflict of faith as thesis and world as antithesis."[8] Clark's refusal of "dualistic oscillation" is particularly astute because it recognizes that, while the discontinuity remains paramount, there is no question of a synchronic relationship between the terms. However, at the same time, Clark cannot help but fold Puritan thought into something resembling a dialectic. A "gesture toward" synthesis would seem to ultimately unite the terms and contradict the "absolute discontinuity" originally identified. In other words, the notion of a synthesis, even an unachieved one, holds on to something like an eventual adequacy between opposed terms that evades more radical possibilities in Edwards's thought.

This problem, so far indentified as a "discrepancy," as "fundamental distrust," and as "absolute discontinuity," surfaces again and again in scholarly accounts of Edwards's theology. Many approach the problem by producing a kind of dialectical unity or synthesis in his thought, an approach exemplified by Joan Richardson's *A Natural History of Pragmatism*. Richardson supposes some form of correspondence or relation of mind and environment subsumed in the "face to face" encounter with an overarching naturalism: "While Edwards believed his insights to have come from God, from our later point of view it is easy to see that his response was animal, that is, the response of a creature struggling to survive in an environment where 'the squirming facts exceed[ed] the squamous mind.' "[9] Likewise, God is seen not as the other to nature, but as the other *in* nature. Edwards "embedded the divine within the empirical."[10] Richardson thus unites the discontinuity between transcendence and immanence on the side of immanence—and this is what motivates her "naturalist" turn. For instance, by way of explanation of the exclusion of Hawthorne and Melville from her study, Richardson writes, "Each was, by his own account, still too haunted by the idea of an 'unnaturalized' Calvinist deity to shed the feeling of a mind inhabited by guilt to be able to put on a new habit, the feeling of what happens to a mind enjoying 'an original relation to the universe.' "[11] Richardson thus "naturalizes" Edwards's thought as a means to unify the discontinuities of his thought and connect him to the genealogy of an organicist romanticism that she finds in Emerson and James—a tradition that also connects Richardson directly to Miller.

Another indispensible study, and one that also follows in Miller's footsteps, is Sang Hyun Lee's *The Philosophical Theology of Jonathan Edwards*. Already in the title, one can see that Lee's approach will also fashion an intriguing unity out of the discontinuity of Edwards's thought. As Lee puts it, "Edwards departed from the traditional Western metaphysics of substance and form and replaced it with a strikingly modern conception of reality as a dynamic network of dispositional forces and habits."[12] Reality is here conceived as the unity of "dynamic movement" that is initiated through God's own dynamic nature: "Edwards' dynamic conception of knowing and being is grounded in his reconception of the divine being as inherently dynamic."[13] As Lee is careful to point out, this movement is not the result of some lack of self-sufficiency on God's part, but quite the opposite: "It is axiomatic in Edwards that God is the absolutely sovereign and eternally perfect ground of all existence and creativity. But the essence of the divine being . . . is now conceived of as a disposition as well as a full actuality. God, therefore, is inherently inclined to enlarge or repeat his primordial actuality through further exercises of his dispositional essence."[14] The question that Lee finds confronted by Edwards is a difficult one: how to conceive of God as "absolutely sovereign and eternally perfect" *and* "inherently dynamic"? More abstractly, we might ask: Does this not also imply that God is both the same *and* different to himself? Lee's ingenious answer suggests as much:

"God is essentially a perfect actuality as well as a disposition to repeat that actuality through further exercises."[15] God, in other words, essentially performs a "self-repetition in time."[16] A repetition, that is, of His own wholeness, perfection, and self-sufficiency *in* time—something that would seem to suggest that the totality of the whole appears through its sequential unfolding and determination.

Lee's analysis goes quite a bit of the way toward the path that will be pursued here, but his conception of the divine as "dynamic" stops well short of considering that idea in its full radical import. Lee insists on a final encompassing unity of the dynamic movement he describes, a unity that becomes most apparent (and most burdened with romanticism and humanism) in his understanding of the role of imagination: "Thus, through the activity of the sanctified imagination, the perceiving self and the perceived world attain their actuality. And such an attainment of their actuality is none other than their participation in God's sovereign work of repeating his internal being in time and space. Through the imagination, then, history and nature come alive and also achieve their union with God."[17] Here Lee offers a humanist conception of consciousness as the imaginary staging ground for uniting God and nature in the form of a relational network: "The shaping and expansive power of the imagination enables the mind to know and love what it experiences as meaningful wholes in their ultimate relational context. In this way, the finite mind is enabled to know and love the world as the temporal repetition of the divine glory."[18] This is a powerful reading of Edwards in the mold set by Miller, but it cannot help but finally domesticate and unify the radical discontinuity that God's "absolute sovereignty" represents. Indeed, God would even seem to be subordinate (even if momentarily) to time and thus to the "relational context" in or through which his self-repetition takes place: God appears inside the system.

One possible means of avoiding the problematic unity or synthesis implied by such readings would be to claim that Edwards simply *affirms* the dualisms of Calvinist thought, something like what Clark above calls a "dualistic oscillation" without a unifying third term. This is more or less the tack taken up in R. C. De Prospo's *Theism in the Discourse of Jonathan Edwards*. Here the "absolute discontinuity" remains fundamental:

> Modern interpretations of Edwards propose that, at least when gripped by those infrequent, heightened affections he hopes are gracious, Edwards

senses a union between the visible and invisible that contradicts dualistic epistemology and anticipates romantic visionary experience, and this despite unmistakable evidence that when Edwards contemplates these emotions, both his own and those of others, in the tranquility of his theological writings, the dualism of his understanding is pronounced, leading him to question feeling in ways that seem precisely to differentiate him both from later romantic visionaries and from supposedly protoromantic contemporaries.[19]

De Prospo's reading of Edwards is especially useful because it resists the temptation to read Edwards's project through the prism of romanticism or notions of "imagination" derived from that tradition. De Prospo thus departs from a common humanist narrative of American intellectual history: "The theist discursive pattern revealed in Edwards's writing represents a single phenomenon differentiated from humanism in American literature."[20]

De Prospo's argument represents an important corrective, but like humanist readings, it cannot avoid resolving the paradox at the heart of Edwards's thought. For instance, he writes,

> Edwards's inability to conceive an identity between Creator and Creation does not blind him to the subtle resemblance between them. . . . Although he holds lesser expectations about the experience of nature than do romantic writers, Edwards perceives a likeness between natural beauties and divine excellency sufficient to inspire a religious enjoyment of the wilderness of eighteenth-century New England. . . . This enjoyment is one of Edwards's attributes that most intrigues modern critics. Remove Edwards's discussion of the logic of Creation, remove also the many qualifications he attaches to his idea of the visibility of divine beauty, and the resulting text, though short, resembles romantic discourse.[21]

This passage is notable because it would seem to suggest that Edwards's thought even resists (though only, it must be said, to a degree) De Prospo's dualistic thesis as well. Indeed, along the lines given by De Prospo, it is difficult to account for the very passages in Edwards that have seemed to so incite the imaginations of modern readers. It seems hard to claim, in other words, that Edwards rests content in a static dualism.

A way forward, a kind of third way, seems to be available in Stephen H. Daniel's *The Philosophy of Jonathan Edwards*. The book's subtitle,

A *Study in Divine Semiotics*, identifies the approach taken by Daniel, one of impressive complexity that nevertheless smuggles in the very synthesis that De Prospo argues against, which is to say that it lapses into yet another version of the "face to face" encounter. Again, the operative distinction is between transcendence and immanence, and Daniel argues decisively for the latter:

> To describe the fall into the mentality of classical modernity, Edwards situates talk of subjectivity and alienation in a discourse that is itself neither subjective nor alien, because it does not claim to be self-validating or to refer to any transcendent principles. The immanent system of signification constituted by the language of God (expressed in nature and Scripture) does not need to refer to itself or anything beyond itself for legitimacy, for the notion of legitimacy is itself a feature of classical modernity describable only in terms of the divine discursive exchange.[22]

In this scheme there is no place for any form of dualism between transcendence and immanence because transcendence ultimately finds itself dissolved by or distributed within immanent systems of signification.

In much the same way as Lee, Daniel evades the distinctions that Edwards would presumably take for granted. For Daniel, "Every communication assumes a relation between that which is said and that which is meant, between a signifier and a signified. The disposition to communicate is the displacement of the signified by a signifier, and thus the designation of the signified as that which is other. The signifier itself identifies the signified as an absence to which the signifier points."[23] This scheme supposes a "system of signification" as the structural ground of a differential field in which relations achieve a kind of immanence or adequation to one another that bridges or mediates the divisions between real and ideal, mind and matter, and, most fundamentally for this discussion, God and Creation: "The subject and predicate of a proposition have no meaning apart from the proposition, and the proposition has no meaning apart from its function in a discourse."[24] This is to say that for Daniel a discourse itself functions autonomously beyond the requirements of difference that the terms *within* the discourse must operate under. The law imposed by the discourse (the system of differences it structures) does not apply to the discourse as a whole. In this sense a discourse can be said to be the immanent, symmetrical, and self-present guarantor of meaning.

It is worth pausing here to compare Daniel's divine semiotics with Gregory Bateson's intriguing description of God in *Steps to an Ecology of Mind*, a description that can be said in some respects to resemble the God that Daniel finds in Edwards:

> The individual mind is immanent, but not only in the body. It is imma-nent also in pathways and messages outside the body; and there is a larger Mind, of which the individual is only a subsystem. This larger Mind is comparable to God and is perhaps what some people mean by "God," but it is still immanent in the total inter-connected social sys-tem and planetary ecology. Freudian psychology expanded the concept of mind inward to include the whole communication system within the body—the automatic, the habitual and the vast range of unconscious processes. What I am saying expands mind outward. And both of these changes reduce the scope of the conscious self. A certain humility becomes appropriate, tempered by the dignity or joy of being part of something bigger. A part—if you will—of God.[25]

Needless to say, such sentiments are decidedly impious for Calvin-ism, which insists on the absolute division between transcendence and immanence. Daniel's semiotic immanence switches out the humanist or romanticist "face to face" encounters of Miller for the immanence of semiotic meaning. But along with De Prospo, we may insist that for Edwards such encounters would seem impossible because they discover God's immanent presence, however indirectly and however transiently, in the world itself.

Niklas Luhmann's critique of semiotics bears directly on this point by applying the structuring difference between signifier and signified to the semiotic system itself: "A sign must first and foremost distinguish itself from something that cannot be distinguished: from emptiness, unmarked space, the white of paper, the silence that is assumed in every perception of sound. And this is true especially when a sign is supposed to be noth-ing more than a distinction between signifier and signified."[26] Semiotics, in other words, falls short of a totalizing description because there must remain a *non*signified from which it distinguishes itself. By contrast, Dan-iel's semiotic understanding of Edwards's theology finds a higher unity in immanent "discourses" or "communicative exchanges" *within* which the distinction between signifier and signified takes place, and therefore semiotic discourse itself evades the requirement of what Luhmann calls the "unmarked space"—the difference that allows the system to emerge in the first place. For semiotics this presumed unity (the unity of the distinction signifier/signified) is necessary for its continued operation. It cannot, however, justify that unity on its own terms. If God is the ground of a distinction, the immanence in which the distinction takes place, is it then not true that even the designation "God" is the product of a distinction and therefore a comprehension, limitation, determination, definition, or constraint upon that which *cannot* be comprehended, limited, determined, defined, or constrained? The maddening circularity of this problem is what Luhmann calls the paradox of "self-reference," a concept that will have special resonance for understanding Edwards.

Paradoxical self-reference points the way to a new understanding of Edwards's theology. Here the "absolute discontinuity" will be understood as a self-referential distinction, which in another manner of speaking can be seen as a *one-sided* or asymmetrical distinction. This is to approach the difference *itself*. The presence of the immediate or unmediated "face to face" encounter is occluded and already given over to the material or mechanical as the "fallen" conditions of its emergence, thus recasting such experiences through the act of distinction, a distinction that can observe one side only under the condition that the *other* side remains unobservable. The condition of immanence is its splitting or breach by an ungraspable and unobservable transcendence. We can thus agree with Daniel when he writes, "Instead of being transcendent pronouncements about the relation of God and creation, Edwards's suppositions themselves enact the same logic that governs the possibility for any and all meaning and existence."[27] This self-referring logic, however, is not a structural framework that governs the possibility for meaning but the paradoxical absence of that very framework that makes any form of determinant meaning ultimately contingent.

Self-Reference, Mysticism, and Romanticism

God don't fully obtain his design in any one particular state that the world has been in at one time, but in the various successive states that the world is in, in different ages, connected in a scheme. 'Tis evident that he don't fully obtain his end, his design, in any particular

state that the world has ever been in; for if so, we would have no
change. But God is continually causing revolutions.

JONATHAN EDWARDS, "THE MISCELLANIES"

Connections between systems theory and traditional theology are not difficult to find. This is so, as Luhmann points out, because theology took
as its aim the twin and contradictory duties to simultaneously represent
God and remember that God is unrepresentable, and it was therefore in
the business of continually investigating its own paradoxical foundation.
As Luhmann writes by way of describing Nicholas of Cusa's theology,

> God is beyond all distinctions, even beyond the distinction between distinc-
> tions, and beyond the distinction between distinctness and indistinctness.
> He is the *non-aliud*, that which is not different from anything different. In
> him, everything that transcends distinctness coincides insofar as it tran-
> scends distinctness—i.e., that which cannot be conceived as greater, as
> smaller, as quicker, as slower (*coincidentia oppositorum*); . . . that God
> in this way makes himself comprehensible in his incomprehensibility; and
> that truth, although finally incomprehensible, consists for human beings in
> the correspondence of their distinctions with those of things.[28]

Luhmann's observations show that the goal of traditional theology was
not so much the representation of God as the perceiving of God as that
which cannot be perceived. Or as he cryptically puts it in a different context,
"Reality is what one does not perceive when one perceives it."[29] That is, perception involves the self-referential observation of the distinction between
perception and reality as perception's *other* just out of the corner of its eye.
    As Stefan Rossbach has argued, Luhmann's systems theory uses self-
reference as a means to contemplate the "oneness" beyond all worldly
distinctions: "It is the systems theory itself that evokes a consciousness
of the pre-cosmic unity. . . . Any observation is a self-limitation."[30] The
means by which Luhmann's theory accomplishes this contemplation,
however, are unique because the theory is designed in order to foreclose
itself. The theory seeks to close its own loop. Luhmann's self-referential
systems theory is designed to focus on its own internal limitations and
conditions, thus recalling in many respects Cusa's "learned ignorance."
The contemplation of the other side of the distinction (say, the far side

of perception/reality) is the attempt to see that one cannot see what one cannot see (and so on, and so on). It is this hidden and unseeable "unknown" unity that recalls the Gnostic beyond in Rossbach's view— an unknown that, and this is the critical point, appears *outside* of the theory, not within it. For my own purposes, this means that systems theory is the best way to apprehend Edwards's searching notions of the beyond because Edwards is quite attuned to the space on the far side of his distinctions.

Edwards seems concerned, in other words, not with God's immediacy or mediation but with the continual *failure* of God's mediation in worldly forms—a kind of constitutive failure that Edwards even self-referentially applies to his own Calvinist doctrine. Miller observes this same tension in Edwards when he writes, "Holding himself by brute will power within the forms of ancient Calvinism, he filled those forms with a new and throbbing spirit. Beneath the dogmas of the old theology he discovered a different cosmos from that of the seventeenth century, a dynamic world, filled with the presence of God, quickened with divine life, pervaded with joy and ecstasy."[31] Adding to Miller's insight, I will argue that Edwards has a keen sense of the distorting power of perception, and thus his idea of God has much in common with Luhmann's idea of reality as the foundational blind spot of any observing system. The quickening of divine life is not simply the present manifestation of God but the repetition of the difference made by a self-referential observation coping with what it *cannot* see. God remains transcendent even when immanent, both the same *and* different—a distinction, moreover, that takes place already on the side of difference. Even the forms of Calvinism, as Miller perceptively notes, are not sufficient to contain God, and Edwards's theology presses hard at these boundaries in order to indicate divinity through the limitation and failure of its observing forms, demonstrating in turn God's unlimitedness outside itself. As Rossbach puts it, "The infinite unity of the 'world' reappears in the theory in the absence of limits of problematization."[32]

This argument now brings us to a point at which we may begin to grapple with Edwards's complex relationship to romanticism. As already noted, De Prospo ably dismantles any argument that would identify Edwards as a romantic, but it is in fact the glimmers of romanticism that many scholars see in Edwards which point the way toward systems theory. Luhmann suggests that romanticism may be interpreted as an attempt to grapple with the autonomy brought on by modernity's ongoing differentiation into a variety of system-specific references at the expense of an encompassing totality—a predicament Luhmann theorizes as the continual re-entry of the system/environment distinction. In this way, a systems-theoretical analysis "frees us . . . from the mystifications previously attached to concepts such as 'meaning' (*Sinn*) or 'mind' (*Geist*). They enable us to see today more clearly why and how something like 'imagination' is required and in what sense construction/deconstruction/reconstruction as an ongoing process, an ongoing displacement of distinctions (Derrida's *différance*), is necessary in order to dissolve paradoxes in and as time."[33] Upon reading this, one cannot help but recall Lee's thesis concerning God's "self-repetition in time," but with a theoretical rigor that can evade the supposition of humanism. It is not my intent to submit that Edwards is a proto–systems theorist any more than he is a protoromantic; it is instead to argue that his attempt to show that the world of creation is necessarily indebted to a Creator, which is to say that creation is founded on an exclusion that it paradoxically *cannot* see, can be more easily understood with the help of theories that deal explicitly with self-reference.

De Prospo writes that for Edwards, "Form in nature signifies a principle of order both superior and opposed to matter."[34] This agrees with the idea that Edwards is concerned with *form*, an act of distinction that makes observation of the world possible by marking itself (that is, the observation itself) as different from what is observed. Through this self-acknowledged limitation or closure, a self-referential distinction refers to the intrinsically chaotic character of nature that is reducible in itself to no forms, that is so exceedingly complex, so infinite, that it exists on another plain entirely from the observable. This means that the infinite is not simply an extrapolation or extension of the finite, but totally heterogeneous to it. This also suggests that the infinite, God, or the environment can be most accurately described (though still so far from accuracy as to be mostly false) as an undecidable state of pure possibility, in which multiple possibilities exist at the same time, in which, for instance, something can be both true *and* false. This realm, however, is not observable without a cut or a distinction, without a form to reduce the complexity of the environment, and so it is not available for observation but persists, out of the corner of the observer's eye, as the infinite possibilities that must be occluded for an observation to actualize or determine what it is observing. As Perry Miller writes,

God did not create the world, said Edwards, merely to exhibit His glory;
he did not create it out of nothing simply to show that He could: He
who is Himself the source of all being, the substance of all life, created
the world out of Himself by a diffusion of Himself into time and space.
He made the world, not by sitting outside and above it, by modeling it
as a child models sand, but by an extension of Himself, by taking upon
Himself the forms of stones and trees and of man. He created without
any ulterior object in view, neither for His glory nor for His power, but
for the pure joy of self-expression, as an artist creates beauty for the
love of beauty. God does not need a world or the worship of man; He is
perfect in Himself. If He bothers to create, it is out of the fullness of His
own nature, the overflowing virtue that is in Him.[35]

Much as in Lee's helpful formulation, the most ingenious aspect of
this idea of Creation is that it suggests that God created the world as
a means to actualize Himself through determinant forms. For God to
actualize His own overdetermined possibilities, he differentiates Himself in forms. This actualization is not a limitation, however, because
it only takes place through partiality, finitude, and contingency—and
therefore actualization is at the same time something like *non*actualization, nonidentical even to itself. In this way, actuality and the infinity signified by pure possibility are presented simultaneously, but only
through their *difference* and not through their identity or unity in
something like consciousness or imagination. God and his actualization in forms are the repetition of a difference or distinction: a continual splitting apart of part and whole. And it is in this last sense that
God becomes both the first and the last of Creation, the first "uncaused
cause" *and* the final actualization of the universe, as if creation begins
and ends with the infinity of God, as if the world as we know it begins
and ends in contingency.

The Forms of Creation

As there is an infinite fullness of all possible good in God—a fullness of every perfection, of all excellency and beauty, and of infinite happiness—and as this fullness is capable of communication,
or emanation *ad extra*; so it seems a thing amiable and valuable in

itself that this infinite fountain of good should send forth abundant
streams, that this infinite fountain of light should, diffusing its excel-
lent fullness, pour forth light all around.

JONATHAN EDWARDS, "CONCERNING THE END FOR WHICH GOD
CREATED THE WORLD"

Two early pieces, "Of Being" (1721) and "The Mind" (1723), suggest that
Edwards hit upon certain critical ideas at a precocious age and developed
them in further complexity throughout his life. "Of Being" is concerned
with the perennial problem of universal continuity. How can the world be
both differentiated and one, both parts and whole? Edwards writes, "We
fancy there may be figures and magnitudes, relations and properties, without anyone's knowing of it. But it is our imagination hurts us. We don't
know what figures and properties are."[36] What are figures, properties, and
relations (that is, differences) if they are not real existing qualities of the
universe? In answer, Edwards writes a passage worth quoting at length:

> Let us suppose the world deprived of every ray of light, so that there
> should not be the least glimmering of light in the universe. Now all
> will own that in such a case, the universe would be immediately really
> deprived of all its colors. One part of the universe is no more red, or
> blue, or green, or yellow, or black, or white, or light, or dark, or trans-
> parent, or opaque than another. There would be no visible distinction
> between the world and the rest of the incomprehensible void—yea, there
> would be no difference in these respects between the world and the infi-
> nite void. That is, any part of that void would really be as light and as
> dark, as white and as black, as red and as green, as blue and as brown,
> as transparent and as opaque as any part of the universe. Or, as there
> would be in such case no difference between the world and nothing in
> these respects, so there would be no difference between one part of the
> world and another. All, in these respects, is alike confounded with and
> indistinguishable from infinite emptiness.[37]

My gambit is that Edwards supposes a *distinction* as the fundamental act
of perception. Since the universe itself contains no differences (the universe
or the whole is not different from itself) but is instead continuous, there are
no differences but that we make them so. To see is to see only a difference.

Shapes and colors and magnitudes, therefore, are not a matter of the inherent qualities of a substance, but exist only in an act of interested observation. As the cyberneticist Heinz von Foerster puts it, " 'Out there' there is no light and no color, there are only electromagnetic waves; 'out there' there is no sound and no music, there are only periodic variations of air pressure."[38] Or more generally, "The environment as we perceive it is our invention."[39] The environment, that is, is a difference produced within the system.

Daniel comes to a similar understanding of Edwards by connecting his thought to medieval suppositional logic: "Instead of assuming that things are significant prior to their incorporation into the rhetoric of creation, Edwards's supposition theory defines each thing in terms of its supposition of something other than itself. In literally supposing a thing we imply the existence of God as the other always already removed in supposing any thing."[40] As already noted, Daniel's semiotic framework seems to suggest that God is in some sense synonymous with the totality of discourse—that the differential mechanisms of semiotics can have meaning only when placed *within* "the rhetoric of creation," something one presumes is like the class of all classes. Does this mean that God is then responsible for connecting signs with their meanings? This gives the term "discourse" a rather weighty theological role, for it would then escape from its own suppositional logic. As if in answer, Daniel later writes, "To say that the world exists means that it points to its displacement as that which gives it meaning. Accordingly, God is not that which supposes or displaces the world, for that would mean that the world exists independently from God. Rather, God is the supposition of the world, the world's having been supposed or displaced."[41] This is a critical insight because it confronts God as pure difference. God may be described as the other "always already removed" (that is, the discourse of discourses within which the play of difference takes place), but when one wants to suppose the world itself as a whole ("the world exists"), God manages to elude us like Russell's barber. The binary God/world subordinates God to the immanence of that distinction and suggests equivalence between God and creation, an impossibility for Edwards. There is therefore no overriding discourse in which the distinction between God and world can take place, no discourse that gives that distinction any meaning because there is no possibility of uniting the terms in any kind of symmetrical relationship. They cannot become adequate to each other lest God be subordinated to the relationship between God and his creation.

How then to understand God? Building from Daniel's insights, we may suppose that God is the unity of the distinction between the world and its other. This idea introduces inside the concept of "unity" a re-entry of the distinction between unity and disunity: what can now be described as a distinction between "unity" and "identity." The unity of a distinction is a *non*identity, the difference itself, a double consciousness. God is not the world's other, for the world cannot exist independently from God (as De Prospo notes, self-creation is impossible for Edwards, and the continuity of the world is sustained only by the will of God). Neither is the world identical to God (this is impious pantheism). God is neither the world nor the not-world. To recall Luhmann: "He is the *non-aliud*, that which is not different from anything different." Or Miller: "Puritan thinking on the subject of the Deity always confronted the ini-tial difficulty that in one sense thinking about Him was impossible."[42] Or Derrida: "God is the name of the absolute metonymy, what it names by displacing the names, the substitution and what substitutes itself in the name of this substitution."[43] God is neither in nor out of the sys-tem. God is the unity of the distinction world/not-world, not anything identifiable by means of the distinction but the distinction itself and therefore the fact of the re-entry of the distinction into itself that points, paradoxically, even mystically, to the unity of the distinction. God is the unity (but not the identity) of the distinction. This is self-referential paradox as religious meditation.

Self-reference removes consciousness from its place as an objective observer (the starting point for modern science and philosophy) and places it squarely in the thick of things as an active participant in what is constructed before it. All views are partial views (even, it goes with-out saying, this one). For Edwards, the human mind has a stake in cre-ation. In Miller's words, he "asserted the radical conception of man as an active, interested, passionate being, whose relation to objective reality is factual to the extent that he is concerned about it, whose anxieties and not his clear thinking make his destiny."[44] A fallen human consciousness, in other words, is a *part* of the world, fully within and not above it. The only unity is a unity beyond the makings of any distinctions, thus out of sight but held together as continuous by the infinite observing pow-ers of God, the unobserved observer: "God is by definition a Being who perceives not separate entities in succession, but the totality of being in a single, eternal glace."[45]

The observer and the observed are both the same, and not the same, with the perceiving act distinguishing itself from the perceived in a form of self-referential closure that references an unseen "other" as a necessary part of the observation. This leaves the possibility that one may, through the vacillations of self-reference and the re-entry or repetition of the distinction, catch what escapes perception through an acknowledgment of that very exclusion. We cannot see *what* we cannot see, but we can see *that* we cannot see. In religious terms, this is translated into a distinction between immanence and transcendence that takes place on the side of immanence. As Miller writes, "Because the source of ideas is external, and yet every idea is a self's manner of conceiving, there must come a time when the redeemed self realizes that a sensation cannot be clutched to his bosom as a private luxury, but belongs to a system of impressions that has a logic deeper and more beautiful than any incidental advantages (or disadvantages) that accrue to him."[46] Reality, in other words, is what one perceives when one does not perceive it. As we will see, Edwards's most developed version of this idea occurs in *The Nature of True Virtue*, yet the theme persists at varying levels of prominence throughout his writing.

Consider, for instance, the idea of spiritual perception in *A Treatise Concerning Religious Affections* (1746). As Michael J. McClymond has noted, there are two mutually exclusive ways to interpret spiritual perception in *Religious Affections*. Either one may argue that it is "discontinuous" with material reality and thus represents something like a "sixth sense," or one may follow Miller and argue for "continuity": "Those who make a case for continuity describe Edwards's spiritual sense as the apprehension of a content that is already accessible and known through everyday experience. . . . Grace is sensible, not supersensible. . . . Perry Miller originated this 'continuous' interpretation of the spiritual sense."[47] However, Miller's work has suffered due criticism, particularly for his enthusiastic recasting of Edwards as an empirical psychologist in the Lockean mode. As James Hoopes puts it, Miller made "persistent attempts to make Edwards not only 'modern' but also a materialist like Miller himself."[48]

In contrast to Miller, McClymond argues,

> Edwards sought duality without duplicity, and it is not surprising that
> his later readers have tended to lay hold of one or the other side of

his formulations. . . . He insisted on God's immediate presence to each believer and on the indispensability of divine grace. Yet, simultaneously he asserted that the spiritual sense was a kind of evidence for God's reality and that the perception of God's beauty and truth enabled the human mind to perceive truth and beauty wherever it appears.[49]

Again, we find something like a synthesis of contrary terms: "Spiritual perception," according to McClymond, "links idea and emotion, the cognitive and the affective. It meshes experiential manifestation with philosophical reflection. It brings together God and nature."[50] This argument solves the continuity versus discontinuity debate by robbing both "idea" and "emotion" of their distinct power, their difference. On the contrary, Edwards does not simply mesh the two terms together, finding one as a reflection of the other, but uses their attraction and repulsion to each other as a spiritual practice in itself, seeing the vacillation or re-entry (the process itself) of the excluded third as a reference to meaning or complexity, or, in Edwards's own terminology, as a reference to God. Edwards seeks unity as a spiritual practice, but only as the by-product of the processional march of worldly differentiation.

That is to say, spiritual sense does not offer any *determinate* mode of conduct. It does not go to work in the world as itself. Instead, it refers only to itself. It leads to its own reproduction, a repetition of its difference from the material world and determinate modes of conduct. Feelings lead to actions, but religious feeling also leads back to itself as forever different from any particular action. As Edwards writes in a dense and difficult passage,

> This new spiritual sense, and the new dispositions that attend to it, are no new faculties, but are new principles of nature. I use the word "principles," for want of a word of a more determinate signification. By a principle of nature in this place, I mean that foundation which is laid in nature, either old or new, for any particular manner or kind of exercise of the faculties of the soul; or a natural habit or foundation for action, giving a person ability and disposition to exert the faculties in exercises of such a certain kind; so that to exert the faculties in that kind of exercises, may be said to be his nature. So this new spiritual sense is not a new faculty of understanding, but it is a new foundation laid in the nature of the soul, for a new kind of exercises of the same

faculty of understanding. So that new holy disposition of heart that attends this new sense, is not a new faculty of will, but a foundation laid in the nature of the soul, for a new kind of exercises of will.[51]

Spiritual feeling is "new" because it effects a change in natural habits *without being identified with those particular habits*. It is the newness, what Emerson calls "onwardness," that matters, and only in this sense is Christian practice identified. As argued throughout this chapter, the operation of this practice can then be best clarified by understanding it as a self-referential distinction. Religious feelings are the repetition of a difference from the habits they give rise to, a re-entry of the distinction into itself. True religion, then, is an engagement, not a doctrine: "That religion which God requires, and will accept, does not consist in weak, dull and lifeless wishes, raising us but a little above a state of indifference: God, in his Word, greatly insists upon it, that we be in good earnest, fervent in spirit, and our hearts vigorously engaged in religion."[52] One does not grasp religious feeling; one is grasped by *it*, enfolded by *it*. It is not in us, it seems, but we are in *it*. The signs of saintliness are demonstrated only in Christian practice, and so not in actual habitual practice at all. One cannot set one's watch by God, who dispenses His grace as He sees fit: "It was never God's design to give us any rules, by which we may certainly know, who of our fellow professors are his, and to make a full and clear separation between sheep and goats: but that on the contrary, it was God's design to reserve this to himself, as his prerogative. And therefore no such distinguishing signs as shall enable Christians or ministers to do this, are ever to be expected to the world's end."[53] Spiritual feeling persists as the unmarked side—the *unactualized* side—of every distinction, and there is no final sign.

On the Nature of True Virtue

'Tis no solid objection against God's aiming at an infinitely perfect union of the creature with himself, that the particular time will never come when it can be said, the union now is infinitely perfect.

JONATHAN EDWARDS, "CONCERNING THE END FOR WHICH GOD
CREATED THE WORLD"

According to R. C. De Prospo, Edwards (as well as Puritan thought generally) conceives of the universe as a cascading series of "frames"—each descending frame a step farther from grace: "The being of God is diffused throughout Creation in regular stages, or, as Edwards terms them, 'frames' of existence. These frames ascend hierarchically according to the amount of divine being they contain."[54] This informs what Edwards understands by his favored term "excellency" because while some idea of excellency may be perceived down here on the lower frames of existence, as when Edwards writes in "The Mind," "All beauty consists in similarness of identity of relation,"[55] true excellency is nevertheless constituted by a more general identity of relation, a larger framework: "The more the consent is, and the more extensive, the greater is the excellency."[56]

How then may we understand the greatest excellency? For Edwards, this is accomplished only by consent to "being in general," a concept for the totality of relations that nevertheless applies that same logic to itself:

> One alone without any reference to any more cannot be excellent; for, in such case, there can be no manner of relation no way, and therefore no such thing as consent. Indeed, what we call "one" may be excellent because of a consent of parts, or some consent of those in that being that are distinguished into a plurality some way or other. But in a being that is absolutely without any plurality there cannot be excellency, for there can be no such thing as consent or agreement.[57]

One alone has no excellency because that quality grows only with the progress of consent, the relation of parts to a greater whole. Edwards often calls this progress a form of "virtue" or "love," which successively rises up from one frame to another, ultimately toward God: "For, so far as a thing consents to being in general, so far it consents to Him. And the more perfect created spirits are, the nearer do they come to their Creator in this regard."[58] What's most interesting about this idea is that it seems to suggest that the concept of excellency as consent to being in general names at the same time a difference from being in general *and* an sameness to it—an elusive unity: the sameness of what is different.

In his late masterwork *The Nature of True Virtue*, Edwards lays out a perspective on being in general that, in Sharon Cameron's perceptive reading, outstrips any possibility of virtue or love for a real human being, or any particular thing at all:

When Edwards defines "virtuous love" as exempt from a private system, and defines a "private system," no matter how expansive, as anything less than what comprehends "the universality of existence"—when he insists moreover that all nonuniversal love "put in the scales with it, has no greater proportion to it" than love for a single person—it is safe to say that any person's love is excluded from qualifying as virtuous. Thus while Edwards deliberates the differences between a private system and a common morality, with its ever-enlarging circumference, he finally lumps these together, drawing a line between love based on any sense of exclusion (all love had by all persons) and that extended without limit everywhere. The latter—specified in this treatise by opposition, negation, and inference—repeatedly defined as what persons cannot muster, constitutes the only nontrivial principle of justice.[59]

Cameron's interpretation of *The Nature of True Virtue* expertly points out what is most remarkable about it: Edward's definition of virtue seems to be devoid of any practical content. It seems to suggest that whatever one might do, toward whatever one might give love, and no matter how wide and general a love it may be, it is not "true virtue" because it is limited or "nonuniversal." True virtue is forever distinct from worldly virtue: "Edwards is not proscribing what we can do. The impediment is part of the point."[60] The point being, by implication, our distance from the infinity of divine love: "The infinite is preserved as an ideal not in spite of our being unable to arrive at it, but precisely because we can't empirically arrive at it."[61]

True virtue is, for Cameron, essentially impossible. It is not something "we can do," and in this respect it conforms to the strict adherence to an absolute dichotomy between transcendence and immanence. From this point, however, it is possible to put our finger more precisely on the meaning of this impossibility and the paradox it points to. I want to suggest that "true virtue," while not achievable for an individual, is nevertheless something that still *happens*. True virtue represents the means by which we are held accountable for the private and limited frames that we adopt. It is the means by which we are pulled toward greater consent to being in general, not by the logic of our private systems but by the nonidentity or asymmetry that irrupts from within them.

In "The Mind," Edwards writes, "We have said already that it is naturally agreeable to perceiving being that being should consent to being, and the contrary, disagreeable. If by any means, therefore, a particular and restrained love overcomes this general consent, the foundation of that consent yet remaining in the nature exerts itself again, so that there is the contradiction of one consent to another."[62] We may take this to mean that any "particular and restrained" love is always already *disagreeable* to the general consent—or agreeable insofar as it consents and disagreeable insofar as it does not. What Edwards calls the "foundation of that consent" represents this distinction, the fundamental *nonidentity* of the particular and of its paradoxical difference from the whole while nevertheless being a part of it. This passage suggests that true virtue is not simply impossible, not simply the mark of transcendence, but the repetition of the distinction between transcendence and immanence *in* that distinction. It is possible as impossible—which is to say, it is not possible for an individual or part because it is precisely Edwards's point to hold those limited domains accountable for what they leave out, namely, being in general.

Again, it is Niklas Luhmann who can help us understand the distinction Edwards makes between a private and a general system of virtue:

> Communication systems develop a special way to deal with complexity, i.e. introducing a representation of the complexity of the world into systems. I call this representation of complexity "meaning"—avoiding all subjective, psychological or transcendental connotations of this term. . . . The function of meaning is to provide access to all possible topics of communication. Meaning places all concrete items into a horizon of further possibilities and finally into the world of all possibilities. Whatever shows up as an actual event refers to other possibilities, to other ways of related actions and experience within the horizon of further possibilities. Each meaningful item reconstructs the world by the difference between the actual and the possible. Security, however, lies only in the actual. It can be increased only by indirection, by passing on to other meanings while retaining the possibility of returning to its present position. Again, a self-referential, recursive structure is needed to combine complexity and security.[63]

Luhmann describes religion as a system that takes upon itself the task of representing the unity of all distinctions to itself, and so it becomes a system in which the oscillations of self-reference are most acute. God is continually causing revolutions: "Religious forms incorporate, so to speak, paradoxical meanings; they differentiate religion against other fields of life; they involve the risk of refusal; they inaugurate deviant reproduction, i.e. evolution."[64] What Cameron correctly identifies in *True Virtue* as an impediment, what might be termed an uncrossable (or one-sided) boundary, can also be seen with the aid of Luhmann's systems theory as a form of openness, the sense in which the system is exposed to the environment and forced to evolve. This is, as Cary Wolfe has observed, the "openness from closure" principle: "The very thing that separates us from the world *connects* us to the world, and self-referential, autopoietic closure, far from indicating a kind of solipsistic neo-Kantian idealism, actually is generative of openness to the environment."[65] It is in this respect that "private systems" make themselves accountable to *other*, or more general, systems through that very closure.

The Nature of True Virtue is Edwards's most sophisticated attempt to create what might be called an open-ended or process-oriented ethics—an ethical system that holds *itself* accountable. Edwards makes a crucial distinction very early in *True Virtue*:

> There is a general and particular beauty. By a particular beauty, I mean that by which a thing appears beautiful when considered only with regard to its connection with, and tendency to, some particular things within a limited, and as it were a private sphere. And a general beauty is that by which a thing appears beautiful when viewed most perfectly, comprehensively and universally, with regard to all its tendencies, and its connections with every thing to which it stands related.[66]

One may read this distinction as having no value for embodied and particular persons, but the shear impossibility of grasping what Edwards identifies as general beauty can be overcome when it is indentified as what Luhmann above calls "meaning." General beauty, then, represents the limitedness of any particular beauty, its particularity or actuality, and thus acts as a reference to *further*, infinitely further, determinations of that beauty as part of a larger system of the world, "or beautiful in a comprehensive view."[67] A particular object can be beautiful in itself, but only insofar as it references the unrepresentable whole, a crucial analogy for understanding what Edwards means by "true virtue," which consists in *"benevolence to being in general."*[68] He goes on, "When I say true virtue consists in love to being in general, I shall not be likely to be understood, that no one act of the mind or exercise of love is of the nature of true virtue, but what has being in general, or the great system of universal existence, for its direct and immediate object: so that no exercise of love, or kind affection to any one particular being, that is but a small part of this whole, has any thing of the nature of true virtue."[69] Any particular act is limited and one-sided, it has *no part* of true virtue, it is entirely distinct from it, and this imbalance leads it inevitably toward a "larger" symmetry or unity that in turn cannot be seen because it too is inevitably one-sided. True virtue escapes the private systems it continually generates.

Edwards sees this process as circular: "If virtue consists primarily in love to virtue, then virtue, the thing loved, is the love of virtue: so that virtue must consist in the love of the love of virtue—and so on in infinitum. For there is no end of going back in a circle. We never come to any beginning or foundation; it is without beginning, and hangs on nothing."[70] He continues, "Therefore, if the essence of virtue of beauty of mind lies in love, or a disposition to love, it must primarily consist in something *different* both from complacence, which is a delight in beauty, and also from any benevolence that has the beauty of its object for its foundation. Because 'tis absurd to say that virtue is primarily and first of all the consequence of itself. For this makes virtue primarily prior to itself."[71] The difference that Edwards speaks of can best be understood as a self-referential distinction, a kind of symmetry-breaking that references Being by marking itself out as false to it.

Self-referential closure opens out on to the infinite possibilities of meaning. Derrida's words in *The Gift of Death* offer a contemporary point of comparison: "On what condition does goodness exist beyond all calculation? On the condition that goodness forget itself, that the movement be a movement of the gift that renounces itself, hence a movement of infinite love. . . . I have never been and never will be up to the level of this infinite goodness nor up to the immensity of the gift, the frameless immensity that must in general define a gift as such."[72] The frameless immensity appears within the frame as a *gift* for Derrida, an asymmetrical movement toward the other, and likewise for Edwards the nature of the love of virtue and thus the law of spiritual growth raises us up toward grace. Edwards writes, "As to that excellence that created spirits partake of, that it is all to be resolved into love; . . . that to love is to fulfill the royal law; and that all the law is fulfilled in this one word, love."[73] Virtue is the unity, but not the identity, of the distinction between private and general systems, between part and whole. It is the infinite within the finite and fallen systems of our love.

— 4 —
Neither Here nor There

Grief and Absence in Emerson's "Experience"

Yesterday night, at fifteen minutes after eight, my little Waldo ended
his life.

RALPH WALDO EMERSON, *JOURNALS*, JANUARY 28, 1842

It seems as if I ought to call upon the winds to describe my boy, my
fast receding boy, a child of so large & generous a nature that I cannot paint him by specialties, as I might another.

RALPH WALDO EMERSON, *JOURNALS*, JANUARY 30, 1842

The movement of love is circular, at one and the same impulse projecting creations into independency and drawing them into harmony.

CHARLES S. PEIRCE, "EVOLUTIONARY LOVE"

Ralph Waldo Emerson wrote "Experience" (1844) shortly after the death
of his son, and yet the essay is notorious for the fact that Emerson pointedly refuses to demonstrate his grief. It would seem, from his words and
the cursory manner in which he treats it, that the loss does not affect
him: "In the death of my son, now more than two years ago, I seem to
have lost a beautiful estate,—no more."[1] Instead, "Experience" finds its
author adrift on an ocean of signifiers that do not find their mark. Unable
or unwilling to speak his son's name, Emerson is preoccupied with the
inadequacy of the very act of naming, and consequently the claim in
Nature (1836) that "words are signs of natural facts" can no longer be
sustained.[2] Rather than perform a eulogy that systematically remembers
the names of the dead, it seems as if "Experience" turns around to inter-
rogate the constitutive faultiness of language, its inability to refer to an
actual world beyond the words themselves.

Not surprisingly, "Experience" is often linked to a decisive shift
away from the optimistic and affirmative transcendentalism espoused in
Nature, particularly the idea that we are fundamentally at home in the

world. In fact, it would seem that Emerson's stance on naming in "Experience" does not differ in spirit from the Calvinist philosophy regarding representations of God, as seen in the Puritan poet Edward Taylor's lament: "Whether I speake, or speechless stand . . ./I faile thy Glory."[3] Not only do these words express the inadequacy of language, but they imbue that inadequacy with the double bind of an ethical charge to accurately represent the unrepresentable. To stand speechless does not discharge the duty. Emerson's silence in "Experience" can be seen to enact similar problems, with his prose continually hinting at what it cannot, or will not, say despite itself: "An innavigable sea washes with silent waves between us and the things we aim at and converse with. Grief too will make us idealists."[4] If we cannot speak the unspeakable, and cannot remain silent, what can we say? Here Niklas Luhmann considers the problem under very nearly the same terms as Taylor:

> The other possibility is silence—a silence that no longer wants to be understood as communication (but forever understood, is understandable only in this way). This does not only mean to opt for silence within the distinction between speaking and silence, but to avoid the distinction as such, so that the problem does not arise in the first place. . . . But then, doesn't one still have the problem that in a world in which one speaks, silence is possible only within self-drawn boundaries, i.e., as the production of difference?[5]

Emerson's silence speaks volumes, but his words would have it that his son is utterly lost along with the world itself, not to be recovered even in grief. And yet, as Sharon Cameron's influential essay on "Experience" poignantly argues, Emerson's pointed elisions offer a "testament to the pervasiveness of a loss so inclusive that it is inseparable from experience itself."[6]

While the arguments of this chapter would not be possible without Cameron's important insights, I will depart slightly from her analysis of "Experience" in order to take Emerson more plainly at his word. I will take Emerson's claim that "I cannot get it nearer to me"[7] in reference to the loss of his son at something closer to face value: a total refusal of representation and not simply a coy or indirect representation of hidden grief. In retrospect, the breakthrough of Cameron's idea is that she provides the interpreter of "Experience" with the ability to see Emerson's grief everywhere at once in the text, and thus liberates a potential for readers of "Experience" to incorporate into their interpretations exactly the thing that Emerson excludes. This is significant. If it is axiomatic for criticism that "every system excludes or expels something which does not let itself be thought within the terms of the system, and lets itself be fascinated, magnetized, and controlled by this excluded term, its transcendental's transcendental,"[8] then Cameron brilliantly shows that "Experience" is a text that is uniquely, and paradoxically, *about* its excluded term.

However, that powerful analysis can occur only at the expense of a confrontation with the more radical effects of Emerson's denial of feeling. For Cameron, the dead son is not left behind or forgotten in his singularity, but quite the reverse: grief is so substantially present that it stands behind every word in the essay—as if every word says the child's name—while subsuming all particulars under a guiding transcendental term. Cameron's interpretation of "Experience" has the curious effect of flattening an essay of extraordinary depth since the particular experience of grief "migrates so that it is recognizable as the property of *all* experience independent of particularity."[9] Even the title of Cameron's essay, "Representing Grief," assumes the very thing Emerson seems at pains to question. She heroically rescues the child from the oblivion of death, while Emerson seems only too willing to leave him there.

Some of the force of Emerson's meaning in "Experience" is thereby lost if we accept wholesale Cameron's reincorporation of his absent grief, and yet at the same time it cannot be denied that an understandable and unavoidable melancholic longing for the dead child persists in all subsequent readings of "Experience." This dilemma can be resolved by arguing that Emerson's refusal of grief rejects any internalized representation of his son in favor of accepting his son, and therefore his relationship to his son, as finally external and independent from himself—such is the lesson of death. This interpretation reconciles Cameron's discovery of Emerson's grief within or behind his words with the more explicit denials of grief found in the text, thus insisting that the excluded term *remain* excluded—what amounts to the reincorporation or repetition of a fundamental absence.

"Knowledge as such is a space of transformation,"[10] writes Michel Serres, and with that statement in mind we may approach "Experience" through Charles S. Peirce's concept of Thirdness, the logical category for signs. The determined actuality of a sign, as Peirce has it, is always related at the same time to an undetermined future being, and so the meaning of a sign (Thirdness) is forever playing itself out as a relationship between the actual (what Peirce calls Secondness) and the possible (Firstness). This means that the final meaning of a sign is ultimately something that *remains* to be determined: "The rational meaning of every proposition lies in the future."[11] Floyd Merrell puts it most ably: "To know what a sign *is* entails knowing at least in part what it *is not*, but *might otherwise have been*. Without some inkling of the unknown and unactualized, whatever is known at a given moment would be no more than a self-sufficient, unrelated whole."[12] This state of affairs, in which propositions are confronted with their own limitation or constitutive partiality, calls for an attempt to get beyond the traditional being/nonbeing binary that grounds Western metaphysics in order to introduce a logical description of contingency, what Luhmann has called "a third value of undeterminability."[13] As he writes,

> The concept of contingency is quickly and clearly defined within the apparatus of modal logical concepts. Anything is contingent that is neither necessary nor impossible. The concept is therefore defined by the negation of necessity and impossibility. The problem lies in the fact that these two negations cannot be reduced to a single negation. This would not really be a problem if negation were considered an identical operator and then simply applied to different statements. Here, however, *one* concept is *constituted* by *two* negations that must then be used in the singular in the subsequent employment of the concept. In the Middle Ages this led to the notion that the contingency problem could not be adequately addressed using a two-valued classical logic predicated on ontology (being/nonbeing).[14]

We may take Peirce's "triadic logic" as an attempt to accomplish exactly this. As he puts it, "*Potentiality* is the absence of Determination (in the usual broad sense) not of a mere negative kind but a positive capacity to be Yea and to be Nay; not ignorance but a state of being."[15]

This sense of a sign representing a "third value" provides a means for interpreting Emerson's grief as neither incorporated in *nor* excluded from the text. Reading "Experience" is itself an experience mediated by a mood of intense grief for an object so conspicuous in its absence that it overflows and surges past the representational schemes demanded by mourning. The idealism of the "glass prison" that permeates the opening pages gives way not to a strict metaphysical realism but to a semiotic understanding of the world as independent and undetermined, a realm of infinite potential awaiting determination and actualization. Grief may make us idealists, but the absence of Emerson's grief in "Experience" leads to a third way between idealism's glass prison and a naïve realism.

In order to make this argument, I will expand on Cameron's breakthrough text by introducing a Derridean reading of the term "experience" as aporia, thus connecting Emerson's essay to an experience of the liminal or that which is permanently between. At the same time, I also take Emerson's suspicion of representation following the death of his son to derive from an inheritance of the Calvinist suspicion of mourning, which discourages any naming of the dead due to the risk of improper worldly attachments. In order to make this connection, I will compare Emerson's text to the captivity narrative of Mary Rowlandson, a powerful Puritan text of grief and homelessness, as well as to Mitchell Breitwieser's provocative reading of Rowlandson's text. Finally, with the framework made available by the introduction of the Calvinist material, I will argue that Emerson is ultimately reconciled to the loss of his son through an understanding of his son as a relation or sign in the Peircean sense: neither here nor there, neither present nor absent, neither mind-dependent nor mind-independent. This is somewhat like what Stanley Cavell observes in his important essay on "Experience" as "an acceptance of separateness,"[16] except that separateness is itself a necessary condition for any attachment at all.

Reading "Experience" in this way involves a kind of ventriloquism, a strategy of putting names into Emerson's mouth to substitute for the name he will not speak. In place of that name is offered a series of necessarily inadequate substitutions: Nietzsche, Freud, Derrida, Cameron, Rowlandson, and Peirce. These proper names bring along a context of associations and presuppositions that are less important for themselves than for their eventual displacement and substitution. In reading "Experience" this way, in effect mimicking Emerson's relentless substitutions of the "Lords of Life," it is hoped that the effect achieved will help to clarify the argument. Following the course of these names, we will find ourselves first on one side (an internalization of the lost object) and then on the other (a rejection of internalization) in order to better grasp the third way pursued in "Experience." This strategy admits the necessity of binaries while at the same time using them to indicate what the law of the excluded middle leaves out.

Experience as Aporia

You have no idea what you are experiencing; you run through life as if you were drunk and once in a while fall down a staircase. But thanks to your drunkenness, you don't break your limbs in the process; your muscles are too slack and your head too dull for you to find the stones of these stairs as hard as the rest of us do! For us, life is a greater danger: we are made of glass—woe unto us if we bump against something! And everything is lost if we fall!

FRIEDRICH NIETZSCHE, *THE GAY SCIENCE*

In this vivid passage from *The Gay Science*, a comic image of drunkenly falling down stairs forcefully suggests the treacherous danger of the ground beneath our feet. Very early in "Experience," we find ourselves in a similar scenario: "We wake and find ourselves on a stair; there are stairs below us, which we seem to have ascended; there are stairs above us, many a one, which go upward and out of sight."[17] A staircase, a space without stable or determinate foundations, evokes the homelessness or tension inherent in liminal spaces: always between, areas of transition in which rest or stasis is impossible. Staircases, moreover, are relational, as a line may be diagonal only in comparison with the straight or horizontal. They are temporary, as a staircase only begins on one level ground and ends on another, suspended in mid-air just as the staircase suspends, or places in suspense, those that traverse it.

Nietzsche characteristically casts metaphysical confusion in the terms of an imminent risk to life and body. Emerson, also characteristically, doesn't seem to recognize the threat of falling at all, and focuses instead on the dreamlike feeling that accompanies confusion: "All things swim and glitter. Our life is not so much threatened as our perception."[18] Indeed, Emerson seems to see the human condition as akin to permanent inebriation: "But the Genius which, according to the old belief, stands at the door by which we enter, and gives us the lethe to drink, that we may tell no tales, mixed the cup too strongly, and we cannot shake off the lethargy now at noonday."[19] The lethe (notably in Greek the opposite of *aletheia* [to uncover]) casts a shroud over all perception, yet it also inebriates to the point that no pain is felt as we bump our way along. For Nietzsche, it is our sober commitment to truth that threatens our lives, but Emerson's target in "Experience" is not so much the problem of truth as the threat of an enervating skepticism. Nietzsche questions how one is to survive and navigate the staircases, the abyssal transitional moments between the level grounds of decision and action. Emerson's task is to cope with a permanent lack of foundation, an infinite staircase with no level ground in sight.

Indulge me a bit further in imagining that Emerson sits dejected and sleepy on the staircase while Nietzsche wonders in passing at his drunken imperviousness. Emerson's stupor suggests nothing so much as what Freud defined as melancholia, an affective condition closely connected to mourning that provides for the possibility of inhabiting the staircase. More abstractly, it presents the individual with the possibility of being *between* indefinitely. In this state, Freud writes, we find "profoundly painful dejection, abrogation of interest in the outside world, loss of capacity to love, inhibition of all activity"—all due to an inability to conclusively detach oneself from the lost object.[20] With the form of melancholia that occurs in mourning, especially with the loss of a loved one, we find a "loss of a capacity to adopt any new object of love, which would mean a replacing of the one mourned, the same turning from every active effort that is not connected with thoughts of the dead."[21] Here the melancholic individual cannot yet return to the world because the lost object persists as a gap that cannot be papered over and therefore cannot ever be fully represented: "The patient cannot readily perceive what it is that he has lost."[22]

As Freud would have it, the proper course of mourning entails a finality and consummation of the project that finally lets go of the lost object through the accomplishment of introjection: a complete integration of a representation of the lost object into the self. However, it is easy to imagine that the loss of a young child, a being of seemingly limitless potential, is a loss especially difficult to mourn due to an inability to define or delimit just what, exactly, has been lost. The death of a child, that is, seems in some sense to represent a loss of the future itself, thereby leaving the subject trapped in a kind of endless (and thus vacant and meaningless) present tense. Melancholic mourning, in contrast to successfully completed mourning, leads the subject to experience the lost object as conspicuous in its absence. For the melancholic subject, mourning cannot be completed because there is no possibility for an adequate representation of the lost object, no correct name that can call it to presence. Along similar lines, Cameron asserts that "Emerson preserves the sanctity of his feeling, preserves by keeping hidden or unconscious (that is, dissociated) his sorrow for the child, as if hidden the feeling escapes the words that debase it."[23] That is, only through a putative silence can Emerson truly mourn.

However, Cameron's reading of "Experience" seems to me to make too strong a claim when she writes that the essay is "governed by Emerson's relation to the dead child." Cameron argues that grief is present and behind every word in the essay, and she reconciles this with Emerson's explicit silence on the matter by supposing that Emerson's grief is present *in* the essay but hidden away in a secret place. This is a major breakthrough for making sense of a notoriously difficult text, but at the same time it presumes a symmetrical relationship between the essay and its excluded term, and therefore something like a negative adequacy of language is retained in Cameron's reading of the essay as what she calls "a powerful and systematic representation of grief."[24] In this reading, language becomes adequate to its transcendental exclusion through the tactics of substitution, silence, and secrecy—an adequacy and introjection accomplished through mere negativity. But isn't this speaking too? Doesn't this "fail" as well? By contrast, I want to argue that Emerson's silence suggests that his grief for his son is neither in nor out of the essay—it evades the binary logic of representation altogether, a logic of incorporation or exclusion that obscures other possibilities.

We can begin to approach this possibility by considering the most explicit philosophical theme of "Experience," what Emerson calls "the secret of illusoriness," which derives from "the necessity of a succession of moods or objects." Emerson offers the memorable metaphor of a "glass prison" to describe our condition, which brings a "vague guess at new fact" but "is nowise to be trusted as the lasting relation between that intellect and that thing."[25] He writes, "Dream delivers us to dream, and there is no end to illusion. Life is a train of moods like a string of beads, and, as we pass through them, they prove to be many-colored lenses which paint the world their own hue, and each shows only what lies in its focus. From the mountain you see the mountain."[26] From any

particular mood or perspective, one may only see what that mood or perspective reveals, which is to say that perspective, the necessary condition
for seeing at all, is inherently limited and partial.

The boundaries between different points of observation are uncrossable yet nevertheless visible; they are, to borrow from Jacques Derrida,
aporias. An aporia is not so much the space *outside* a particular perspective (how then would one know it is there?) as the inside edge of the
boundary of that perspective's limit—a fully internal indication of the
outside space. Derrida asks, "Can one speak—and if so, in what sense—
of an *experience of the aporia*? An experience *of the aporia as such*? Or
vice versa: Is an experience possible that would not be an experience of
the aporia?"[27] His questions are about the possibility of limit experiences, about the potential for *crossing over* the interval: "What would
such an *experience* be? The word ["experience"] also means passage,
traversal, endurance, and rite of passage, but can there be a traversal
without line and without indivisible border?"[28] Experience, in Derrida's
reading, names the act of traversing the aporia, or confronting the limit
of a mood's revealing powers, or holding still where one should not hold
still, as on a staircase:

> It had to be a matter of the nonpassage, or rather from the experience of
> the nonpassage, the experience of what happens and is fascinating in this
> nonpassage, paralyzing us in this separation in a way that is not neces-
> sarily negative: before a door, a threshold, a border, a line, or simply the
> edge or approach as such. It should be a matter of what, in sum, appears
> to block our way or to separate us in the very place where *it would no
> longer be possible to constitute a problem*, a project, or a projection, that
> is, at the point where the very project or the problematic task becomes
> impossible and where we are exposed, absolutely without protection,
> without problem, and without prosthesis, without possible substitution,
> singularity exposed in our absolute and absolutely naked uniqueness,
> that is to say, disarmed, delivered to the other, incapable even of shelter-
> ing ourselves behind what could still protect the interiority of a secret.[29]

The aporia thus exposes an absolute "singularity" that, in the terminology
of *Being and Time*, is connected to the anticipation of death. But Derrida
proceeds to overturn the singularity that grounds Heidegger's fundamental
ontology: "If death names the very irreplacability of absolute singularity

(no one can die in my place or in the place of the other), then all the *examples* in the world can precisely illustrate this singularity. Everyone's death, the death of all those who can say 'my death,' is irreplaceable."[30] In "Experience," Emerson seemingly denies this "irreplaceable" quality to his dead son, now no more than a lost "estate,—no more."[31] These seem to be callous words precisely because they deny Emerson's unnamed son his ability to say, as *Dasein*, "my death." Instead, it would seem Emerson is quite willing to usher his son, and his possession of whatever his son may have become, into a system of material economic exchanges where death is rendered as "bankruptcy"—a move that makes the child entirely replaceable and enacts the exact paradox that Derrida points to: every death is equally irreplaceable, and so any particular death is only as unique as every other. What is interesting about this move is that while it resists a modern approach to mourning—which points to the aporia Derrida describes—it also closely resembles a radical strain of early modernist thought: namely, Calvinism and, in particular, the early American Puritans.

If we follow through on this somewhat fanciful association, we will find that Emerson's lack of grief resembles the social taboo on excessive mourning or grief in Puritan culture. Of course, it need hardly be said that Emerson never became a Calvinist after abandoning Unitarianism, but "Experience" shows a dramatic turning in his thought, even if it is only relegated to a few sentences: "It is very unhappy, but too late to be helped, the discovery that we have made, that we exist. That discovery is called the Fall of Man."[32] This provocative statement raises a question: Who has made this discovery, and when? If "Experience" issues in the wake of unbearable trauma, then these words mark a fall twice over, a loss both personal and epistemological. As he puts it, "I know that the world I converse with in the city and in the farms, is not the world I *think*. I observe that difference and shall observe it. One day, I shall know the value and law of this discrepance."[33] The question of how one can observe a difference (the different *itself*) brings us once again to the brink of an aporia. What else is the sign of discrepancy but the inside limit that hints at what is unrepresentable?

Perry Miller's influential work on Puritanism provides an ideal departure for discovering the Puritan elements in Emerson's suppression of mourning. In his important essay "The Marrow of Puritan Divinity," Miller sums up the Puritan intellectual experience as an attempt to reconcile the irreconcilable:

Here, then, was the task which seventeenth-century Calvinists faced: the task of bringing God to time and to reason, of justifying His ways to man in conceptions meaningful to the intellect, of caging and confining the transcendent Force, the inexpressible and unfathomable Being, by the laws of ethics, and of doing this somehow without losing the sense of the hidden God, without reducing the Divinity to a mechanism, without depriving Him of unpredictability, absolute power, fearfulness, and mystery. In the final analysis this task came down to ascertaining the reliability of human reason and the trustworthiness of human experience as measurements of the divine character—in short, to the problem of human comprehension of this mysterious thing which we today call the universe.[34]

This description of the task of Calvinism clearly shares much with the descriptions of "Experience" offered earlier. But perhaps what's most important in this passage is the notion that the Puritans attempted to stay loyal to a God that surpasses human understanding, a God that always represents a potential "more than" which exceeds any present determination of meaning. The task of Calvinism, if we follow Miller, was to mark the discrepancy between the world as it is and the world as we think it. In this schema our observations are all incomplete, and necessarily so in our sinfulness. This flaw in our perception is reflected most emphatically in death, and so death does not represent a singularity to be recovered into the fold of the subject but a final irrecoverable *lack* that exposes the subject to original sin and the judgment of God. As Gordon Geddes puts it, "In their experience of death, the Puritans found themselves face to face with the original curse."[35]

As Ronald Bosco points out,

Owing partially to the sheer presence of death in the New England landscape, the Puritan was not much moved or struck by death as a fact. Confirming him in what may seem to twentieth-century readers to be an excessively cold or casual attitude toward death was the instruction in the ways of death that he received from the pulpit. Except to acknowledge the passing of New England's most illustrious men . . . the Puritan ministry positively discouraged, and during the 1640s and 1650s civil law forbade, public notice of death in any significant way.[36]

This involved in particular a "prohibition against speaking the name of the dead by others outside the family during the period of mourning."[37]

And, as if to drive this point home, Bosco notes that the typical Puritan funeral was, to put it mildly, a sparse affair: "A person died, was wrapped in whatever goods might be available for that purpose, was carried away by a few relatives or friends, and was buried without ceremony in a shallow and often unmarked grave." To do much more was seen as a "misapplication of emotion."[38]

In practical terms, these practices were in place to keep people *working*, since to fall into prolonged periods of grief would render one unable to work and so threaten the survival of the community. The harsh violence and natural hardships of the environment that the typical Puritan had to contend with made them acutely aware of the tenuousness of any intimate relationship, what Emerson might call the *absence* of a "lasting relation between that intellect and that thing." Furthermore, a strong emphasis on the survival of the community (the "shining city on a hill") at the expense of any particular individual along with the overall denigration of all things "worldly" pointed out quite forcefully the irrelevance of any one death within the larger scheme. To grieve too much, or too emphatically, was to publicly question God's plan.

In his book *Welcome Joy*, Gordon Geddes writes, "In mourning, as in other areas of Puritan life, the goal was not repression but control, or, as they termed it, moderation. . . . The goal of mourning was triumphant affirmation of God's will, but the path began with the harsh reality of death as an evil."[39] To the extent that they overstep the bounds of moderation set by Puritan society, grief and mourning must be suppressed and pushed underground to a private realm of sinfulness. Public rites of mourning gave little thought for the individual who died: "The major themes explored in these expressions of public mourning focused on either the blessedness to be enjoyed by saints after death or on the lesson that death should hold for the living."[40] There was to be no remembrance for the names of the dead. Writing along similar lines, Mitchell Breitwieser suggests that the Puritan approach to these matters was

in large measure an attempt to sublimate mourning, to block and then redirect its vigor to various social purposes: to sublimate something, one must start by encouraging it to be, to consolidate its vigor, before appropriating it; but such cultivation risks the possibility that the sublimated thing might remain in itself, rather than accept transference to the proffered sublimatory surrogate; and, in the case of mourning, such

a failure of sublimation would be antithetical to the ideology that seeks
to appropriate it, because mourning is a project of constructing a per-
sonally sufficient memory of what has died, and thus tends to show a
certain stubbornness when required to view the dead and the death clear
specimens of a general moral type.[41]

This suggests that the "sublimatory surrogate" is subject to the risk of
failure, an inability to contain or constrain its object. On this reading,
Emerson's explicit denial of grief for his son, along with the refusal to
name his son, is evidence of encouragement and appropriation in Breitwieser's sense. The unnamed son, as Stanley Cavell says (summariz-
ing Cameron's argument), is "not forgotten but generates the ensuing
topics of the essay."[42] In this reading, Emerson's sublimation of grief is
the force that propels "Experience" into existence. But again, as already
argued, this interpretation lingers over an implicit adequation between
terms, a sense in which the essay somehow meets its object through that
very silence and negativity, in which, for the text at least, absence is as
good as presence.

The binary we confront is a forced choice between inclusion and exclusion. As we've seen, for psychoanalysis the goal of mourning is a complete introjection of the lost object. For Calvinism, by contrast, the goal
was detachment from worldly things in favor of a biblical typology—a
total rejection of the temptations of a private internalized subject in favor
of the shared external meaning of the community or, less provisionally,
God's absolute sovereignty. This is the difference between a thoroughly
modern idealism—which removes the world but in return provides the
relative stability and knowledge of one's own mind—and a premodern
suspicion of subjectivity as the seat of sin. The Puritan, perhaps uniquely
perched on the precipice of modernity, is faced with the emergence of
the modern subject, on the one hand, and, on the other, the terrors of
an outside world symbolically represented by the chaotic wilderness of a
new "uncivilized" continent.

The individual Puritan was placed in a situation that encouraged and
appropriated the emergence of the modern subject but was encouraged
to harness and control that emergence for the greater community. These
subjective energies had to be directed into appropriate communal chan-
nels. "Experience," however, embraces the Puritan suspicion of mourning without recourse to external determinations of meaning. Ultimate

meaning finds no purchase on the *outside* because it remains finally inaccessible. Emerson does not achieve psychoanalytic catharsis, nor does he surrender himself to skepticism. What he achieves, then, is a middle way. Given the context thus far, perhaps the best way to make sense of all this is through comparing "Experience" to a well-known early American text that deals powerfully, if also indirectly, with grief.

In 1676, Mary Rowlandson was taken captive by Pocasset Indians during King Philip's War. She lost several family members in the process, including a six-year-old daughter named Sarah, whose name never actually appears in Rowlandson's written account. Rowlandson's narrative helped establish the genre of the American captivity narrative, which was studied so famously by Richard Slotkin, among others. A standard interpretation of Rowlandson's narrative might see it as a typically pious and homiletic Puritan text written under the authoritarian direction of the Puritan minister Cotton Mather. However, in a fascinating book, Mitchell Breitwieser seeks to reinterpret Rowlandson's narrative as being "among the more intense and unremitting representations of experience as a collision between cultural ideology and the real in American literature before Melville."[43]

Breitwieser argues that Rowlandson's grief for her recently deceased daughter disrupts the Puritan typology she has been instructed to apply to her experience. The singularity of what she mourns places itself *outside* all available systems of meaning. This situation not only isolates and individuates Rowlandson but also allows her to encounter the possibility of a space outside traditional typologies, especially in her encounters with Native Americans. Mourning *unfixes* the structure of Rowlandson's perception and allows her to experience the "Indian" as a true human other "at the margin of perception."[44] It creates for her not a new system of meaning, but a limit or boundary (an aporia) for the meanings she attempts to apply to her experience. Mourning foregrounds the "lost object," which then becomes the unthought or unseen of every system.

This quality of mourning as bearing witness to the outside arises *because* of the Puritan injunction against it: mourning is already outside any accepted code of right behavior. Again, the aim of the Puritans was not to eliminate mourning but to control it, to erect a boundary not to be crossed. The inevitable outcome of this strategy is that mourning brings into view the boundary itself which therefore indicates the outside: "With the assistance of narratives such as Rowlandson's, Puritanism could once again govern by virtue of explanatory cogency, the entire range of human experience: nothing was outside of it; there was nothing that happened that was not a clear *example*."[45] None of this is possible, of course, if there is not also that which can be targeted as something that is *not* an example, something clearly anomalous that can then be assimilated and brought into the fold of Puritan typology: "For the Puritans themselves, there was an *other-to-the-type* that, though it could be labeled sin or error, was nonetheless a real factor in signification, and had considerable force."[46] In other words, Puritan hermeneutics was the systematic detection and elimination of singularity, but with the existence of such singularities being a necessary part of the typology: for there to be an "inside," there must be an "outside."

What, then, of the ultimate singularity? It remains as a *lack*: "Death, then, is to be a lesson in the protocols of perception: it teaches that the gross is really a shadow, that the lost object is not in itself of note, an embodiment of value, but rather an accommodation (commodity) of a transcendental value, a luminescence, certainly, to the rude mind, but, from the highest perspective, a color laid over truth."[47] This is the task of Puritan hermeneutics. How does one take the death of the *other* and bring it into the fold of a systematized and iterable meaning? This is the heart of Rowlandson's narrative purpose as well as the aporetic limit on which Puritanism defines its boundaries. As Rowlandson writes near the end of her story: "Our family being now gathered together (those of us that were living)."[48] The clause divides itself in two, one part typical of the redemptive typology she assigns to her narrative, the other tellingly a parenthetical (thus outside the official meaning) that indicates what is left out or passed over. It does not, however, *name* what is excluded.

The Puritan diagnosis of suffering offers little consolation: "We are afflicted by loving too much."[49] The only recourse is to deny love in order to prevent or forestall mourning. This is, in philosophical terms, a form of skepticism: "Skepticism, were it within range, would sacrifice happiness to gain freedom from fright—a bargain, it seems to a still grieving self, because the better part of happiness lies back in the past anyway."[50] If, as Cavell has argued, "Experience" is an encounter with skeptical idealism in the Kantian tradition, then perhaps Emerson strikes this bargain. We could take it even further: "Experience" expresses the *impossibility* of mourning a singularity, and is thus a testament to the absolute distance of the world, where even grief is out of reach—a testament that serves to reinforce both solipsistic idealism and the terrors of skepticism.

But that conclusion is exactly what "Experience" resists. Despite the pressures of grief ("Grief too will make us idealists"), Emerson's task, especially in the latter portions of the essay, is to deny idealism while acknowledging the distance between thought and reality. What is the measure of this discrepancy? What is the meaning of an idea that is neither fully within the mind nor absolutely external to it? Peirce writes,

> If you ask what mode of being is supposed to belong to an idea that is in no mind, the reply will come that undoubtedly the idea must be embodied (or ensouled; it is all one) in order to attain complete being, and that if, at any moment, it should happen that an idea . . . was quite unconceived by any living being, then its mode of being (supposing that it was not altogether dead) would consist precisely in this, namely, that it was about to receive embodiment (or ensoulment) and to work in the world. This would be a mere potential being, a being in futuro.[51]

This suggests that the discrepancy of a representation is a reflection of the fact that it is a sign that stands for something *other than itself* and so its constitutive inadequacy is the performance of an internal difference or nonidentity that defaces itself for that which it is pointing to. As Max H. Fisch puts it, "Essentially, Peirce seems to be saying that triadic logic may be interpreted as a modal logic which is designed to deal with the indeterminacies resulting from that mode of being which Peirce has called 'Potentiality' and 'Real Possibility.' Under such an interpretation, dyadic logic becomes a limiting case of triadic modal logic resulting from removing indeterminacy and being determined entirely by 'Actuality.' "[52] Reincorporating "indeterminacy" thus involves the reintroduction or reentry of the excluded middle *as* that which is excluded in any determinate or dyadic logic. This means that when dealing with "possibility" or "indeterminacy," the representational tenants of our thinking take on a developmental character or forward momentum: "So, then, the essence of Reason is such that its being never can have been completely perfected. It always must be in a state of incipiency, of growth."[53] In Emerson's words, "This onward trick of nature is too strong for us."[54]

Peirce famously wrote, "All this universe is perfused with signs, if it is not composed exclusively of signs."[55] That quality is perhaps most poetically reflected by the sliding, swimming, glittering words of Emerson's prose in the opening pages of "Experience." In perhaps the most quoted passage of the essay, Emerson depicts a world of shifting appearances: "I take this evanescence and lubricity of all objects, which lets them slip through our fingers then when we clutch hardest, to be the most unhandsome part of our condition."[56] In the closing pages, however, a radically different tone is struck. Names fail, our words recede from the objects they point to, and in this process it can feel as if our handle on the solid, real, and graspable world is precarious or even absent. But, if we pay careful attention, we will find ourselves not isolated in innavigable seas but adrift in interminable oceans.

We do not hold an adequate picture of the world in our mind, and Emerson peers into the gap between representation and reality: "We do not see directly, but mediately."[57] It is the sense of the sign as existing not beyond but in an aporetic sense *between* dyadic categories—neither ideal nor real, neither being nor nonbeing—that best describes the role of Emerson's son in "Experience." The question at issue is, as John Deely asks in a different context, "When a child dies, in what sense is the child's parent a parent?"[58] In other words, in what sense are relationships real if they are only passing? As Emerson writes, "What help from thought? Life is not dialectics. We, I think, in these times, have had lessons enough of the futility of criticism. . . . Intellectual tasting of life will not supersede muscular activity. . . . Do not craze yourself with thinking, but go about your business anywhere. Life is not intellectual or critical, but sturdy."[59] The mystery marveled at in "Experience" is the difference between the encroaching threat of idealism and the "sturdy" reality that seems to happen anyway: "So it is with us, now skeptical, or without unity, because immersed in forms and effects all seeming to be of equal value, and now religious, whilst in the reception of spiritual law."[60] This vacillation contains the pain and grief of our losses as well as the joy of our attachments, as one would seem to be the absolute condition of the other.

We see that as early as *Nature* Emerson states, "I am nothing; I see all,"[61] or that in "Circles" he says, "I am God in Nature, I am a weed by the wall."[62] In these statements, we can already see him attempting to reconcile the paradox of idealism, the sense of all the world falling into the subject, with the persistence of a sturdy outside reality. This is a vacillation of power and powerlessness, of sight and blindness: "To-day, I am full of thoughts . . . but yesterday, I saw a dreary vacuity in this direction in which I now see so much."[63] In "The Poet," he writes, "For poetry was all written before time was, and whenever we are so finely organized that we can penetrate into that region where the air is music, we hear those primal warblings, and attempt to write them down, but we lose ever and anon a word, or a verse, and substitute something of our own, and thus miswrite the poem."[64] These statements point to the distorting power of expression, how every statement "miswrites" the original. In "Experience" the generative power of these paradoxes finally comes into view: only by observing our separateness ("discrepancy") from Nature is any union with it possible. Only through a miswriting is any writing possible. The problem of "Experience" is not the absolute distance of the world, but the fact that it is sometimes near and sometimes far. That which is closest and dearest to us, that which seems to be the most irreducibly present and real part of us, can fall away and leave not even the faintest trace of a scar.

"Experience" is constructed to mirror this back-and-forth vacillation. It is a series of affirmations buried in negations and vice versa, with the disillusionment of the opening paragraphs giving way to an expectantly victorious embrace of the universe. The professions of his son's abstractness in the early parts of "Experience" only serve to suggest his singularity as a shadow that trails the rest of the essay. Likewise, the affirmations that appear throughout are haunted by their negation. Is not the lost object the generative *condition* of affirmation? Why else is there a need for affirmation unless something required affirming—as if it cannot stand on its own? And does not affirming "new creation" merely repeat the act of mourning by inscribing within each new creation what is lost, the original "defeat"? To designate the "new" includes knowledge of what is now "old," what is lost or left behind. All new philosophies "must include the oldest beliefs" even if barely acknowledged. We find that "an innavigable sea washes with silent waves between us and the things we aim at and converse with," but are not the infinite waters between the self and the other what make the cherishing love of something beyond the self possible? If it were not so, Emerson would merely love his idea of his son, and not his son. Love does not bind, but pushes and pulls.

Emerson can appropriate his son as an idea in his head, which belongs to him alone and which will perish when he perishes, or he can cast his son into an outside world that cannot ever be known or touched. He chooses a middle way, as on a staircase. To what extent is the parent of a dead child still a parent? "If the child dies, the physical relation between them ceases, but it remains that the erstwhile parents must be *thought of* as having been the parent of that child if the parent is to be understood according to the full extent of its intelligible being."[65] But who, exactly, is made to think about it? A melancholic longing for the dead son persists in all readings of "Experience"—a loss is felt, and a sign carries an inexhaustible well of possibility forward into the future as what it paradoxically leaves behind in every contingent actualization of its meaning. It is thus no secret grief that we feel at Emerson's loss, and so "Experience" becomes exactly the memorial Cameron proclaims it to be, but only to the extent that the reader connects the dots by observing what remains *outside* the text—only if the text is itself observed *as* the reproduction of that very difference. Emerson's relation to his dead son survives even his own death by his refusal of introjection and representation—and so the relation, as well as the child it points to, is continuously affirmed and acknowledged as the absence, the exclusion, that makes any presence possible.

Throughout the pages of "Experience" Emerson repeatedly comes back to the always inadequate task of naming: "In our more correct writing, we give to this generalization the name of Being, and thereby confess that we have arrived as far as we can go. Suffice it for the joy of the universe, that we have not arrived at a wall, but at interminable oceans."[66] This is not containment, but expansion. The innavigable sea has become interminable oceans, bursting out from inside itself and so metamorphosing of its own accord from melancholy disillusionment to joyful hope. And back again, inevitably. An ocean of unsteady signs: "Illusion, Temperament, Succession, Surface, Surprise, Reality, Subjectiveness,—these are the threads on the loom of time, these are the lords of life. I dare not assume to give their order, but I name them as I find them in my way."[67] And more: "Fortune, Minerva, Muse, Holy Ghost,— these are quaint names, too narrow to cover this unbounded substance. The baffled intellect must still kneel before this cause, which refuses to be named,—ineffable cause, which every fine genius has essayed to represent by some emphatic symbol, as, Thales by water, Anaximenes by air, Anaxagoras by thought, Zoroaster by fire, Jesus and the moderns by love: and the metaphor of each has become a national religion."[68]

If not one of these names, this obsession with naming, ever suffices, then perhaps the only name that matters, the one that finally identifies what is lost (the "ineffable cause," pure potential, pure absence), is that name that for the sake of a grief-stricken love is never spoken and always withheld, always deferred as the displacement at the heart of significa-tion. It is worth comparing Emerson's words with Derrida's, yet again: "There will be no unique name, even if it were the name of Being."[69] But eventually, as our names tend to under- and overshoot their targets, there is some kind of recognition through displacement or substitution, a recognition that is adequate solely through the simultaneous admission of its inadequacy. Then onward, "Onward and onward!"[70] To the next name, the next substitution, to the name that cannot (yet) be said.

This is why Emerson can write in another essay, "With thought, with the ideal, is immortal hilarity, the rose of joy. Round it all the Muses sing. But grief cleaves to names, and persons, and the partial interests of to-day and yesterday."[71] It is in this context that the closing sentence of "Experience" finally begins to resonate: "Never mind the ridicule, never mind the defeat: up again, old heart!—it seems to say,—there is victory yet for all justice; and the true romance which the world exists to real-ize, will be the transformation of genius into practical power."[72] That statement resonates in turn with Peirce, using words that may console a grieving heart: "Thus, whether you accept the opinion or not, you must see that it is a perfectly Intelligible opinion that ideas are not all mere creations of this or that mind, but on the contrary have a power of find-ing or creating their vehicles, and having found them, of conferring upon them the ability to transform the face of the earth. . . . They have life, generative life."[73]

— 5 —
Every Language Is Foreign
Self and Cybernetics in the Event-Machine

What distinguishes a man from a word? There is a distinction
doubtless. . . . Man makes the word, and the word means nothing
which the man has not made it mean, and that only to some man.
But since man can think only by means of words or other external
symbols, these might turn round and say: "You mean nothing which
we have not taught you, and then only so far as you address some
word as the interpretant of your thought." In fact, therefore, men
and words reciprocally educate each other, each increase of a man's
information involves and is involved by, a corresponding increase of
a word's information.

CHARLES S. PEIRCE, "SOME CONSEQUENCES OF FOUR
INCAPACITIES"

One of the most extreme and most lamentable of my incapacities is
my incapacity for linguistic expression. . . . I have suffered grievously
from it since childhood; and I cannot tell you how assiduously I have
laboured to overcome it. I myself am conscious of the badness of my
style, although I am probably not fully conscious of it. I can imagine one of my readers saying to another "Why can he not express
himself naturally?" I can supply the answer to that. It is because no
linguistic expression is natural to him. He never thinks in words,
but always in some kind of diagrams. He is always struggling with a
foreign language; for him, every language is foreign.

CHARLES S. PEIRCE, "PREFACE TO MEANING," MANUSCRIPT 632

To take him at his word, Charles S. Peirce's incapacity for "linguistic expression" drives a wedge between what he considered to be the
true substance of his thought and the voluminous writings (much of
it unpublished and unfinished) that he left behind before his death in
1914. Nevertheless, a hopeful expectation persists among students of his

thought that as more and more of his writings finally see the light of day the cloudy obscurities of his great system may at last disperse and give way to a degree of clarity that has so far eluded it. At the same time, however, Peirce's incapacity for expression—an inability to make himself clear that kept the creator of pragmatism at arm's length from his own creation—must give us pause because taking him at his word would seem to be the very thing he claims we cannot do.

In this way, Peirce finds himself excluded from a metaphysical tradition that identifies the possession of a self with the power of voice and expression, a tradition for which having a self automatically, as it were, presumes the capacity for language. Of course, it is precisely this distinction between "voice" and *écriture* that Jacques Derrida famously targets with deconstruction in *Of Grammatology*: "Natural writing is immediately united to the voice and to breath. . . . There is therefore a good and a bad writing: the good and natural is the divine inscription in the heart and the soul; the perverse and artful is technique, exiled in the exteriority of the body."[1] This includes the idea that one may simply access the power of expression as the consequence of having a self at all.

From here it is but a single step of inference to arrive at the conclusion that Peirce's inability to join together his voice to his language corresponds to a more fundamental incapacity of *selfhood*—an absence or incapacity that surfaces again and again in his writing, not least in his frequent and bracing pronouncements that the individual is no more than a negation: "The individual man, since his separate existence is manifested only by ignorance and error, so far as he is anything apart from his fellow, and from what he and they are to be, is only a negation."[2] We may presume that when Peirce looks inside himself he doesn't find the presence of a true or "natural" self but the mechanization of diagrams, the blueprint of a machine rather than evidence of a personal soul. In the second epigraph above, a moving admission of his perceived personal shortcomings which cannot help but carry the weight of the tragedy of his entire life as well as the unending series of missed opportunities and unfulfilled potential that mark his thought as a magnificent edifice in perpetual disarray (as if it were being built and torn down all at once), Peirce manages to lose himself: *I* becomes *He*. He never thinks in words.

Seeing quite keenly Peirce's difficulties, William James—himself clearly endowed with the gift that Peirce decidedly lacked—asked his friend to express himself naturally, without technical baggage: "Your intensely mathematical mind keeps my non-mathematical one at a distance."[3] Intending to steer Peirce toward a style that would be more conducive to having and keeping a popular audience, and in this way to provide him with the stable employment that eluded him for most of his life, James encouraged Peirce to avoid excessive excursions into logic and mathematics in his work. Told by James that he is "teeming with ideas" and that he only need find the right way to express them, Peirce's characteristically testy response is most revealing: "My philosophy . . . is not an 'idea' with which I 'brim over'; it is a serious research to which there is no royal road."[4] Here there is a conflict about what and where ideas are: does the word inform the man or does the man inform the word?

For his part, James takes selfhood to be constituted through a primary act of possession: "It seems as if the elementary psychic fact were not *thought* or *this thought* or *that thought*, but *my thought*, every thought being *owned*," as he writes in *The Principles of Psychology*: "On these terms the personal self rather than the thought might be treated as the immediate datum in psychology."[5] A Peircean response would surely resemble the following: "Few things are more completely hidden from my observation than those hypothetical elements of thought which the psychologist finds reason to pronounce 'immediate' in his sense."[6] Peirce effectively reverses James's position, not in the service of placing language prior to the self but in order to insist instead on the distinction, the difference between self and language *as such*. Peirce is not able to *own* his thoughts because they are *already* foreign at the moment of their inception, already given over to the iterative cycles of semiosis as the very condition of their "expression." Indeed, in this way he is continually *losing* his thoughts, losing himself in a language that does not issue forth from the inner heart or soul but through the exteriority or exposure of the body, as if it were the interaction of a tool or instrument with its object.

"The beginning word," writes Derrida, "is understood, in the intimacy of self-presence, as the voice of the other and as commandment."[7] The first word is the word of the *other*, it comes from outside the self and holds it accountable. In this context it is especially interesting that Peirce imagines the call to language as the call to account for himself, even ventriloquizing the voice of the other in order to hold himself responsible. The self is called to being only by the other in the form of an unlimited community constituted by an externalizing movement of negation:

When we come to study the great principle of continuity and see how all is fluid and every point directly partakes the being of every other, it will appear that individualism and falsity are one and the same. Meantime, we know that man is not whole as long as he is single, that he is essentially a possible member of society. Especially, one man's experience is nothing, if it stands alone. If he sees what others cannot, we call it hallucination. It is not "my" experience, but "our" experience that has to be thought of; and this "us" has indefinite possibilities.[8]

Called to selfhood through the call to a linguistic communality, a commandment to respond and account for oneself before an indefinite other, the individual finds himself only through the lack, negation, or exposure that enables the formation of a community. But does this not imply that the other, the fellow member of community, is also negated? Wouldn't the facelessness of the other—the other's *own* negation in its singularity—then need to be less, or more, than fully human? Is there a negation of selfhood on both sides? To borrow again from Derrida: "Must not this place of the Other be ahuman? If this is indeed the case, then the ahuman or at least the figure of some—in a word—*divinanimality*, even if it were to be felt through the human, would be the quasi-transcendental referent, the excluded, foreclosed, disavowed, tamed, and sacrificed foundation of what it founds, namely, the symbolic order, the human order, law and justice."[9]

If we have seen that sacrificial foundation take the figurative form of a lost child (for Ralph Waldo Emerson) or virtue (for Jonathan Edwards), then for Peirce it would seem to be the self and its power of expression that is the sacrificial condition of community and therefore the possibility of communication. Here it is worth quoting Derrida at length on the metaphysical tradition of selfhood, which Peirce's thought helps to overturn:

This presence to oneself, this self of the presence to itself, this universal and singular "I" that is the condition for the response and thus for the responsibility of the subject—whether theoretical, practical, ethical, juridical, or political—is a power, a *faculty* that Kant is prudent or bold enough not to identify with the power *to speak*, the literal power of *uttering* "I." This personal subject *is capable* of its selfness, is capable of doing it without saying it, if I can say so; it can affirm itself in its selfness and in its dignity, which is to say its *responsibility*, its power to respond,

to answer for itself, before others and before the law, "even when he cannot yet say 'I'" He has this "I" in his thinking, and that defines thinking
itself as what gathers itself, there where it remains the same, gathered
and present to itself through this power of the *I*, through the *I can* of
this *I*, this *I can I* as an "I think" that accompanies every representation.
Even where the ipseity of the I cannot speak itself and utter itself as such
in the world *je, Ich, I, ego*, it *effects itself* in every language, provided it is
human. . . . Every human language has at its disposal this self "as such,"
even if the word for it is lacking.[10]

What distinguishes a man from a word? As Derrida notes, for the metaphysical tradition that distinction is founded on a faculty or capability, an
"able to." For Peirce, this faculty is absent—it is an incapacity that reveals
itself in and through the call to the impersonal machinery of language,
a call to community. In place of this faculty is found what Derrida terms
"nonresponse": "a language that doesn't respond because it is fixed or
stuck in the mechanicity of its programming, and finally lack, defect,
deficit, or deprivation."[11]

Why don't you express yourself naturally? Peirce cannot respond,
and his language remains stuck in the mechanicity of what he calls "diagrams," and it is this incapacity of response that brings us to what Derrida refers to as "the question of how an iterability that is essential to
every response, and to the ideality of every response, can and cannot fail
to introduce nonresponse, automatic reaction, mechanical reaction into
the most alive, most 'authentic,' and most responsible response."[12] Every
response, that is, depends on nonresponse. The capacity of response
that can only take place in language entails an essential "iterability" that
overtakes it and introduces "mechanicity," a *lack* of voice, presence, or
"natural" writing. Language betrays the ideal of natural expression, for
language is a communicative realm that must exclude the expression or
presence of consciousness.

This sacrificial condition of communication means that there is no
natural expression free from language as a technical instrument, no
word or communicable intent not "perfused with signs," no immediacy
without meditation. If natural expression evokes a purity that then subjects itself to something like mechanical repetition in order to signify at
all, then this purity is only produced through the impurity of a copy or
citation. Again, Derrida's seminal analysis of the effects of a signature

bears on this point: "But the condition of possibility of those effects is simultaneously, once again, the condition of their impossibility, of the impossibility of their rigorous purity. In order to function, that is, to be readable, a signature must have a repeatable, iterable, imitable form; it must be able to be detached from the present and singular intention of its production. It is its sameness which, by corrupting its identity and its singularity, divides its seal."[13] All communicational forms operate by means of iterability, "the possibility of disengagement and citational graft,"[14] which even applies, as it by now goes without saying, to the citation of an "I" or self: "Nothing is in fact more irreducibly singular than 'I,' and yet nothing is more universal, anonymous, and substitutable."[15] Every language is foreign, "always already translation," as David Wills pus it.[16]

Throughout his work, Derrida circled around some of the very same themes that I want to explore here, specifically the thought of what *Of Grammatology* called "a double movement of protention and retention," which is characteristic of the cybernetic machine.[17] This thought requires a logic that resists synthesis, which resists moreover any *identity* whatsoever. This is a double movement or mutually causal process: the word informing the man and the man informing the word, a logic of the quasi-machine that continuously and repeatedly refuses the binary logic of a machine-like reductionism. In a late essay, "Typewriter Ribbon," Derrida describes this logic of an "event-machine":

> One of our greatest difficulties, then, would be to reconcile with the machine a thinking of the event, that is, a thinking of what remains real, undeniable, inscribed, singular, of an always essentially *traumatic* type, even when it is a happy event: an event is always traumatic, its singularity interrupts an order and rips apart, like every decision worthy of the name, the normal fabric of temporality or history. How, then, is one to reconcile, *on the one hand*, a thinking of the event, which I propose withdrawing, despite the apparent paradox, from an ontology or a metaphysics of presence (it would be a matter of thinking an event that is undeniable but without pure presence), and, *on the other hand*, a certain concept of machineness? The latter would imply at least the following predicates: a certain materiality, which is not necessarily a corporeality, a certain technicity, programming, repetition or iterability, a cutting off from or independence from any living subject—the

psychological, sociological, transcendental, or even human subject, and so forth.[18]

This logic does not in Hegelian fashion repossess or recontain the excluded middle that makes it possible, but sacrifices or forecloses that possibility continually—the event is only possible *by* the machine but remains at the same time irreducible to it. Here I want to follow Cary Wolfe's lead and connect this thought of the event-machine to contemporary systems theory, particularly how systems theory understands communication, in order to better understand how Peirce's thought leads us to a posthumanist theory of the subject or self.

Wolfe links deconstruction to the systems theory of Niklas Luhmann: "Luhmann's handling of systems theory accomplishes just the sort of 'conservation' of the logic of the *grammé* that Derrida calls for, a conservation that is crucial to any posthumanism whatsoever."[19] In this respect, the most salient convergence of deconstruction and systems theory is a "disarticulation of consciousness and communication."[20] Systems theory totally excludes consciousness or "mind" from systems of communication. In essence, this means that the metaphysical construct of the human or subject is excluded from the act of communication. As Luhmann quite memorably (and bluntly) puts it, "Humans cannot communicate; not even their brains can communicate; not even their conscious minds can communicate. Only communication can communicate."[21] From this basis we may argue that semiosis no longer requires a human subject or consciousness to bring forth the final interpretant that guarantees the meaning of the sign. Instead, Peirce pursues a logic of the event-machine through the continual foreclosure ("negation") of the individual self or consciousness for the sake of communication.

In Two Places at Once: Thought and Embodiment

There is a famous saying of Parmenides, . . . "being is, and not-being is nothing." This sounds plausible, yet synechism flatly denies it, declaring that being is a matter of more or less, so as to merge insensibly into nothing.

CHARLES S. PEIRCE, "IMMORTALITY IN THE LIGHT
OF SYNECHISM"

Peter Skagestad offers an intriguing analysis of some of Peirce's writings that attempt to account for the material embodiment of thought in communication. He begins by quoting the following fascinating passage from Peirce:

> A psychologist cuts out a lobe of my brain (*nihil animale a me alienum puto*) and then, when I find I cannot express myself, he says, "You see, your faculty of language was localized in that lobe." No doubt it was; and so, if he had filched my inkstand, I should not have been able to continue my discussion until I had got another. Yea, the very thoughts would not come to me. So my faculty of discussion is equally localized in my inkstand. It is localization in a sense in which a thing may be in two places at once.[22]

Again, Peirce describes an incapacity for expression, but this time he attributes it to the lack of an effective technical means for communicating. He suggests that mental processes cannot be expressed unless embodied (that is, somehow actualized or determined) in a material form: "The idea must be embodied (or ensouled; it is all one) in order to attain complete being."[23] At the same time, he mocks the idea that the faculty of language is confined or localized in the brain alone. Skagestad remarks:

> One thing Peirce is doing in the passage quoted is, of course, to ridicule the idea that the faculty of discussion, or any other mental faculty, is localized in the brain or anywhere else. . . . We might now be tempted to dismiss the reference to the inkstand as only a joke: localization in the sense in which a thing can be in two places at once is, of course, the same thing as no localization at all. So, it might be argued, what Peirce is doing is using the very ludicrousness of the idea of the mind being localized in an inkstand as a way of highlighting the equal ludicrousness of supposing the mind to be localized in the brain, or anywhere else.[24]

This would mean of course that the faculty of linguistic communication is not *in* the brain any more than it is *in* the inkstand. Instead, Peirce seems to suggest that communication takes place only through some form of interaction between states of consciousness and their embodiment or materialization in language or something like it.

As Skagestad goes on to argue, Peirce "simply did not regard cognition as consisting of such conscious states. Cognition consists in the manipulation of signs which may be externally embodied; as each sign is what it is by virtue of its possible later interpretations—i.e., virtually—so the mind itself is virtual."[25] On this account, thought is thought only insofar as it is embodied in a technical apparatus and the mind thus emerges only *through* that interaction: "In Peirce's view you do not find the mind inside the brain, any more than you find electricity inside copper wires—an analogy explicitly cited by Peirce. You find the mind where there are inkstands or other means of expressing thoughts, paper or other vehicles for preserving and conveying thoughts, and of course brains capable, through the intermediary of eyes and hands or the equivalent, of interacting with external tools and media."[26] The mind is in two places at once, then, in the sense in which it is produced through the interaction between a possible thought and its actual or material embodiment. As Skagestad concludes, "To be a reasoner is to be a user of machines, be they soft machinery, like alphabets, numerals, logical notations, and typefaces, or hard machinery, like logic machines, alembics, cucurbits, and inkstands."[27]

Although insightful, this interpretation leaves an unanswered question: How do these forms of embodiment *express* thoughts? Like a copper wire conducting electricity? At this point, it seems that Skagestad smuggles in a form of Cartesian representationalism by suggesting that we are "users of machines," that we express thought *through* machines. Here the role of "reasoner" takes on exactly the "I think, I *can*" that designates the subject through the self-possession of a space of control. By way of comparison, consider Cary Wolfe's critique of Daniel Dennett's theory of consciousness and language: "The problem is that it is not clear how such prosthetic processes and devices can be said to constitute— to 'store, process, and *re-present*' (in Dennett's words)—'our' thinking. After all, if we pay attention to the material, social, technical, and cultural complexities of such devices, then in what sense can the internal psychic states Dennett calls 'our thinking' be said to be 're-presented' by such devices?"[28] Put simply, how can the forms of its embodiment *represent* thought? As Wolfe puts it, the evasion of this dilemma suggests that Dennett—and, I wish to argue by extension, Skagestad—"uses a fundamentally representationalist concept of language that reinstalls the disembodied Cartesian subject at the very heart of his supposedly embodied, materialist functionalism."[29]

To put an even finer point on it, when Skagestad claims that the mind is found in its technical or mechanical expression, one is tempted to reply that, rather, it *isn't* found. To be in two places at once is to be in no place at all, neither here nor there. It's always in the place you *don't* look. Isn't this instead the reproduction or repetition of the difference or distinction between thought and its embodiment? As in a passage from Peirce also quoted by Skagestad: "What I say is that the mind is virtual . . . not capable of existing except in a space of time—*nothing* in so far as it is at any one moment."[30] *Nothing* because the mind at any one moment, any particular state of consciousness, is foreclosed, excluded, or sacrificed to the machine at the moment of communication. Minds cannot (are not *able to*) communicate.

A different though also highly informative reading of Peirce is offered by Vincent Colapietro, yet it manages to also import a form of Cartesianism into Peirce's thought, thus demonstrating just how ingrained and pervasive the metaphysics of selfhood is. Colapietro argues that a theory of the subject is not by necessity excluded from a formal theory of signs: "We cannot fully understand any of these fundamental dimensions of human subjectivity apart from an elaborate theory of semiotic processes. However, is the reverse true? Can we understand the nature of varieties of semiosis apart from any consideration of the subject?"[31] For Colapietro, the answer is most definitely no: "The self is alternately a speaker and a listener, a source *from whom* discourse flows and a being *to whom* discourse is addressed. . . . The self as speaker is someone *through whom* others speak. . . . The subject is, among other things, a medium through which forces and persons other than the subject speak."[32] Here the subject is determined as a mode of address, localization, and embodiment as "the means *through which* the self is able to address and be addressed by some other."[33] The self is something like a performative or positional necessity, produced through semiotic activity as the object or agent of an address, and in this way it essentially represents the power or capacity for addressing and being addressed. To be sure, the subject does not appear *in* semiosis but acts as its inferred medium or "source." This is an advance, but it still holds on to the subject as a kind of *capacity* for communicating, which is to say that Colapietro ultimately grounds the possibility for semiosis *in* the subject. Put another way, the distinction between the subject and semiosis is unified within the subject as the very capacity or *able to* of communication.

I want to argue instead that Peirce's thought offers a rigorous challenge to this line of thought. For Peirce this *able to* is also at the same time a *not able to* because the subject can be observed or investigated only as an originary cleft or breach. The subject is precisely that which *cannot* address or be addressed. The subject is *already* (and not prior to) that through which the other speaks, the other that calls the subject to language and constitutes it as other. The subject is an *I* that through its (non) response, (in)ability to respond, and (in)capacity for language becomes a *He*. This means that if Peirce defines the self as a "possible member of society," then that self only becomes actualized or determined through a community, through paradoxically negating itself as an individual. This is the subject *as* difference, in two places at once.

Colapietro seems to recognize as much when he points to what seems to be a paradox in Peirce's understanding of the self: "If the self can only realize itself through its commitments to ideals and if the commitment to ever higher ideals necessarily requires ever greater surrenders of the self, then the true self can emerge only when the futile ego dissolves."[34] The self, in other words, emerges only through its effacement. This is to render the power of the self as *nonpower*, despite attempts to reconcile it to a more traditional ontological notion of the subject for which the self "*is* an organically embodied center of purpose and power."[35] Peirce's *power*, by contrast, is thoroughly impersonal: "not the sham power of brute force . . . but the creative power of reasonableness, which subdues all other powers, and rules over them with its sceptre, knowledge, and its globe, love."[36] As Colapietro points out, "The ideal of reasonableness requires a radical openness to what may confront the individual, either in the guise of another person or of an inner thought, as utterly foreign: 'The idea of other, of *not*, becomes a very pivot of thought.'"[37] To be radically open to the utterly foreign, though, undermines the individual subject as the seat of power and agency, a surrender or exposure to the law of community in opposition to a Kantian notion of *giving* oneself the law.

Bees and Crystals: The Impersonality of Signs

I should like to write a little book on "the conduct of Thoughts" in which the introductory chapter should introduce the reader to my existential graphs, which would then be used throughout as the

apparent subject, the parable or metaphor, in terms of which everything would be said,—which would be far more scientific than dragging in the "mind" all the time, in German fashion, when the mind
and psychology has no more to do with the substance of the book
than if I were to discourse of the ingredients of the ink I use.

CHARLES S. PEIRCE, *SEMIOTICS AND SIGNIFICS*

The German philosopher Jürgen Habermas runs in rather the opposite
direction from Skagestad and Colapietro in order to accuse Peirce of
wanting to "conceptualize the interpretation of signs abstractly, detached
from the model of linguistic communication between a speaker and a
hearer, detached even from the basis of the human brain. Today this
makes us think of the operations of artificial intelligence, or of the mode
of functioning of the genetic code; Peirce had crystals and the work of
bees in mind."[38] He refers to the following suggestive passage: "Thought
[that is, the development of signs] is not necessarily connected with a
brain. It appears in the work of bees, of crystals, and throughout the
purely physical world."[39]

According to Habermas, such passages show that Peirce embraces a
"cosmology of the sign" that can "encompass nature and not just our
interpretation of nature. . . . This semeiotic idealism requires, of course, a
naturalization of semeiosis. The price Peirce had to pay for this is the anonymization and depersonalization of the mind in which signs call forth their
interpretants."[40] Habermas protests that this "naturalization" neglects to
theorize the moment of one mind meeting another in something like a
face-to-face encounter: "[Peirce] neglected that moment of Secondness
that we encounter in communication as contradiction and difference, as
the *other* individual's 'mind of his own.' "[41] That is, Peirce's semiotics flat-
tens the difference between individual minds and thus creates a whole and
self-sustaining materialist system with no place for the human subject:

What remains after this abstraction are currents of depersonalized
sequences of signs, in which every sign refers as the interpreter to the
previous sign, and refers as the interpretandum to the following sign.
To be sure, these linkages are established only through the mediation
of a mind in which signs are able to call forth interpretations: "intelligent consciousness must enter into the series." Still, this *mind* remains

anonymous, because it consists of nothing other than that three-placed relation of representation in general, *it* is absorbed by the structure of the sign.[42]

Habermas remains intent on avoiding what he calls the "anonymization" of the interpreter because otherwise we are led to a theory of communication in which "universalization asserts itself, only from *one* side: communication is not for the sake of reaching initial understanding between ego and alter ego about something in the world; rather, interpretation exists only for the sake of the representation and the ever more comprehensive representation of reality."[43] In Peirce's system semiosis encompasses and objectivizes even the subject. The encounter with a true "other" would in this system be impossible because it represents only the automatic and depersonalized programming of a machine.

According to Habermas, the critical flaw in this approach is that a sign can only refer to other signs, an infinite regress or self-reference that seems to shut down the possibility of communication altogether if there is no point at which the mind can appear on the scene and complete the communicative act by assigning or construing the final meaning of the sign. The sign-to-sign relationship thus has no room for mind as the *other* to the sign relationship—it is as if signs are somehow left to interpret *themselves*. As Habermas writes, "Such an infinite regress would come about only if the process of interpretation were to circle from within itself, as it were, without continual stimulation from outside, and without discursive processing."[44] Habermas takes the flaw of Peirce's semiotics to be the *internal* development of a sign, the fact that it elides an "intersubjective relationship that requires [Ego and alter ego] to orient themselves toward each other as first person is oriented toward second person. That means, however, that each must distinguish himself from the other in the first-person plural from others as third persons."[45] For Habermas, communication requires consciousness to appear as something like a "here I am" with the capacity to respond and interpret the meaning of a sign.

Yet this critique performs a flattening of its own through the positing of intersubjectivity *in* consciousness as the bridge, as it were, between communication and its other. As Habermas writes, "By being absorbed into an all-encompassing nexus of communication, the conversation among humans loses just what is specific to it."[46] This is an important point for Habermas because if there is nothing specific to the conversation among humans, then an intersubjective theory of communication loses its bearing. It would be forced to universalize intersubjectivity, thus leaving us in the strange position of positing intersubjective communications in the natural world, of depersonalized objects or animals encountering one another in the "first person." But at the same time, it is hard to see how attributing intersubjective specificity to human conversation avoids what Habermas disparages as "the philosophy of consciousness" and "the epistemic self-relation of the representing subject."[47] How, in other words, does intersubjectivity escape the very critique Habermas applies to Peirce? How does it avoid something like idealism? As Klaus Oehler puts it, "[Habermas] makes intentionality depend on consciousness and reason, and divorces it radically from physical processes. This dualism of mind and nature is not merely foreign to Peirce's thought. Peirce opposed it. He would charge Habermas with Cartesianism, and it is difficult to see how Habermas can survive this criticism."[48] Habermas keeps the difference between mind and nature but ultimately unifies it in and through human consciousness. The difference between mind and other is made available as a unity on the side of mind, and so that difference is then overcome *in* consciousness as intersubjectivity. It's precisely this humanist gesture, however, that Peirce's semiotics is designed to overcome.

How can the mind, self, or subject be reconceived from the point of view of Peircean semiotics? Colapietro quotes an intriguing passage from the unpublished manuscripts: "A *mind* may, with advantage, be roughly defined as a *sign-creator in connection with a reaction-machine.*"[49] Could it be that thinking the subject in semiosis entails thinking together the event and the machine? Thinking them at once as a *difference*, as a unity but not an identity? Colapietro writes, "It is one thing to say that a *general* and *formal* theory of signs does not necessarily take into account the subject of semiosis, and it is quite another to assert that such a theory of signs *cannot* in principle investigate the subject. It is as though the investigator of semiotic phenomena has a form of the Midas touch in which everything touched turns to—signs, the object of the mind's desire. And, in becoming a sign, it ceases to be what it was prior to the glance of the semiotician."[50] Colapietro's complaint is well founded because the *becoming sign* of the subject abandons or sacrifices the subject to the mechanization of language or of any general semiosis. Minds become like bees and crystals, even to themselves.

The Existential Graphs: A Blueprint of the Event-Machine

It seems a strange thing, when one comes to ponder over it, that a sign should leave its interpreter to supply a part of its meaning; but the explanation of the phenomenon lies in the fact that the entire universe—not merely the universe of existents, but all that wider universe, embracing the universe of existents as a part, the universe which we are all accustomed to refer to as "the truth"—that all this universe is perfused with signs, if it is not composed exclusively of signs.

CHARLES S. PEIRCE, "PRAGMATISM AND PRAGMATICISM"

To come back to our beginning: How do we think the event and the machine at once? Colapietro notes a fascinating essay by Larry Holmes on Peirce's idea of self-control, which Holmes divests of any need for a philosophy of the subject: "We can take self-control to mean not the control of a self (substantively), but simply auto-control, the control from within of whatever kind of organism the human being is found to be."[51] The principal breakthrough of Holmes's essay is to make explicit a connection between the Peircean account of scientific inquiry and feedback mechanisms as described in cybernetics:

In cybernetic terminology, there is a corrective feedback, which tends, as the action is considered and repeated, to reduce the oscillations—one's violent wayward impulses—and to bring the action closer to the ideal. There is also a similar process with respect to norms or ideals, until a stable one emerges; although Peirce appears to hold that in the overall development of reason no norm is entirely stable, which indeed seems consistent with an evolutionary pragmatism applied to a developing organism. As Norbert Wiener writes, "The stable state of a living organism is to be dead."[52]

Indeed, Peirce explicitly describes his own theory of inquiry as a quest for stability within vacillating limits: "If experience in general is to fluctuate irregularly to and fro, in a manner to deprive the ratio sought of all definite value, we shall be able to find out approximately within what limits it fluctuates."[53]

On this account, there is no need for a subject of semiosis since it merely describes the automatic functioning of a machine. There is no reflexive "self" because there is "no commitment about anything there at which the reflexive is aimed."[54] Holmes points to the following passage from Peirce's unpublished manuscripts as particularly suggestive:

> Assuming that all of each man's actions are those of a machine, as is indubitably, at least approximately, the case, he is a machine with an automatic governor, like any artificial motor; and moreover, somewhat, though not quite, as the governor on an engine, while it automatically begins to turn off steam as soon as the machinery begins to move too fast, is itself automatically controlled for the sake of avoiding another fault, that of too sudden a change of speed, so, and more than so, man's machinery is provided with an automatic governor upon every governor to regulate it by a consideration not otherwise provided for. For while an automatic governor may be attached to any governor to prevent any given kind of excess in its action, each such attachment complicates the machine. . . . [But] in the human machine,—or, at least, in the cortex of the brain, or in whatever part it be whose action determines of what sort the man's conduct shall be,—there seems, as far as we can see no limit to the self-government that can and will be brought to bear upon each such determining action, except the lack of time before the conduct which was to be determined must come into actual play.[55]

Here we find somewhat, approximately, though not quite, an automatic machine. Why the relentless qualifications? Why these quasi-machines? In one sense, Peirce is surely attempting to avoid reductionism (the very quality of his thought that Habermas seems to miss). But in another, more fundamental sense, Peirce is pursuing the logic of the Derridean event-machine. As Holmes goes on to say,

> The "control of control" that Peirce describes here and in many other passages is what is known as second-order feedback. It is of particular interest because it can be shown that such a system is self-correcting (ordinarily without requiring further higher orders of control) in a manner essentially free from disruptive feedback (to use Ross Ashby's term)—the wild oscillation or "hunting" that throws any system, cybernetic or moral, out of whack. Moreover, the self-correction takes

place by a means that is self-structuring, and consistent with Peirce's pragmatic method of inquiry: a point with some relevance to the question of whether a substantive self is needed to explain self-control.[56]

Holmes opens the door to a consideration of the cybernetic machine alongside semiosis, but stops well short of describing how the mechanisms of feedback and self-corrective behavior may operate in semiosis, and particularly how they may operate in communication systems. How, in other words, do these not-quite-automatic machines *communicate*, with themselves or others? Holmes gestures toward an answer in his discussion of Peirce's idea of the "review process" of action and inquiry: "The review is made more efficacious by breaking up the reasonings so finely, and arranging the critique so mechanically, that there is little chance for error or doubt. The system of existential graphs is designed, he says, to accomplish just this purpose."[57] These graphs are the diagrams that Peirce is forever alluding to as the real substance of his thought, and it is there that the logic of the event-machine takes shape.

The graphs are essentially an effort to diagrammatically break down reasoning into its most basic characteristics. As Don D. Roberts writes, "What are the smallest steps into which a reasoning can be dissected? Insertions and omissions. According to Peirce, if each elementary operation of a symbolic logic is either an insertion or an omission, then the operations of that logic are 'as analytically represented as possible.'"[58] The graphs are placed on a "Sheet of Assertion," a blank page that Peirce defines as the universe of all that may be said to be true. Drawing a single circle, or "cut," on the Sheet of Assertion makes the assertion or indication represented by that cut, the space *inside* of the circle, "false." As Peirce puts it, "To enclose a graph or any portion of a graph in a lightly drawn oval shall be understood as assertively separating it from the universe of truth, that is as denying it."[59] This difference or distinction belongs to the indexical category of Secondness, what Peirce sometimes called the "not" and what Anne Freadman takes to be for Peirce "the very sign of difference, and hence, the formal condition for any classification."[60] An index neither "represents" something as a symbol does nor stands for itself as an icon does. It merely points to something else, as if to say, "not this, *that*." Therefore, to indicate a unique proposition as "true" (rather than simply joined with the undifferentiated Sheet of Assertion), one must then draw another circle inside the first one, thereby indicating that the original indication of "false" is itself false, and thus true (as if to say, "it's not *not* true").

To approach truth as the function of a kind of double negative may seem unorthodox to say the least but it is in fact the critical move of the graphs. The two circles cancel each other out in order to suggest that what is indicated as true is simultaneously continuous with the undifferentiated Sheet (insofar as it is true) as well as differentiated from it (insofar as it is false). Truth, in a manner of speaking, is split in half, and in order to indicate any individual proposition as true, one must keep drawing new circles. This has the effect of redescribing truth as a process of making distinctions—the "real" is only revealed paradoxically through the progressive enfolding of distinctions that may be said to simultaneously hide as much as they reveal. As Louis H. Kauffman points out, "As a Sign of itself, the circle has only itself as a part. That part, equal to the whole, makes the distinction that is the referent of the Sign."[61] That is, the circle indicates itself as different from itself—it is a self-referential paradox. Consequently, we have a determinative oscillation or feedback loop comprising negations or "nots." This process has much in common with Derrida's description of the "cut" in *Without Alibi*: "This *cut* assures it a sort of archival independence or autonomy that is quasi-machinelike (not machinelike but *quasi*-machinelike), a power of repetition, repeatability, iterability, serial and prosthetic substitution of self for self."[62] The cut represents, if you will, the *quasi-* of the quasi-machine, the hyphen in "event-machine," a sort of abyss we fall into and cannot escape except by taking shovel in hand and digging infinitely deeper. This is not a "circle of circles" but circles *within* circles.

One of the more immediately interesting aspects of the Existential Graphs concerns what happens when one draws just one circle, indicating "false." This is equivalent to the famous Liar's Paradox: "This statement is false." What follows of course are the familiar oscillations of a self-referential paradox. This suggests that the very foundation of any indication, of any statement or predication at all, can be understood as a self-referential distinction, a distinction that indicates only one side and not the other. The initial cut that defines any particular indication must *first* distinguish itself as *false* to the Sheet of Assertion, and only then may it establish its "truth" in a series of insertions and omissions. In other terms, the cut may represent an irruption of symmetry-breaking or disequilibrium—an *event*. With Peirce's terminology, it is just as appropriate to describe this cut as falsity or negation. Can it be that the negation or falsity of individual existence refers, in some strict abstract way, to this other falsity? If so, the "cut" or distinction would seem to be synonymous with what Peirce means by individual existence, and it points the way toward a Peircean account of the subject.

The work of the eccentric British mathematician George Spencer-Brown clarifies the relevance of cybernetics and systems theory for interpreting Peirce's work.[63] Spencer-Brown's *Laws of Form* presents a system of diagrams for understanding how distinctions work that is in many functional respects "isomorphic" to the Existential Graphs.[64] Like Peirce, Spencer-Brown begins by suggesting that any act of observation is an act of *distinction*. As Michael Schiltz and Gert Verschraegen put it, *Laws of Form* "is most acutely referred to as a protologic."[65] Like the Existential Graphs, it is an attempt to arrive at the most fundamental or elementary level at which anything may be said, indicated, or reasoned about at all. Spencer-Brown writes, "The theme of this book is that a universe comes into being when a space is severed or taken apart. . . . By tracing the way we represent such a severance, we can begin to reconstruct, with an accuracy and coverage that appears almost uncanny, the basic forms underlying linguistic, mathematical, physical and biological science, and can begin to see how the familiar laws of our own experience follow inexorably from the original act of severance."[66]

Part of what *Laws of Form* is attempting to do is to justify and legitimize the use of imaginary values that can be both positive and negative, if not at the same *time*, then at least sequentially: "For Spencer-Brown, the question is thus purely a mathematical one. His interests lie with showing the *validity* of imaginary values. . . . As they can be used meaningfully for the solution of equations which cannot be solved otherwise, we must accept 'imaginary' as a 'third' category independent from (1) true (tautology: $x = x$) and (2) untrue (contradiction: $x = -x$)."[67] It begins with a command to act: "Draw a distinction!" Make something different from something else—or more precisely, make something different from *itself*.

As an immediate consequence of a distinction, one part of the world can now indicate another: "The notation . . . thereby expresses that topological *asymmetry* as well. Simultaneously with the drawing of a distinction, one of the sides is indicated."[68] This is the reason for calling the distinction self-referential. As Niklas Luhmann comments, "The distinction is made with the pragmatic intent to designate one side but not the other. What is distinguished, therefore, has to be distinguished from the distinction."[69] The unmarked state that is produced with every distinction is absolutely unobservable, while the actual presence of the so-called marked and observable state continually slips away from any stable observation because of the revealing/obscuring action of making a distinction: "Self-referentially operating systems should thus be understood as the *operational difference* between themselves and their environment, a difference that is made through some sort of self-referential oscillating between the two sides of the distinction (i.e. system and environment)."[70] Spencer-Brown calls this oscillation "re-entry"—an "event" in which the form of the distinction (say, inside/outside) re-enters into the distinction. Thus, the distinction inside/outside will find itself on the "inside" of the original distinction and not, crucially, as an identity or unity made available to one side of the distinction but *as the distinction*—as a paradox! As Luhmann writes, "The unmarked space is the indispensible other side, a reference to possibilities that, for their part, point to an infinity that cannot be contained in one place."[71] One might even claim in Peircean terms that the *other* side as a negation merely represents for the system as yet *unactualized* possibilities, an indeterminate future. Finally, once a distinction is made, there is an "oscillation" in the form, as each subsequent distinction switches the value of the form. As Kauffman puts it, "Yet inevitably, there comes through the possibility of seeing anything at all the possibility of seeing a separate part. And so does the part become divided from the whole while still enfolded within it."[72]

To return full circle to our beginning (though it will not be quite the same now), the effects of this kind of "diagrammatic thinking" were already described by Derrida in *Of Grammatology*: "Even before being determined as human (with all the distinctive characteristics that have always been attributed to man and the entire system of significations that they imply) or nonhuman, the *grammé*—or the *grapheme*—would thus name the element. An element without simplicity."[73] Along the same lines, the following passage from a letter that Peirce wrote to Lady Welby in 1908 is particularly illuminating: "I define a Sign as anything which is so determined by something else, called its object, and so determines an effect upon a person, which effect I call its Interpretant, that the latter is thereby mediately determined by the former: My insertion of 'upon a person' is a sop to Cerberus, because I despair of making my own broader conception understood."[74] Concerning this passage, Max Fisch asks, "What was that broader, that more generalized, conception? Negatively, it is apparent that it did not involve 'the mind of an interpreter' or 'an effect upon a person.' Did it also not involve an utterer, a sign-giver? In the last account of his theory of signs which Peirce had published, as a framework, within which to introduce his existential graphs, the place of the sign-utterer or sign-giver had been taken by the Graphist."[75] Fisch then points to the following fascinating passage from Peirce: "Moreover, signs require at least two *Quasi-minds*; a *Quasi-utterer* and a *Quasi-interpreter*; and although these two are at one (i.e. *are* one mind) in the sign itself, they must nevertheless be distinct. In the Sign they are, so to say, *welded*. Accordingly, it is not merely a fact of human Psychology, but a necessity of Logic, that every logical evolution of thought should be dialogic."[76] As Fisch notes, "The sop to Cerberus was lapsing from sign-talk into psych-talk—from semeiotic into psychology."[77]

Peirce's substitution of *graphist* for mind leads to the expulsion or overtaking of voice or mind by the machine of writing, and thus no sense of "natural expression" can be maintained because it is at its point of origin marked or marred by the unnatural or technical conditions of its emergence. More precisely, Peirce's graphs disrupt the " 'natural' bond between *phoné* and the sense"—leading to what Derrida refers to as a "non-intuition" that departs decisively from "a psychology of intuitive consciousness."[78] This results in the "*empty* symbolism of the written notation . . . which exiles us far from the *clear* evidence of the sense, that is to say from the full presence of the signified in its truth, and thus opens the possibility of crisis."[79] This "crisis" that is not amendable to the system is, as we have seen, the possibility of the event. What Derrida calls this "structure of nonpresence," which represents "an emergence that makes the *grammé* appear *as such*,"[80] is represented in Peirce's semiotics as the repetition of difference in the form of the re-entry of a self-referential distinction: a circle drawn within itself.

A Great Catholic Church: Infinity, Community, Continuity

> All communication from mind to mind is through continuity of being.
>
> CHARLES S. PEIRCE, "IMMORTALITY IN THE LIGHT
> OF SYNECHISM"

Niklas Luhmann's theory of social systems offers an account of communication in which consciousness is totally foreclosed from the act of communication. This is so, as Luhmann puts it, because "we have absolutely no idea how to comprehend that conscious minds can bring about communication."[81] Luhmann assumes the complete self-referential closure of both consciousness and communication systems. Meaning and rationality are then generated only from the internal organization of the system without an external reference. In this way, Luhmann's grand theory attempts a revision of our understanding of rationality. It becomes one-sided, taking place only, as it were, *inside* the circle of an Existential Graph.

As Luhmann writes in *Observations on Modernity*:

> Traditional concepts of rationality lived off of *external* presumptions of meaning, whether they were based on the copying of natural laws, given objectives, or given values for the choice of objectives. Such suppositions lose their foundation, as do the secularization of a religious ideology and the loss of the representation of uniquely correct points of departure. Judgments concerning rationality must therefore be separated from external presumptions of meaning and transferred to a consistently *system-internal unity of self-reference and external reference.*[82]

Peirce's rejection of a Cartesian or an Archimedean point of departure ensures that his own philosophy adopts a similar starting point. Peirce starts already within semiosis, with signs that are always partial: "Peirce's sign is not the figure of impartial *judgment*; it is the figure of partial representation."[83] Another way of putting this is that the distinction between part and whole takes place on the side of the part *as a distinction*—this is a fully internal rendering of the distinction between internal and external, a distinction that can only appear within the system as a paradox that must be unfolded through the selection of one side or the other.

Anne Freadman offers a useful link to Luhmann's theory because she advances an account of semiosis without a subject:

> Peirce argues consistently throughout his career that the necessary formal conditions for something's being a sign must not rest on the presuppositions of persons engaged in thinking. On the contrary, it has the function

of explaining the processes of thinking: it is the "law" that underpins the "event." . . . When Peirce describes real cases of semiosis, the thinghood and the eventhood of the sign, and hence of its interpretant, must be specified, and on occasion—particularly those occasions when he is tracing the operations of inquiry—this does indeed involve persons in "conversation"—bodies, things in the world, the locus of experience are the sine qua non of action. This is the machinery of talk.[84]

There is no detachment of semiosis "in itself" from what Freadman calls the *genre* (or classification) of its production. We may also suggest that Freadman's concept of *genre* represents the circle of an Existential Graph, and in that way it represents the local "constraints" made on a semiosis that cannot be separated from the technical conditions of its emergence: "If a technical apparatus is in principle the condition of possibility for any sign, this displaces the locus of activity from cerebration, from concepts, from the universal scope of the theory of knowledge in general, on to local contrivances, with their constraints, their limited and specific capacities, and their local applicability."[85] This means that there is no final or ultimate level of semiosis (no final circle) that can encompass all the others. Ultimately, this leads Freadman to reject the necessity of a subject for semiosis as such because the production of a subject is entailed only for particular semiotic practices. As she puts it, "Thought is nothing without its instruments."[86]

Likewise, Luhmann's distinction between consciousness and communication posits as necessary what Peirce seems to lament as his own incapacity: "Systems of the mind and systems of communication exist completely independently of each other. At the same time, however, they form a relationship of structural complementarity. They can actualize and specify only their own structures and thus can change only themselves. They use each other for a reciprocal initiation of these structural changes."[87] The man informs the word and the word informs the man, a "complementarity" that shows itself in the fact of a double movement that demonstrates a "superiority of consciousness to communication (which, of course, corresponds in inverted system-reference to a superiority of communication over consciousness)."[88] In other words, we must always ask: which system reference (word or man) is being used? If both minds and communications are seen as captive to one-sidedness, to their own encircling self-referential distinctions, then they can be seen as inhabiting the "other side" or unmarked space of each other's operations—the side of the paradox that *isn't* chosen: "The mind cannot instruct communication, because communication constructs itself. But the mind is a constant source of impulses for the one or the other turn of the operative process inherent in communication."[89] To amend Habermas: mind is the necessary *other* to communication and communication is the necessary *other* to the mind.

Here it is important to recall that Peirce aims at a final consolidation or recuperation of continuity in the form of an asymptotic approach toward reality, the "ultimate opinion" of the unlimited community: "Reality is independent, not necessarily of thought in general, but only of what you or I or any finite number of men may think about it; and that, on the other hand, though the object of the final opinion depends on what that opinion is, yet what that opinion is does not depend on what you or I or any man thinks."[90] To affirm the contrary—that there will always remain questions for which no answer can be found—is in Peirce's mind quite unneighborly. Or, what amounts for him to the same thing, unphilosophical:

> Do these things not really exist because they are hopelessly beyond the reach of our knowledge? And then, after the universe is dead . . . and all life has ceased forever, will not the shock of atoms continue though there will be no mind to know it? To this I reply that, though in no possible state of knowledge can any number be great enough to express the relation between the amount of what rests unknown to the amount of the unknown, yet it is unphilosophical to suppose that, with regard to any given question, . . . investigation would not bring forth a solution of it, if it were carried far enough. . . . Who can be sure of what we shall not know in a few hundred years? Who can guess what would be the result of continuing the pursuit of science for ten thousand years, with the activity of the last hundred? And if it were to go on for a million, or a billion, or any number of years you please, how is it possible to say that there is any question which might not ultimately be solved?[91]

In Luhmann's terms, this is somewhat like an affirmation that the system may eventually become adequate to its environment. In Hegel's, it is a way of construing the endless recursive "bad infinity" of semiosis as eventually adequate to the "good infinity" of the Absolute, "a circular totality, a coherent and formed whole containing finitude rather than being opposed to it."[92] Peirce starts from the blank sheet, a continuum containing no actual information until a cut or distinction is introduced. Each new circle represents an increase of determination or information. In this respect the infinite *potentiality* of Thirdness as progressive determination ultimately corresponds to the infinite *possibility* of Firstness as absolute and indeterminate continuity. Peirce construes the Hegelian totality as continuity and reincorporates that continuity by means of its infinite semiotic deferral. Infinity, in this way, reappears on either side of a determination (an individual sign or distinction) *as* semiosis: the object is "unexpressed" and thus prior to the sign, and the interpretant (the yet to be determined) always comes after it.

This allows for the "infinite hope" that we may at last fully determine the universe, what Emerson terms the ultimate "victory" that accomplishes the "transformation of genius into practical power." However, Peirce makes it clear that this hope is not a consequence of dialectical necessity but a decision, a choice to reject (take as a unity) the distinction between Hegel's "good" (an absolute and perfect totality) and "bad" (recursive, endless) infinities because it is the unity of that distinction, in the final analysis, that constitutes the paradoxical unity of a sign or Existential Graph. It is the unfolding of that very unity, in other words, which puts semiosis in motion. Peirce thus commits himself to *semiosis*—to the Sheet of Assertion as the sign of continuity—and it is for this reason that he must hold that nothing, in principle, is unknowable or incommunicable: "Underlying all such principles there is a fundamental and primary abduction, a hypothesis which we must embrace at the outset, however destitute of evidentiary support it may be. That hypothesis is that the facts at hand admit of rationalization, and of rationalization by us. . . . *That* we are bound to assume, independently of any evidence it is true."[93] This foundational commitment to "rationalization" is then for Peirce the contingent operational assumption of philosophical research and communication—what must be assumed, what is already assumed, for philosophy to occur at all.

But here we may turn things around again: Who is this "we" that is bound to the assumption? "Man's highest developments are social," he reminds us, but this sociality cannot be other than the "indefinite" and "unlimited" community, the "great catholic church" that Peirce founds only on a pure and selfless love of the *other*: "Its ideal is that the whole world shall be united in the bond of a common love of God accomplished by each man's loving his neighbor. Without a church, the religion of love can have but a rudimentary existence; and a narrow, little exclusive church is almost worse than none. A great catholic church is wanted."⁹⁴ But if love is only to be given to the *other* and not the self, who ultimately belongs to such a church? Doesn't this idea of an "indefinite" and "unlimited" community bar the admittance of any actual, specific individual? Isn't Peirce's community then where we *don't*, as individuals at least, belong? Peirce seems to gesture toward as much when he writes that "the supreme commandment is to complete the whole system even until continuity results and the distinct individuals weld together. . . . In fulfilling this command, man prepares himself for transmutation into a new form of life, the joyful Nirvana in which the discontinuities of his will shall have all but disappeared."⁹⁵ Peirce suggests that the further determination of the system is what, paradoxically, ultimately dissolves it. Doesn't this then also mean that an "unlimited" community then finds itself with no way to determine who (or what) belongs and who doesn't?

In light of these dilemmas, it is worth considering how the notion of re-entry as theorized by Spencer-Brown allows for a more radical confrontation with contingency, which need not be committed to Peirce's "supreme commandment." As Luhmann describes it, "A unity is put into operation; in the instance of the beginning, it cannot yet be analyzed. Only later . . . does it become apparent that a hidden paradox had already been present at the beginning. This paradox is the distinction contained in the distinction."⁹⁶ This unity that "cannot yet be analyzed"—which is to say, it may only be analyzed after the fact—may be considered as equivalent to Peirce's "primary abduction" (the unity in question being here the beginning sign or distinction which presumes that the totality of the universe *can* eventually be determined in semiosis), but Luhmann then takes an extra step by looping back around to find the hidden paradox that was unfolded at the beginning. At the end, the beginning finds that it was not identical even to itself, and this was how it was able to act as a beginning at all.

In effect, this second-order gesture of the self-inclusion of the initial distinction allows for the use of a hidden or unmarked space within the system. The unmarked space returns after the fact in the manner of the re-entry of the beginning distinction. As Kauffman writes,

Spencer-Brown's work can be seen as part of a continuous progression that began with Peirce's Existential Graphs. In essence what Spencer-Brown adds to the existential graphs is the use of the unmarked state. That is, he allows the use of empty space in place of a complex of Signs. This makes a profound difference and reveals a beautiful and simple calculus of indications underlying the existential graphs. Indeed Spencer-Brown's true contribution is that he added Nothing to the Peirce theory![97]

To amend Peirce, this is a principle for which Nothing remains unknowable. There is no ultimate totality, no single Sheet of Assertion that finally smothers all distinctions in formless continuity, because the Sheet is itself the product of a prior distinction, the "hidden" unity put in play at the beginning that can only become visible again at the end. In this way, Spencer-Brown's calculus brings more clearly to bear the paradox (already implicitly present in Peirce) that what is *known* (marked) simultaneously presents what is *unknown* (unmarked). Something (or someone) is always left out, and even a great catholic church will have its heretics.

One is tempted to follow this particular theme into the rabbit hole (perhaps never to emerge), but short of that we may observe what is at stake in the distinction. As Kauffman notes, Spencer-Brown's innovation can be interpreted as a radicalization of a latent element of Peirce's thought, an insistence that in every single case we must accept that our beginnings (and endings) are arbitrary: contingency comes both before and after the system, as if it were positioned between two infinities. Things could always be otherwise, and this is the condition for them to be anything at all. On this basis it can be seen that we don't *have* to assume something like Peirce's "primary abduction," but I already find myself arguing that assuming it—assuming without cause that what one needs to say *can*, indeed, be said—would seem to be a requirement of communicating at all. To find, or more properly to *lose*, oneself in communication is to discover that such a commitment was made before a word was uttered. Peirce's admission of his "primary abduction" after the fact closes the loop of his own system and points to its own *other* despite itself. As this point Peirce's thought achieves a kind of openness through its closure, an openness *only* achieved through the closure entailed in the "primary abduction" that marks the boundaries of semiosis. Indeed, how can semiosis conceive of what is not amendable to semiosis? After all, to traverse the abyss of continuity (to introduce a mark or difference within the unmarked space) in order to communicate is to *already* find one's self negated after the fact and in this way one is made accountable to someone (or something) else. To communicate at all is then to choose (or *have chosen*) the *other* or external side of the self—even in silence. Communication is self-negation, and Peirce's semiotic community is one with no members and no parts, one to which you—as *you* at least—can't, in fact, belong.

We can now see that Peirce's continuity is itself a paradox: perceptible as *im*perceptible, observable as unobservable, only dimly felt before it has flown. Only present as both already past and what is yet to come, it must, like all paradoxes, be unfolded in the meantime. In an uncharacteristically lyrical moment, Luhmann muses,

> If we were to make an effort to really observe our own consciousness in its operations from thought to thought, we would certainly discover a peculiar fascination with language, but also the noncommunicative, purely internal use of linguistic symbols and a peculiar, background depth of the actuality of consciousness, a depth on which words swim like ships chained in a row but without being consciousness itself, some- how illuminated, but not light itself.[98]

Peirce construes that hidden light, that which illuminates without being illuminated, as the white light of the continuity of being. We cannot look but we fail to see it.

— 6 —
The Cybernetic Imaginary
Musement and the Unsaying of Theory

There is, however, nothing more wholesome for us than to find
problems that quite transcend our powers and I must say, too, that
it imparts a delicious sense of being cradled in the waters of the
deep,—a feeling I always have at sea.

CHARLES S. PEIRCE, LETTER TO WILLIAM JAMES

In 1892, Charles S. Peirce had what his biographer calls a "sudden and
overwhelming mystical experience."[1] He was called as if by a force outside himself into church to receive communion: "I have never before been
mystical; but now I am."[2] According to Joseph Brent, this was a transfor-
mative experience for Peirce and accounts at least in part for the dramatic
change in his philosophy evident in the remarkable series of essays he
wrote for the *Monist* from 1891 to 1893. As Brent writes, "The *Monist*
essays forcefully and unexpectedly proclaimed an objective idealist, as
well as realist, metaphysics that seemed written by a different man."[3] In
the second of those papers, "The Law of Mind," Peirce addressed that
change directly:

> I may mention, for the benefit of those who are curious in studying
> mental biographies, that I was born and reared in the neighborhood of
> Concord,—I mean in Cambridge,—at the time when Emerson, Hedge,
> and their friends were disseminating the ideas that they had caught from
> Schelling, and Schelling from Plotinus, from Boehm, or from God knows
> what minds stricken with the monstrous mysticism of the East. But the
> atmosphere of Cambridge held many an antiseptic against Concord
> transcendentalism; and I am not conscious of having contracted any of
> that virus. Nevertheless, it is probable that some cultured bacilli, some
> benignant form of the disease was implanted in my soul, unawares, and
> that now, after long incubation, it comes to the surface, modified by
> mathematical conceptions and by training in physical investigations.[4]

What is most tantalizing about this passage is that while Peirce intellectually disowns not only Ralph Waldo Emerson but even the likes of Friedrich Schelling and Plotinus, he simultaneously draws them into his orbit, a double gesture that recalls the "circular" movement of love described in "Evolutionary Love" (the capstone of the *Monist* series) as "at one and the same impulse projecting creations into independency and drawing them into harmony."[5]

Peirce's "mental biography" discloses a tension in his thought. On one side is the "virus" of the commanding Emersonian strain in American thought—a transcendentalism that goes at least as far back as Jonathan Edwards and that Peirce perceptively connects to both the romanticism of Schelling and the Neoplatonic mysticism of Plotinus, which is the template for the type of apophatic (or "negative") theology that unites the likes of John Scottus Eriugena, Nicholas of Cusa, Meister Eckhart, and the anonymous author of *The Cloud of Unknowing*, among many others.[6] Moreover, Peirce's incorporation and simultaneous disavowal of Emerson—not to mention the fact that Emerson's name appears so infrequently in Peirce's enormous body of work as to be somewhat conspicuous in its absence—cannot help but suggest to the suspicious critical mind a philosophical rendering of the "anxiety of influence."[7]

On the other side, of course, is Peirce's long-standing commitment to the rational domains of mathematics, science, and logic—an inheritance attributable to the influence of his actual father, the Harvard mathematician Benjamin Peirce. Resolving this tension between "Concord transcendentalism" and the scientifically minded environment of Cambridge may be seen to be a major concern of not only the *Monist* papers but a large portion of Peirce's subsequent philosophical output. This is a concern to harmonize personal experience and scientific determinism—or more generally the venerable modern categories of "subject" and "object"— that aims at what Emerson describes in "Self-Reliance" as "that source, at once the essence of genius, of virtue, and of life, which we call Spontaneity or Instinct. We denote this primary wisdom as Intuition, whilst all later teachings are tuitions. . . . Its presence or its absence is all we can affirm. Every man discriminates between the voluntary acts of his mind, and his involuntary perceptions, and knows that to his involuntary perceptions a perfect faith is due."[8]

However, while Peirce would find much to agree with in this early statement from Emerson, he wasn't interested in merely asserting religious intuition as the ultimate pragmatic arbiter of "truth." As he emphatically put it in the Harvard lectures of 1903, "I do not approve of mixing up Religion and Philosophy."[9] Instead, religious experiences are not exactly demoted by Peirce but relativized within scientific inquiry as the function of a hypothesis—a term alternately referred to by Peirce as "abduction" and "retroduction." Even faith must be questioned, must be sacrificed and offered up for rational scrutiny. The upshot is that *personal* religious experience is neither the source nor the embodiment of truth but must, in a sense, be externalized through the activity of *impersonal* inquiry. In other words, the internal generation of hypotheses, what he refers to in Emersonian fashion as "spontaneous conjectures of instinctive reason,"[10] must be rendered determinate through the functions of scientific inquiry, functions that cannot add anything *new* to inquiry, but may only take something away: "Observe that neither Deduction nor Induction contributes the smallest positive item to the final conclusion of the inquiry. They render the indefinite definite . . . and neither Deduction nor Induction contributes a single new concept to the structure."[11] That is, while "every plank of its advance is first laid by Retroduction alone," the path of inquiry requires the inside to be turned inside out: "Retroduction does not afford security. The hypothesis must be tested."[12]

Those words come from "A Neglected Argument for the Reality of God," an eccentric essay from 1908 that represents, according to Michael Raposa, "both the maturest form of his thought and one of the very few extended treatments of a religious topic produced by him during a lifetime of philosophizing."[13] The "Neglected Argument" is best known for introducing the practice of "Musement," a peculiar notion that sits uneasily in Peirce's wider body of work. Musement is a carefully cultivated form of personal experience that leads, inevitably in Peirce's estimation, to an external, objective, or impersonal "argument" for the reality of God. Musement, that is, represents a hypothesis of a very special kind, one that introduces a sign for God "so 'capitalized' (as we Americans say)" as "*the* definable proper name, signifying *Ens necessarium*: in my belief Really creator of all three Universes of Experience."[14] This seems almost straightforward (for Peirce at least) on its face, but what he intends by the designation "*the* definable proper name" hints at something other than a strictly determinate meaning. If nothing else, it suggests that God's most prominent characteristic is the ability to endure and absorb without exhaustion the descriptions and definitions that are assigned to him.

The word "God" is a particular kind of sign, and a sign is defined as having "its Being in its power of serving as intermediary between its Objects and a Mind. Such, too, is a living consciousness, and such the life, the power of growth of a plant. Such is a living institution,—a daily newspaper, a great fortune, a social 'movement.'" The name or sign of "God" is more abstract still; it is a type of "argument" that is defined as "any process of thought reasonably tending to produce a definite belief. An 'Argumentation' is an Argument proceeding upon definitely formulated premises."[15] What makes the "Neglected Argument" unique is that it proceeds from a premise that is anything but definite, as if it were an argument distinct from argumentation, or the possibility of definability in the first place:

> Because it involves no purpose save that of casting aside all serious purpose. . . . In fact, it is Pure Play. Now, Play, we all know, is a lively exercise of one's powers. Pure Play has no rules, except this very law of liberty. It bloweth where it listeth. It has no purpose, unless recreation. The particular occupation I mean,—a *petite bouchée* with the Universes,—may take either the form of esthetic contemplation, or that of distant castle-building (whether in Spain or within one's own moral training), or that of considering some wonder in one of the Universes or some connection between two of the three, with speculation concerning its cause. It is this last kind,—I will call it "Musement" on the whole,—that I particularly recommend, because it will in time flower into the N.A. One who sits down with the purpose of becoming convinced of the truth of religion is plainly not inquiring in scientific singleness of heart, and must always suspect himself of reasoning unfairly. So, he can never attain the entirety even of a physicist's belief in electrons, although this is avowedly but provisional. But let religious meditation be allowed to grow up spontaneously out of Pure Play without any breach of continuity; and the Muse will retain the perfect candor proper to Musement.[16]

It seems that Musement, as the contemplation of ultimate causes, is not something to be sought and acquired, or something one can be reasoned into—though one can reason *out* of it. It is a quality of thought not unlike the practice of meditation, in which the mind may observe its own internal semiotic or linguistic processes without fully identifying with them. As Peirce puts it, "If one's observations and reflections are allowed to specialize themselves too much, the Play will be converted into scientific study; and that cannot be pursued in odd half-hours."[17] The Zen paradox of the thinking of nonthinking (or thinking *beyond* thinking) is rendered by Peirce as the paradoxical "law of liberty." Musement is thinking *about* thinking—a second-order thinking—that is accomplished by momentarily liberating itself of the rules that constitute rational thought. It is a thinking that *rejects* the one-sided demands of specialization and determination. As Floyd Merrell puts it in his valuable essay on the "Neglected Argument,"

> Musement is a state of indifference, with no particular purpose or end. It is a moment of purposeful purposelessness, mindless awareness, passive indeterminacy, all-embracing nothingness . . . suspension between zero and infinity. For Peirce it is the lively exercise of detached contemplation, when there is neither affirmation nor denial, and at the same time there is both affirmation and denial. There is everything and there is nothing; there is neither choice nor nonchoice, only floating dreaminess.[18]

Merrell attaches Musement to Peirce's idea of "vagueness." Likewise, in *Peirce's Philosophy of Religion*, Raposa writes that, for Peirce, "seemingly paradoxical utterances about the Deity might be explained in terms of their vagueness, by appealing to a logic that defines the 'vague . . . as that to which the principle of contradiction does not apply.' "[19]

Such descriptions have the effect of putting Peirce's disparagement of the "monstrous mysticism of the East" into ironic relief while suggesting that the virus of Concord perhaps at long last subdued its host. However, it is still quite difficult to imagine how this thinking of the vague or indeterminate "without any breach of continuity" can lead to a concrete idea of God, let alone how such thinking is possible in the first place. Does not this seeming suspension of differential semiotic processes, this Jamesian "reinstatement of the vague," have to take place *within* semiosis? Is this not then the standard humanist gesture that represents totality—here the totality of semiosis, or God as the sign of the Universe—*within* consciousness? Is not Musement then a "transparent eyeball" or intuitive transcendental gesture that calls into question the argument of this very book?

Yes and no. Musement is not, to be sure, a posthumanist gesture but the moment at which posthumanist theory encounters its own limit, the boundary line at which posthumanism applies itself to itself and *unsays* itself. After all, the law of liberty—the paradox of law in the moment of its instantiation—suggests that the progression from Pure Play to the specialization of scientific study is by no means always a necessary or predictable one. Musement seems to broach the event of the instantiation of the rule of reason, the moment at which the self or subject is foreclosed and given over to the law. Reason, that is, seems for Peirce to be founded upon the traversal of a lack or abyss, upon *non*reason—a predicament he acknowledges when he comments that "the only thing that is really desirable without a reason for being so, is to render ideas and things reasonable. One cannot well demand a reason for reasonableness itself."[20] Indeed, one cannot *demand* it, but to give oneself over to some sense of "reasonableness" suggests for Peirce something similar to the "primary abduction" discussed at the conclusion of the last chapter—a commitment to *communicate*, to offer up the nothing or negation that is all the self has to offer.

Jacques Derrida quotes those very same words from Peirce before performing his own investigation into the ground of reason:

> Are we obeying the principle of reason when we ask what grounds this principle which is itself a principle of grounding? We are not—which does not mean that we are disobeying it, either. Are we dealing here with a circle or with an abyss? The circle would consist in seeking to account for reason by reason, to render reason to the principle of reason, in appealing to the principle in order to make it speak of itself at the very point where, according to Heidegger, the principle of reason says nothing about reason itself. The abyss, the hole, the Abgrund, the empty "gorge" would be the impossibility for a principle of grounding to ground itself.[21]

I want to argue that it is precisely this distinction between circle and abyss that is at issue for Musement. That is to say, Musement presents to semiosis that very distinction: circle/abyss. In much the same way, "A Neglected Argument for the Reality of God" as a whole (for which Musement, it must be remembered, is only a part) can be seen to be about the reason of reason, or more precisely the hinge on which or displacement through which the unrelated and singular wholeness of a quality of feeling is broken up into the mechanical parts of a semiotic system. The question—"circle or abyss?"—then becomes the question faced by any theoretical system when it confronts the paradox of its own (absent) ground. The choice that distinction presents to the system is either to follow through with the infinite self-referential recursions of the system (circle) or to find a way out (abyss). In this way, Musement may be seen as the movement by which the thought of reason, in a double gesture, calls itself to account while at the *same time* unfolding the circular paradox that constitutes it. This possibility of self-negation is a function of reason's autonomy, its deconstructive "circle," and the mark of its modernity.

In this particular respect, the "Neglected Argument" finds precedent in what Hans Blumenberg calls "the dark lacuna of the Middle Ages."[22] As Blumenberg vividly tells it, this involves the deeply perilous traversal of the abyss between medieval theology and modern rational philosophy:

> The crisis-laden self-dissolution of the Middle Ages can be linked to the systematic relations in the metaphysical triangle: man, God, world. This presupposes an ambivalence in Christian theology. On the one hand, theology's theme is *anthropocentric*: the biblical God's concern, within history and beyond its eschatological invalidation, for man's salvation is transformed with the help of the received Stoic idea of *pronoia* [providence] into an idea of world government and the coordination of nature, history, and man, which is fully unfolded in the Scholastic system of pure rationality. On the other hand, there is the *theocentric* motive: the dissolution of Scholastic rationality through the exaggeration of the transcendence, sovereignty, hiddenness, fearsomeness of its God. The first motive holds the metaphysical triangle of theology, anthropology, and cosmology together; the second tears it apart. The ability of the second motive to prevail shows at the same time that the systematic consistency of the structure constituted by the first motive is insufficient, that it is superficially harmonized heterogeneity.[23]

If we accept Blumenberg's description of the advent of early modernity, then it becomes possible to argue that the "Neglected Argument" is about nothing less than the legitimacy of modernity itself, a concern that links Peirce to the theologies of the transitional period described above. In particular, the mystic theologian Nicholas of Cusa's own mathematically inflected thought and asymptotic realism find a great deal of overlap with Peirce.

Blumenberg places Cusa at the beginning of the medieval crisis of knowledge. From that position, his thought seeks to repair the totality of the medieval cosmos on its own terms. This means holding reason accountable to theology, but without "the mere negativity of the language of mysticism."[24] In other words, Cusa attempted to integrate the anthropocentric and theocentric movements of early modernity from the "side" of the theocentric: "Transcendence is no longer related to an objective topography, a cosmic ground plan. It appears precisely when man, in the manner of Scholasticism—as though upon the ladder of the hierarchical cosmos—wants to pursue his argumentation to a successful conclusion and in the process has an opportunity to experience the incomprehensibility of the world's form, the infinity of the finite; transcendence is a mode of negation of definitiveness of theory."[25] Cusa's thought brings about the negation of reason *through* reason, a means by which "faith is offered to reason as not the unreasonable demand that it sacrifice itself but rather the disclosure of the possibility of its self-fulfillment. That is clearly an attempt to restore the Middle Ages by means of their own substance."[26] Faith, or nonreason, is then the outcome of reason, or reason's confrontation with its own contingency. Here transcendence is rendered not as the positive representation of the whole within the part but as the negation or rejection of the constitutive distinction between transcendence and immanence: the only way out is through.

This precedent for the self-negation of theory leads us in turn to consider what Raposa calls Peirce's "logic of vagueness." As he puts it, "If such vague symbols are the models most appropriately employed for the representation of a real indeterminacy, then a better understanding of the special logic of their usage seems crucial to the development of a general theory of religious language."[27] It seems to me that the best model for understanding this special logic is the tradition of apophatic (or negative) theology. In his important and illuminating book on apophasis, Michael A. Sells investigates what he calls "the *aporia*—the unresolvable dilemma—of transcendence."[28] The question is how one can speak of what is by definition beyond immanence and therefore beyond *words*:

> At least three responses to the primary dilemma of transcendence are conceivable. The first response is silence. The second response is to distinguish between ways in which the transcendent is beyond names and ways in which it is not. . . . The third response begins with the refusal to solve the dilemma posed by the attempt to refer to the transcendent through a distinction between two kinds of name. The dilemma is accepted as a

genuine *aporia*, that is, as unresolvable; but this acceptance, instead of leading to silence, leads to a new mode of discourse.[29]

This new mode of discourse that takes its object to be its own unresolvable-ness (a discourse that could then be said to take the distinction or excluded middle between itself and its object *as* its object) is called apophasis. It is a discourse that begins with a refusal of representational adequacy, a discourse that marks itself out as "false" from its very founding gesture. As Sells points out, apophasis can mean "negation," but that designation (appropriately) fails to fully grasp the meaning of the discourse it designates because it remains unavoidably tied to a single or primary act of negation rather than, as Sells prefers, an emphasis on "*apo phasis*" as indicating "un-saying or speaking-away."[30]

Unsaying is then not simply a simple negation or nihilism, or a strict denial of the potential adequacy of representation between a discourse and its object, but it is instead something much more elusive. One cannot unsay the unsaid: "Every act of unsaying demands or presupposes a previous saying. . . . Any saying (even a negative saying) demands a correcting proposition, an unsaying."[31] This is a discourse in which no proposition, not negation and certainly not affirmation, has meaning except through its deferral and substitution: "It is in the tension between the two propositions that the discourse becomes meaningful. That tension is momentary. It must be continually re-earned by ever new linguistic acts of unsaying."[32] Ultimately, "no single, static paradigm is meaningful: 'A then B' leads ineluctably to 'B then A.'"[33] Apophasis, then, remains caught in a circular relationship with its own object:

When Plotinus writes that "it is neither X nor not X," he violates the logical rule of the excluded middle. When he writes that "it is both X and not X," he violates the law of noncontradiction. I argue that these statements are paradoxical in a very strong sense. They are not rhetorical paradoxes or "seeming contradictions" that can be used for effect and then be resolved by further explanation. Real contradictions arise when the delimited, referential function of language encounters a rigorously apophatic notion of the unlimited. Such contradictions are not illogical, however. The rules of non-contradiction and excluded middle apply specifically to delimited language reference. The coming together of opposites (*coincidentia oppositorum*) results logically from any reference to the unlimited.[34]

Interestingly, Peirce's concept of a sign as Thirdness (as seen in chapter 1) does *not* violate the law of noncontradiction because it demands a subsequent determination, a selection of one side at the expense of the other. If we claim that Musement in true apophatic fashion violates *both* the rule of the excluded middle *and* the law of noncontradiction, then Musement is in some sense *not* amendable to semiosis as Thirdness, but something like the condition of the possibility of semiosis in the first place, the contingency *of* semiosis itself. Analogously, Sells puts the matter in the context of ontology, "in order for 'being' to be, the source of being cannot be being."[35]

Apophasis, as should by now be clear, is an extremely demanding form of discourse. Indeed, a key insight provided by Sells is that "the smallest semantic unit is not the sentence or proposition, but the double sentence or dual proposition."[36] Circle or abyss? The transcendental question par excellence is itself subjected to reversal or inversion. As Sells puts it, "The effort to express and affirm transcendence leads to an affirmation of radical immanence. That which is beyond is within. That which is other, is the non-other."[37] Cusa finds a way through by taking the distinction or difference *itself* to be the true object of observation. As Blumenberg puts it, "The perceptible stands *between* the two infinities; it has, as it were, both an outward and an inward transcendence."[38] And in Cusa's own words, "We know of the truth only that we know that it cannot be comprehended precisely as it is. Truth is like the most absolute necessity, which can be neither more nor less than it is, while our intellect is like possibility."[39] Compare this with Peirce, who considers the present as "this living Death in which we are born anew" that constitutes a "Nascent State between the Determinate and the Indeterminate."[40]

All of this raises a difficult question: How to define the indefinite? My contention is that Musement supplies the "indefinite" (and thus apophatic) premise for semiotics, the nonother that is other, the beyond within. Musement provides the founding apophatic gesture of what Sells calls "a moment of receptivity free from the security of referential delimitation."[41] Peirce describes it as a journey out into the calm waters of the mind: "Enter your skiff of Musement, push off into the lake of thought, and leave the breath of heaven to swell your sail. With your eyes open, awake to what is about or within you, and open conversation with yourself; for such is all meditation."[42] For Peirce, such musings inevitably strike upon the phenomenon of "growth," not only in the outward manifestations of the world, but in the progress of thought itself. But how to represent change or growth from within the static binary confines of a linguistic discourse?

Peirce's solution to this problem arrives at what I consider to be the most important moment of the essay, a moment that reflects what Sells calls the heightened moments of "semantic intensity" in which a paradox is unfolded through language, as when Plotinus writes, "The one is all things but no thing."⁴³ How does the infinite appear within the finite? How does "A then B" become "B then A"? "Reason is led," writes Sells, "by its own reasoning, beyond itself, continually, without arriving at a final entity or conclusion."⁴⁴ This is both the instantiating moment of semiosis *and* its unending movement, a unity of two infinities. That moment arrives in the "Neglected Argument" when Peirce attempts to define the particular characteristics of the hypothesis of God:

> The hypothesis of God is a peculiar one, in that it supposes an infinitely incomprehensible object, although every hypothesis, as such, supposes its object to be truly conceived in the hypothesis. This leaves the hypothesis but one way of understanding itself; namely, as vague but as true so far as it is definite, and as continually tending to define itself more and more, and without limit. The hypothesis, being thus itself inevitably subject to the law of growth, appears in its vagueness to represent God as so, albeit this is directly contradicted in the hypothesis from its very first phase. But this apparent attribution of growth to God, since it is ineradicable from the hypothesis, cannot, according to the hypothesis, be flatly false. Its implications concerning the Universes will be maintained in the hypothesis, while its implications concerning God will be partly disavowed, and yet held to be less false than their denial would be. Thus, the hypothesis will lead to our thinking of features of each Universe as purposed; and this will stand or fall with the hypothesis. Yet a purpose essentially involves growth, and so cannot be attributed to God. Still it will, according to the hypothesis, be less false to speak so, than to represent God as purposeless.⁴⁵

Here Peirce dispenses with the protocols of clear and rational argumentation (or puts them in overdrive) to such a degree that it is difficult to take away anything more than a headache. But this passage may be seen to represent nothing so much as a certain well-worn theological tradition of describing God's indescribability. For example, Cusa's theology understands God as the "absolute maximum" but interprets this as process, one not unlike Peirce's triadic semiotics: "The maximum unity, therefore, is not other than indivision, distinction, and connection."[46]

The hypothesis of God understands itself *as* contradiction. "For God," writes Cusa, "causes not-being to enter into being and being to enter into not-being."[47] The hypothesis understands itself as true and definite only insofar as it is false and indefinite. The hypothesis is marked with a distinction (definite/indefinite or false/true) that cannot observe its own unity, but only re-enter itself on one side, on the side of "false" or "definite." And for this reason, the hypothesis cannot rest as itself, but must grow beyond itself and recontain itself in a double gesture. In a passage that could come straight from Peirce's own pen, Cusa writes, "So the intellect, which is not truth, never comprehends truth so precisely but that it could always be comprehended with infinitely more precision."[48] This is because all observations are constituted by a distinction, a hidden or excluded unity between determinate and indeterminate, and so cannot grasp the totality of the world except through its erasure. The "other" side always escapes determination, growth, and even purpose, as if God leaves those qualities behind in a world now marked by his absence. This is the difference, the negation or the exclusion or even the sacrifice, that returns again and again to remake the world anew.

Exit Point

Noise destroys an order, the order of discourse; it also announces another order. Disorder is the end of order and sometimes its beginning. Noise turns around, like a revolving door. The beginning or the end of a system for the former; an entrance or exit for the latter. Exclusion, inclusion.

MICHEL SERRES, *THE PARASITE*

In an early paper from 1940, Gregory Bateson describes a decidedly Peircean premonition of an overarching uniformity in nature, a "vague mystical feeling that we must look for the same sort of processes in all fields of natural phenomena."[49] For Bateson, this feeling means that "the types of mental operation which are useful in analyzing one field may be equally useful in another—that the framework (the *eidos*) of science, rather than the framework of Nature, is the same in all fields."[50] He suggests that this feeling and its encouragement of "loose analogies" may be in fact the very means of scientific progress.[51] At the same time, "loose" thinking keeps science on guard against a stale and abstract formalism that inevitably fails to express the inexhaustible richness of nature. Science, he concludes, must learn to think with a "double habit of mind" that can accommodate both "loose" and "strict" forms of thinking:

> I want to emphasize that whenever we pride ourselves upon finding a newer, stricter way of thought or exposition; whenever we start insisting too hard upon "operationalism" or symbolic logic or any other of those very essential systems of tramlimes, we lose something of the ability to think new thoughts. And equally, of course, whenever we rebel against the sterile rigidity of formal thought and exposition and let our ideas run wild, we likewise lose. As I see it, the advances in scientific thought come from a *combination of loose and strict thinking*, and this combination is the most precious tool of science.[52]

The vacillation between these two opposed types of thinking forms "the whole fluctuating business of the advance of science . . . first the loose thinking and the building up of a structure on unsound foundations and then the correction to stricter thinking and the substitution of a new underpinning beneath the already constructed mass."[53]

As argued in the previous section, Peirce approaches the progress of determination accomplished by science as the continual determination of what Bateson terms "loose" thinking, a one-sided or asymmetric vacillation that refuses the harmony of Bateson's ecological holism by gesturing toward a practice similar to negative theology. "Loose" or mystical thinking continually exceeds the grasp of science as the occluded condition of thought itself. This is, we may remember, the same as Emerson's "unhandsome" condition. Likewise, Peirce's discourse of signs exceeds Bateson's assertion that "the ancient problem of whether the mind is immanent or transcendent can be answered in favor of immanence."[54] The immanent whole is not something arrived at, as Bateson assumes, through the simple addition of "man *plus* environment" but only through a kind of inverted or reverse transcendence as the negation or rejection of those distinctions.[55] The whole is what *isn't* arrived at. Bateson's holistic idea of immanence, by contrast, is captive to a residual humanism that is familiar from William James. After all, where else can the thought of "man *plus* environment" become a unity except in something like the mind of an observer?

Despite this difference, Bateson offers an important link between the posthumanist gestures of Peirce, Emerson, and Edwards and the cybernetic critique of modern science. As Steven Best and Douglas Kellner write, "Modern science, in its classical self-conception, sharply separates 'fact' from 'value,' thereby pursuing a 'value-free' study of natural systems apart from ethics and metaphysics."[56] Bateson's ecological or holistic critique of this perspective is of course well known, particularly the critique of the set of destructive assumptions into which the modern scientific mindset inevitably leads us, assumptions summed up by Bateson as "it's us *against* the environment."[57] That opposition in turn leads to the modern humanist presumption of control that Bateson defines as a one-sided domination of the environment: "We *can* have unilateral control over the environment and must strive for that control."[58]

As Niklas Luhmann notes, such critiques are common enough to have a general form that calls not only modern science but also modernity itself into question: "What is at stake in such a critique is the form of modern science—that is, the difference made by the fact that science exists. . . . It takes aim at a one-sided tendency toward formalization, idealization, technicalization, accounting, etc."[59] Luhmann's use of the term "one-sided" is particularly fortuitous, since Peirce's definition of scientific truth, intended as part of just such a critique, also includes it. For Peirce, truth is true only insofar as it confesses its "inaccuracy and one-sidedness" as an "essential ingredient" of what makes it true.[60] Such statements run directly counter to modern science, which supposes, "If knowledge is true, it is always true."[61]

Of course, science spent much of the twentieth century under epistemological assault even as its practical and technological achievements grew more and more spectacular, a divergence that began in earnest once the discovery of entropy called into question the explanatory power of the modern paradigm. As Ilya Prigogine and Isabelle Stengers write, "The ambition of Newtonian science was to present a vision of nature that would be universal, deterministic, and objective inasmuch as it contains no reference to the observer, complete inasmuch as it attains a level of description that escapes the clutches of time."[62] Dissipative or entropic systems, on the contrary, thrust the observer back into time, into a universe in which change is fundamental: "Irreversible processes may be considered as the last remnants of the spontaneous and intrinsic *activity* displayed by nature when experimental devices are employed to harness it."[63] Scientific observation, that is, takes reversible snapshots of irreversible processes.

Peirce's description of this phenomenon usually involves the intrusion of possibility, chance, or chaos (what he calls "tychism") into otherwise deterministic systems. In an early essay he writes, "The dissipation of energy by the regular laws of nature is by those very laws accompanied by circumstances more and more favorable to its reconcentration by chance. . . . And from this it follows that chance must act to move things in the long run from a state of homogeneity to a state of heterogeneity."[64] This passage is quoted with admiration by Prigogine and Stengers as an early description of the evolution of complexity in dissipative systems. They even suggest that Peirce's notion of "chance" can stand in for what they term "nonequilibrium" as the means by which order emerges from disorder: "How is this possible? How can structure arise from disorder? Great progress has been realized in this question. We know now that nonequilibrium, the flow of matter and energy, may be a source of order."[65]

As Bruce Clarke shows in his essay "Heinz von Foerster's Demons," "No system of any stripe can be adequately treated in the absence of the environment it constitutes for itself by emerging as a system. . . . Although certain systems *do* self-organize, or decrease their internal entropy, they do so only in the presence of conditions provided for elsewhere, by environments that lend a necessary other to the self of self-organization."[66] Like Maxwell's Demon, self-organizing systems defy the second law of thermodynamics by increasing complexity as a reaction to entropy, as if they are running in place only by forever increasing their speed. This is the bargain that a self-organizing system must strike with its environment: organization (operational closure) can only be maintained through increasing complexity. As Heinz von Foerster argues, "This term ["self-organizing system"] becomes meaningless, unless the system is in close contact with an environment, *which possesses available energy and order*, and with which our system is in a state of perpetual interaction, such that it somehow manages to 'live' on the expenses of this environment."[67]

Contemporary systems theory supposes that if the growth and complexity of a system run parallel to (or are equivalent to) its entropic dissipation, then there is a complementary *and* inverse relationship between order and disorder that is best understood through the concept of a self-referential distinction. A self-organizing system is simultaneously structurally *open* to energy but *closed* in terms of its organization. This means that the asymmetrical or one-sided distinction between order (organization) and disorder (energy) can be said to repeat or re-enter itself on the side of order, a continual re-entry that produces a progressive enfolding of disorder within order that increases the ordered autonomy of the system at the same time that it paradoxically increases the system's sensitivity to the "disorder" of the environment. The paradoxical unity of this two-sided form is what I have been calling the hidden God, the double consciousness, the cybernetic imaginary. As Luhmann puts it, "One always carries along the fact that there is another side that is not indicated at the moment and has no operational significance, and on which one is not at the present moment, from which one does not begin or take one's departure, and from which one cannot launch repetitions."[68] In pursuit of absolute autonomy, the system is inevitably thrust back onto its own absolute contingency.

I cannot help but wonder if perhaps this is the reason why religion, particularly mysticism and negative theology, seems like the proverbial bad penny of modernity. The self-descriptions produced by modernity recall their lost theological origins, the "conditions provided for elsewhere," and thus they cannot help but "re-occupy" (Blumenberg's useful term) observational positions that are in fact lost to it. As Friedrich Heinrich Jacobi famously asserted, "God is, and is *outside me, a living, self-subsisting being*, or I am God. There is no third."[69] That double bind is a particularly difficult one, since to reject it is to reject the possibility of grounding knowledge in either the immanence of the self or the transcendent authority of the divine, ultimately the conditions of a secularist and humanist modernity or its theological predecessor. Nevertheless, a rejection of the double bind implied in the distinction between anthropocentric and theocentric visions of the world is exactly the "third" way, the excluded middle, that must be taken up by posthumanist theory. It is precisely in this sense that figures such as Nicholas of Cusa, Jonathan Edwards, Ralph Waldo Emerson, and Charles S. Peirce remain so important for posthumanist thought. Thinking in the shadow of the hidden god, they show that the only way out of the double bind constitutive of modernity is *through* modernity, through the intense demands of a thinking that addresses the *other* side of every distinction it makes.

This thinking has an essential religious heritage, but to reverse Cusa we may take this as a form of religion *within* modernity, a thinking that unsays even the divine authority of theology. In his book on religion, Luhmann describes the concept of God as a "contingency formula" that accomplishes "the transformation of the indeterminable into the determinable."[70] God, that is, *is* the system/environment distinction, the means of selection for the system of religion. This suggests that religion remains in many respects the paradigmatic modern system because it confronts most directly the problem of its own contingent observations. As Luhmann puts it, "Every self-description has to open itself up to logical problems that cannot be solved with classical bivalent logic. . . . But the logical problems have to be resolved somehow, and if not by logic, then by imagination."[71] Elsewhere he writes,

> Everything that is communicated is communicated in society. Everything that happens, occurs in the world. This, too, holds for observations and descriptions, no matter with what kind of authorship (subject, science, etc.) they wish to equip themselves. For this very reason, the unity of society (of the world) cannot be reintroduced into society (the world). It cannot be observed or described as a unity, especially not on the basis of a representation without competition or on the grounds of some didactic authority. For each observation and description requires a distinction for its own operation. The observation of the One within the One, however, would have to include what it excludes (that against which it distinguishes its designation). It would have to be enacted in the system (in the world), just as the distinction between self-reference and external reference is enacted in the system (in the world). Such an enactment is possible, and it gives its paradox the form of a "re-entry," but the solution requires an imaginary space (as one speaks of imaginary numbers), and this imaginary space replaces the classical a priori of transcendental philosophy.[72]

This imaginary space, I have argued throughout, is represented in American thought through the God of Puritan theology. This hidden God, "not revealed even in His own revelation," represents an early description of what the mathematician Louis H. Kauffman has called "the essential circularity and inseparability of the issue, the cybernetic hub of the matter."[73] This is an imaginary space, moreover, made available only as *un*available, a space that reverses itself and in this way represents its own paradoxical *unity* to itself as something to be continually unfolded in time.

This brings us at last to one final detour. Mitchell Breitwieser has noted that Perry Miller's influential scholarship on the American Puritans derives from a fascination with the negative theology of Karl Barth. In particular, what Breitwieser terms a "dialectical negativity" resembles in some respects what I have been calling a double negative:

> Criticism's inquiry into the dialectical negativity of Puritan typologism follows almost inevitably form the work of Perry Miller, whose allegiance to the negative theology of Barth, Tillich, and Niebuhr led him away from what was in his time the prevailing view of Puritanism as a static body of dogmatic affect and into the dialectical energetics that he called the marrow of Puritan divinity. Whether in praise or blame of Puritanism, the critics with whom he chose to disagree failed to perceive, according to Miller, its essential commitment to Calvin's unknown god. . . . Cataclysm rather than code, Miller's unknown god lies beyond the possibility of adequate articulation in word or image—a god to be experienced in awe and dread, but not thought, spoken or translated into practice.[74]

Breitwieser takes Miller's argument to mean that the Puritan must, intellectually at least, take all actual forms and institutions as bereft of the actual truth of God, as "more or less embarrassing capitulations to necessity":[75]

> However much Miller may individually admire the practical compromises made by these theologues caught in the "coils" of present necessity, and however much he may insist that his heroes never forgot the "leap" into the inscrutable, he nevertheless regards the move to administration as the commencement of a decline into the dry rationalism of the bourgeois Enlightenment. The social articulation of the Protestant genius adulterates and betrays it, confining that genius to sporadic subsequent resurrections like those of Edwards and Emerson.[76]

In opposition to Miller, Breitwieser argues that such capitulations were not perceived merely as failures, but involved a "conception of negation as the refinement of holy society through the work of history rather than the incessant demolition of all attempts to socialize the good."[77] In this respect, Breitwieser sees Puritan institutions as involved in something resembling progress without presuming the ultimate appropriation of the hidden God: "I am not challenging Miller's argument that the theology of the unknown god was a durable factor in the ideology of the American Puritans, but rather contending that they chose to see positive institutionalization as a triumphal passage out of the interlude of the negative rather than as a regrettable accommodation to the practical demands of worldliness."[78]

Breitwieser extends his point with a reading of Hegel's contention that the sublimation of grief (which is to say, the sublimation of affective attachments to what is singular in experience) constitutes a necessary sacrificial act that props up the hermeneutic dominance of the social order. Breitwieser's wonderful book, however, is principally about how grief resists sublimation and operates as an outside intrusion into systems of meaning, a disharmonious force on the margins, using a concept he can thematize only as a type of realism:

> Though the idea of a coherent reality distinct from the work that legitimates the work on the basis of a criterion of mimetic adequacy has been discarded, there is nonetheless a largely consistent attention to an X that breaks into or through the work's aspiration to formal and ideological coherence, an aspiration that motivates the work's positing of a guaranteeing or legitimating reality. I feel like I'm trying to pick up a dime with a thick glove here, but I want to suggest that all this attention to a surreptitious getting-through amounts to a different way of seeing literary realism, as a transcription of reality's astonishing and at least discursively hurtful impact on systems of coherent representation. I do not mean that what I call the real at this point has an extradiscursive, extratextual, or extrahistorical authority, all of which propositions ultimately dissolve into logical absurdity, but that it exceeds the specific coherence the writer intends to achieve—even if this exceeding is a contrary intention.[79]

At this point of tension, we may pause to note Hegel's long shadow, which seems to trail even the most assiduous attempts to reach beyond the dialectic. It would seem that even the most self-suspecting of gazes cannot curtail the force of a recuperative effect, a bringing together that erases the turbulent force of astonishment. We cannot remain in suspense for very long. At the same time there is a persistent negativity that perceives all worldly forms as declension, as a continuous falling away from divinity (as if the very act of creation was itself a fall, a difference, or negation from God), and as what Breitwieser argues may be seen as progressive refinement through negativity with God as the unreachable horizon. All at once there is both the falling away and the coming closer, progress and regress, as if moving backward and forward at the same time.

Miller's words mark the dilemma as well as anyone's: "The law, which no man can perfectly fulfill anymore, exists as a 'school-master,' it teaches us what we should do, whether we can or no, and as soon as we realize that we cannot, we flee to Christ for the assistance of grace. And since Christ has satisfied God by fulfilling the law, there is no necessity that we do it also. It is only necessary that we attempt it."[80] If the task at issue was, by Miller's estimation, one of "bringing God to time and reason,"[81] living by an impossible law, then for the Puritan the finite attempt alone (and therefore its failure) is the utmost achievable form. In much the same vein as Miller, Emerson writes, "Every man is an impossibility, until he is born; every thing impossible, until we see a success. The ardors of piety agree at last with the coldest skepticism,—that nothing is of us or our works,—that all is of God."[82] Peirce has a similar flare for self-negation: "Those that have loved themselves and not their neighbors will find themselves April fools when the great April opens the truth that neither selves nor neighborselves were anything more than mere vicinities; while the love they would not entertain was the essence of every scent."[83] Is this not in some sense the imposition of an impossible law? To take leave of the safety of the ego in this way threatens to plunge one into the bottomless depths of an oceanic abyss. And yet the only answer to this threat, the only way to stay afloat, is again something like a repeated self-sacrifice or exposure to the *other*—a commitment to speak even in spite of its "impossibility," in spite of contingency and finitude. There is an abyss on either side, and so we find ourselves at last confronted by the commandment that opens Spencer-Brown's *Laws of Form* and that ensures the terms of our vulnerability: "Draw a distinction!" We are called to account for ourselves, to speak even if what is most necessary and urgent to say can never, finally, be said.

Luhmann holds that one of the great advantages of his theory is its ability to make "transparent decisions."[84] By foregrounding the paradox, one may also foreground the contingency of the pragmatic decision that follows. This makes it possible to retrace our steps:

> Fully constructed theories are complicated formations. In a sense, they are works of art. It is difficult to get involved with them and still know how one will relativize all that again or how one will be able to detach oneself when the time comes. . . . The countermeasure I have in mind is to make the theory decisions as transparent as possible. To do this, it is necessary to single out the following questions at every juncture. What are the different options? What is connected to the decision in favor of *this* concept as opposed to another one? Where is there an exit point?[85]

This is the point at which even systems theory circles back around again to find itself before the abyss of a radically contingent, and thus pragmatic, decision: to sail on or abandon ship? Either choice occludes the other and yet carries it along as the ever-present possibility of making a different decision, of seeing things in a different way: "This is the whole trick of the theory: suspended between two markers, both of them paradoxical, a purely logical operational space is created. As is typical of paradoxes, this one, too, can be dissolved."[86] Endings, like beginnings, find themselves suspended between two infinities. "There is the incoming or the receding of God," muses Emerson, "that is all we can affirm; and we can show neither how nor why."[87] All rivers run to the ocean.

Notes

Introduction

1. Ralph Waldo Emerson, "Experience," in *Emerson's Prose and Poetry*, ed. Joel Porte and Saundra Morris (New York: Norton, 2001), 198.

2. Martin Jay, *Songs of Experience: Modern American and European Variations on a Universal Theme* (Berkeley: University of California Press, 2006), 275.

3. Ibid.

4. Ibid., 263.

5. Ibid., 263–264.

6. Ibid., 261.

7. Hans Blumenberg, *The Legitimacy of the Modern Age*, trans. Robert M. Wallace (Cambridge, Mass.: MIT Press, 1985), 172.

8. Robert M. Wallace, "Translator's Introduction," in *Legitimacy of the Modern Age*, by Blumenberg, xviii.

9. Blumenberg, *Legitimacy of the Modern Age*, 173.

10. Ibid., 162.

11. Jürgen Habermas, "Modernity's Consciousness of Time and Its Need for Self-Reassurance," in *The Philosophical Discourse of Modernity: Twelve Lectures*, trans. Frederick G. Lawrence (Cambridge, Mass.: MIT Press, 1990), 7.

12. Blumenberg, *Legitimacy of the Modern Age*, 66.

13. Ibid., 69.

14. Ibid., 74.

15. William Rasch, "The Self-Positing Society," introduction to *Theories of Distinction: Redescribing the Descriptions of Modernity*, by Niklas Luhmann, ed. William Rasch (Stanford, Calif.: Stanford University Press, 2002), 3.

16. Ralph Waldo Emerson, "Nominalist and Realist," in *Essays and Lectures* (New York: Library of America, 1983), 581.

17. Blumenberg, *Legitimacy of the Modern Age*, 571.

18. Niklas Luhmann, *Observations on Modernity*, trans. William Whobrey (Stanford, Calif.: Stanford University Press, 1998), 1.

19. Niklas Luhmann, *Theory of Society*, trans. Rhodes Barrett (Stanford, Calif.: Stanford University Press, 2012), 1:110.

20. Niklas Luhmann, *Introduction to Systems Theory*, trans. Peter Gilgen (Cambridge: Polity, 2013), 44.

21. Niklas Luhmann, *Social Systems*, trans. John Bednarz Jr. and Dirk Baecker (Stanford, Calif.: Stanford University Press, 1996), 48.

22. Luhmann, *Theory of Society*, 1:110.

23. Niklas Luhmann, *A Systems Theory of Religion*, trans. David A. Brenner with Adrian Hermann (Stanford, Calif.: Stanford University Press, 2012), 89.

24. Jay, *Songs of Experience*, 264.

25. Michel Foucault, *The Order of Things: An Archaeology of the Human Sciences* (New York: Vintage, 1994), 56.

26. Ibid., 345.

27. Cary Wolfe, *What Is Posthumanism?* (Minneapolis: University of Minnesota Press, 2010), 244.

28. Charles S. Peirce, "The Three Normative Sciences," in *The Essential Peirce*, vol. 2, *Selected Philosophical Writings, 1893–1913*, ed. Peirce Edition Project (Bloomington: Indiana University Press, 1997), 199.

29. Blumenberg, *Legitimacy of the Modern Age*, 184.

30. Charles S. Peirce, "Some Consequences of Four Incapacities," in *The Essential Peirce*, vol. 1, *Selected Philosophical Writings, 1867–1893*, ed. Nathan Houser and Christian Kloesel (Bloomington: Indiana University Press, 1992), 29.

31. Perry Miller, "The Augustinian Strain of Piety," in *The New England Mind: The Seventeenth Century* (Cambridge, Mass.: Belknap Press of Harvard University Press, 1983), 21.

32. Ralph Waldo Emerson, *Nature*, in *Essays and Lectures*, 10.

33. Ralph Waldo Emerson, "The American Scholar," in *Essays and Lectures*, 57.

34. Ibid.

35. Ibid., 58.

36. Russell B. Goodman, *American Philosophy and the Romantic Tradition* (Cambridge: Cambridge University Press, 2008), 35.

37. Ibid., 32.

38. Ibid., 57.

39. Perry Miller, "From Edwards to Emerson," in *Errand into the Wilderness* (Cambridge, Mass.: Belknap Press of Harvard University Press, 1984), 203.

40. Perry Miller, "Jonathan Edwards on the Sense of the Heart," *Harvard Theological Review* 41, no. 2 (1948): 123–145, at 127.

41. Emerson, *Nature*, 27.

42. Miller, "Jonathan Edwards on the Sense of the Heart," 127.

43. Stanley Cavell, *In Quest of the Ordinary: Lines of Skepticism and Romanticism* (Chicago: University of Chicago Press, 1994), 53.

44. Ibid., 52.

45. Stanley Cavell, *Emerson's Transcendental Etudes* (Stanford, Calif.: Stanford University Press, 2003), 63.

46. Emerson, "Experience," 200.

47. Wolfe, *What Is Posthumanism?*, 248.

48. Ralph Waldo Emerson, "History," in *Essays and Lectures*, 246.

49. Cavell, *Emerson's Transcendental Etudes*, 63.

50. Ibid., 132.

51. Wolfe, *What Is Posthumanism?*, 250.

52. Ibid.

53. Ibid., 251.

54. Niklas Luhmann, "A Redescription of Romantic Art," *Modern Language Notes* 111, no. 3 (1996): 506–522, at 513.

55. Ibid., 512.

56. Quoted in M. H. Abrams, *Natural Supernaturalism: Tradition and Revolution in Romantic Literature* (New York: Norton, 1973), 226.

57. Ralph Waldo Emerson, "The Method of Nature," in *Emerson's Prose and Poetry*, 84.

58. Ralph Waldo Emerson, "Circles," in *Emerson's Prose and Poetry*, 174.

59. Wolfe, *What Is Posthumanism?*, 239.

60. Michel Foucault, "What Is Enlightenment?," in *The Foucault Reader*, ed. Paul Rabinow (New York: Pantheon, 1984), 43.

61. Ibid., 44.

62. For more on the origins of systems theory, see Steven Joshua Heim, *Constructing a Social Science for Postwar America: The Cybernetics Group, 1946–1953* (Cambridge, Mass.: MIT Press, 1993).

63. Wolfe, *What Is Posthumanism?*, 235.

64. Aside from Louis H. Kauffman, who is cited throughout this study, see especially Søren Brier, *Cybersemiotics: Why Information Is Not Enough* (Toronto: University of Toronto Press, 2008), and "Peirce and Spencer-Brown: History and Synergies in Cybersemiotics," special issue, *Cybernetics and Human Knowing* 8, nos. 1–2 (2001).

65. George Spencer-Brown, *Laws of Form* (Portland, Ore.: Cognizer, 1994), 105.

66. Luhmann, *Social Systems*, 409.

67. Niklas Luhmann, "Deconstruction as Second Order Observation," in *Theories of Distinction: Redescribing the Descriptions of Modernity*, ed. William Rasch (Stanford, Calif.: Stanford University Press, 2002), 94–112.

68. Jacques Derrida, "Remarks on Deconstruction and Pragmatism," in *Deconstruction and Pragmatism*, ed. Chantal Mouffe (New York: Routledge, 1997), 82.

69. Ibid., 81.

70. Jacques Derrida, *Positions*, trans. Alan Bass (Chicago: University of Chicago Press, 1982), 3.

71. Ibid., 43.

72. Jacques Derrida, *Acts of Religion*, ed. Gil Anidjar (New York: Routledge, 2001), 252.

73. Ibid., 265.

74. Luhmann, *Theories of Distinction*, 129.

75. Niklas Luhmann, "Cognition as Construction," appendix to *Luhmann Explained: From Souls to Systems*, by Hans-Georg Moeller (Chicago: Open Court, 2006), 250.

76. Luhmann, *Observations on Modernity*, 25.

77. Ibid., 25–26.

78. Luhmann, "Cognition as Construction," 250–251.

79. Ibid., 252.

80. Blumenberg, *Legitimacy of the Modern Age*, 65.

81. Ibid., 64.

82. Miller, "From Edwards to Emerson," 185.

83. Luhmann, *Observations on Modernity*, 34.

84. Niklas Luhmann, "The Paradox of Form," in *Problems of Form*, ed. Dirk Baecker, trans. Michael Irmscher and Leah Edwards (Stanford, Calif.: Stanford University Press, 1999), 18.

1. The Double Consciousness

1. Ralph Waldo Emerson, "Nominalist and Realist," in *Essays and Lectures* (New York: Library of America, 1983), 585.

2. Ralph Waldo Emerson, "Compensation," in *Essays and Lectures*, 269.

3. Branka Arsić, *On Leaving: A Reading in Emerson* (Cambridge, Mass.: Harvard University Press, 2010), 127.

4. Ibid.

5. Sharon Cameron, "The Way of Life by Abandonment: Emerson's Impersonal," in *Impersonality: Seven Essays* (Chicago: University of Chicago Press, 2007), 99.

6. Ibid. 93.

7. Ibid., 89.

8. Ibid., 102.

9. Ralph Waldo Emerson, "Fate," in *Essays and Lectures*, 943.

10. Ibid.

11. Ibid., 953.

12. Ibid., 943.

13. Ibid., 968.

14. Ibid., 967.

15. Ibid., 943.

16. Gregory Bateson, "Toward a Theory of Schizophrenia," in *Steps to an Ecology of Mind: Collected Essays in Anthropology, Psychiatry, Evolution, and Epistemology* (Chicago: University of Chicago Press, 2000), 208.

17. Anthony Wilden, *System and Structure: Essays in Communication and Exchange*, 2nd ed. (New York: Tavistock, 1980), 120.

18. Bateson, "Toward a Theory of Schizophrenia," 202.

19. Ibid., 203.

20. Gillian Rose, *Hegel Contra Sociology* (New York: Verso, 2009), 48.

21. Ibid., 49.

22. Ibid. The passage is worth reading in full:

> Once it is shown that the criterion of what is to count as finite and infinite has been created by consciousness itself, then a notion is implied which does not divide consciousness or reality into finite and infinite. This notion is implied by the very distinction between finite and infinite which has become uncertain. But it is not pre-judged as to what this notion, beyond the distinction between finite and infinite, might be. It is not pre-judged in two senses: no autonomous justification is given of a new object, and no statement is made before it is achieved. The infinite or absolute is present, but not yet known, neither treated methodologically from the outside as an unknowable, nor "shot from a pistol" as an immediate certainty. This "whole" can only become known as a result of the process of the contradictory experiences of consciousness which gradually comes to realize it.

23. Ibid., 109.

24. Ibid., 110.

25. Ibid., 101.

26. Slavoj Žižek, *Less Than Nothing: Hegel and the Shadow of Dialectical Materialism* (New York: Verso, 2012), 800.

27. Slavoj Žižek, "Class Struggle or Postmodernism? Yes, Please!," in *Contingency, Hegemony, Universality*, by Judith Butler, Ernesto Laclau, and Slavoj Žižek (New York: Verso, 2000), 121.

28. Ibid., 122.

29. Slavoj Žižek, "Holding the Place," in *Contingency, Hegemony, Universality*, 326.

30. John Dewey, "The Development of American Pragmatism," in *The Philosophy of John Dewey*, ed. John J. McDermott (Chicago: University of Chicago Press, 1981), 57.

31. Ibid.

32. Ibid.

33. Emerson, "Fate," 962.

34. Žižek, "Class Struggle or Postmodernism? Yes, Please!," 125.

35. Cary Wolfe, *What Is Posthumanism?* (Minneapolis: University of Minnesota Press, 2010), xxv.

36. Wilden, *System and Structure*, 122.

37. Charles. S. Peirce, "Definitions of Truth," in *The Collected Papers of Charles Sanders Peirce*, vol. 5, *Pragmatism and Pragmaticism*, ed. Charles Hartshorne and Paul Weiss (Cambridge, Mass.: Belknap Press of Harvard University Press, 1935), 564.

38. Ralph Waldo Emerson, "Intellect," in *Essays and Lectures*, 426.

39. Dewey, "Development of American Pragmatism," 47.

40. Wolfe, *What Is Posthumanism?*, xx.

41. Wilden, *System and Structure*, 268.

42. Quoted in Max H. Fisch, "Peirce's Triadic Logic," in *Peirce, Semeiotic, and Pragmatism*, ed. Kenneth Laine Ketner and Christian J. W. Kloesel (Bloomington: Indiana University Press, 1986), 177.

43. For a detailed history of the American origins of systems theory, see Steven Joshua Heims, *The Cybernetics Group* (Cambridge, Mass.: MIT Press, 1991).

44. Wilden, *System and Structure*, 265.

45. Charles S. Peirce, "The Law of Mind," in *The Essential Peirce*, vol. 1, *Selected Philosophical Writings, 1867–1893*, ed. Nathan Houser and Christian Kloesel (Bloomington: Indiana University Press, 1992), 322.

46. Ibid.

47. Charles S. Peirce, *Pragmatism as a Principle and Method of Right Thinking* (Albany: State University of New York Press, 1997), 160.

48. Ibid., 147.

49. Ibid., 179.

50. Peirce, "Law of Mind," 323.

51. Peirce, *Pragmatism as a Principle and Method of Right Thinking*, 186.

52. Floyd Merrell, *Peirce, Signs, and Meaning* (Toronto: University of Toronto Press, 1997), 143.

53. Gotthard Günther, "Cybernetic Ontology and Transjunctional Operation," in *Self-Organizing Systems*, ed. Marshall C. Yovits, George T. Jacobi, and Gordon D. Goldstein (Washington, D.C.: Spartan, 1962), 351.

54. Ibid., 353.

55. Ibid., 382.

56. Ibid., 384.

57. Ibid., 353.

58. Niklas Luhmann, *Theories of Distinction: Redescribing the Descriptions of Modernity*, ed. William Rasch (Stanford, Calif.: Stanford University Press, 2002), 100.

59. Niklas Luhmann, *Introduction to Systems Theory*, trans. Peter Gilgen (Cambridge: Polity, 2013), 220.

60. Luhmann, *Theories of Distinction*, 82.

61. Ibid., 83.

62. Niklas Luhmann, *Social Systems*, trans. John Bednarz Jr. and Dirk Baecker (Stanford, Calif.: Stanford University Press, 1996), 61 (emphasis added).

63. Niklas Luhmann, *Art as a Social System*, trans. Eva M. Knodt (Stanford, Calif.: Stanford University Press, 2000), 107.

64. Emerson, "Fate," 954.

65. Luhmann, *Social Systems*, 62.

66. Luhmann, *Art as a Social System*, 33.

67. Ibid., 27.

68. Ibid., 65.

69. Ibid., 28.

70. Heinz von Foerster, *Understanding Systems: Conversations on Epistemology and Ethics* (New York: Springer, 2003), 26.

71. Ibid., 39.

72. Ralph Waldo Emerson, "The Method of Nature," in *Essays and Lectures*, 119.

73. Charles S. Peirce, "The Basis of Pragmaticism in the Normative Sciences," in *The Essential Peirce*, vol. 2, *Selected Philosophical Writings, 1893–1913*, ed. Peirce Edition Project (Bloomington: Indiana University Press, 1998), 395.

74. Merrell, *Peirce, Signs, and Meaning*, 268.

75. Francisco J. Varela, "Not One, Not Two," *CoEvolution Quarterly*, no. 12 (1976): 62–67, at 64.

76. Emerson, "Fate," 961.

77. Charles S. Peirce, "Design and Chance," in *Essential Peirce*, 1:222.

78. Ibid., 219.

79. Louis H. Kauffman, "The Mathematics of Charles Sanders Peirce," *Cybernetics and Human Knowing* 8, nos. 1–2 (2001): 79–110, at 56.

80. Emerson, "Nominalist and Realist," 584.

81. Ralph Waldo Emerson, "Intellect," in *Essays and Lectures*, 425.

82. Wolfe, *What Is Posthumanism?*, 248.

83. Charles S. Peirce, "What Pragmatism Is," in *Essential Peirce*, 2:338.

84. Ralph Waldo Emerson, "Self-Reliance," in *Essays and Lectures*, 271.

85. Charles S. Peirce, "Evolutionary Love," in *Essential Peirce*, 1:362.

86. Jacques Derrida, *The Gift of Death*, trans. David Wills (Chicago: University of Chicago Press, 1995), 106.

87. Peirce, "Evolutionary Love," 353.

88. Ibid.

89. Von Foerster, *Understanding Systems*, 159.

90. Peirce, "Evolutionary Love," 354.

91. Ralph Waldo Emerson, "Love," in *Essays and Lectures*, 337.

2. Inside-Out

1. Cornel West, *The American Evasion of Philosophy: A Genealogy of Pragmatism* (Madison: University of Wisconsin Press, 1989), 5.

2. Ibid.

3. John J. Stuhr, *Genealogical Pragmatism: Philosophy, Experience, and Community* (Albany: State University of New York Press, 1997), 32.

4. Richard Rorty, *Consequences of Pragmatism: Essays, 1972–1980* (Minneapolis: University of Minnesota Press, 1982), 161.

5. H. O. Mounce, *The Two Pragmatisms: From Peirce to Rorty* (New York: Routledge, 1997), 229.

6. Joseph Brent, *Charles Sanders Peirce: A Life* (Bloomington: Indiana University Press, 1998).

7. West, *American Evasion of Philosophy*, 6.

8. Tom Cohen, *Anti-Mimesis from Plato to Hitchcock* (Cambridge: Cambridge University Press, 1994), 90.

9. Ibid., 89.

10. Cary Wolfe, *Critical Environments: Postmodern Theory and the Pragmatics of the Outside* (Minneapolis: University of Minnesota Press, 1998), 21.

11. Cohen, *Anti-Mimesis*, 90.

12. William James, *Pragmatism*, in *Writings, 1902–1910* (New York: Library of America, 1988), 506.

13. Louis Menand, *The Metaphysical Club: A Story of Ideas in America* (New York: Farrar, Straus and Giroux, 2001), 351.

14. Charles S. Peirce, "What Pragmatism Is," in *The Essential Peirce*, vol. 2, *Selected Philosophical Writings, 1893–1913*, ed. Peirce Edition Project (Bloomington: Indiana University Press, 1997), 335.

15. Charles S. Peirce, "The Continuum," in *The Collected Papers of Charles Sanders Peirce*, vol. 6, *Scientific Metaphysics*, ed. Charles Hartshorne and Paul Weiss (Cambridge, Mass.: Belknap Press of Harvard University Press, 1935), 168.

16. Peirce, "What Pragmatism Is," 345.

17. Robin Robertson, "One Two Three . . . Continuity," in "Peirce and Spencer-Brown: History and Synergies in Cybersemiotics," ed. Søren Brier, special issue, *Cybernetics and Human Knowing* 8, nos. 1–2 (2001): 7–24, at 19.

18. Matthew E. Moore, introduction to *Philosophy of Mathematics: Selected Writings*, by Charles S. Peirce, ed. Matthew E. Moore (Bloomington: Indiana University Press, 2010), xxi.

19. Ibid.

20. Ranulph Glanville and Francisco J. Varela, "Your Inside Is Out and Your Outside Is In (Beatles, [1968])," in *Applied Systems and Cybernetics*, vol. 2, *Systems Concepts, Models, and Methodology*, ed. G. E. Lasker, Proceedings of the International Congress on Applied Systems Research and Cybernetics (New York: Pergamon, 1980), 640.

21. Ibid.

22. John Patrick Diggins, *The Promise of Pragmatism: Modernism and the Crisis of Knowledge and Authority* (Chicago: University of Chicago Press, 1995), 116.

23. Martin Jay, *Songs of Experience: Modern American and European Variations on a Universal Theme* (Berkeley: University of California Press, 2006), 283.

24. Diggins, *Promise of Pragmatism*, 16.

25. William James, *A Pluralistic Universe*, in *Writings, 1902–1910*, 644.

26. Ibid., 652.

27. Diggins, *Promise of Pragmatism*, 130.

28. James, *Pluralistic Universe*, 642.

29. Ibid., 644.

30. Perry Miller, "The Marrow of Puritan Divinity," in *Errand into the Wilderness* (Cambridge, Mass.: Belknap Press of Harvard University Press, 1984), 56.

31. Ibid.

32. Ibid., 51.

33. Herschel Clay Baker, *The Wars of Truth: Studies in the Decay of Christian Humanism in the Earlier Seventeenth Century* (Cambridge, Mass.: Harvard University Press, 1952), 25.

34. Ibid., 9.

35. Ibid., 102.

36. Ibid., 15.

37. Miller, "Marrow of Puritan Divinity," 97.

38. Perry Miller, "The Augustinian Strain of Piety," in *The New England Mind: The Seventeenth Century* (Cambridge, Mass.: Belknap Press of Harvard University Press, 1983), 33.

39. Miller, "Marrow of Puritan Divinity," 51.

40. Baker, *Wars of Truth*, 36.

41. Joan Richardson, *A Natural History of Pragmatism: The Fact of Feeling from Jonathan Edwards to Gertrude Stein* (Cambridge: Cambridge University Press, 2007), 2.

42. Miller, "Marrow of Puritan Divinity," 53.

43. Ibid., 63.

44. Ibid., 70.

45. Ibid., 94.

46. Leigh Eric Schmidt, *Hearing Things: Religion, Illusion, and the American Enlightenment* (Cambridge, Mass.: Harvard University Press, 2002), 179.

47. James, *Pragmatism*, 515.

48. Ibid., 643.

49. Perry Miller, "From Edwards to Emerson," in *Errand into the Wilderness*, 185.

50. Ibid., 184.

51. Ibid.

52. Ibid., 185.

53. Ibid.

54. Richardson, *Natural History of Pragmatism*, 1.

55. Ibid., xi.

56. Ibid., 13.

57. Ibid., 11.

58. William James, *The Varieties of Religious Experience*, in *Writings, 1902–1910*, 15.

59. Ibid., 23.

60. Richardson, *Natural History of Pragmatism*, 11.

61. Ibid., 10.

62. Ibid., 2.

63. Ibid., xi.

64. Ibid., 15.

65. Michael Allen Gillespie, *Nihilism Before Nietzsche* (Chicago: University of Chicago Press, 1996), xiii.

66. Ibid.

67. Ibid., xxii.

68. Ibid., xiv.

69. William James, "The Will to Believe," in *Writings, 1878–1899* (New York: Library of America, 1988), 467.

70. Ibid., 478.

71. James Beniger, *The Control Revolution: Technological and Economic Origins of the Information Society* (Cambridge, Mass.: Harvard University Press, 1989), 175.

72. Ibid., 15.

73. Isabelle Stengers, "William James: An Ethics of Thought?," *Radical Philosophy* 157 (2009): 9–19, at 19.

74. William James, "A World of Pure Experience," in *Writings, 1902–1910*, 1170.

75. Ibid., 1175.

76. Charles S. Peirce, "A Guess at the Riddle," in *The Essential Peirce*, vol. 1, *Selected Philosophical Writings,1867–1893*, ed. Nathan Houser and Christian Kloesel (Bloomington: Indiana University Press, 1992), 248.

77. James, "World of Pure Experience," 1162.

78. Ibid., 1163.

79. Ibid.

80. James, *Pragmatism*, 509.

81. James, *Pluralistic Universe*, 760.

82. James, *Pragmatism*, 510.

83. James, "World of Pure Experience," 1146.

84. Ibid.

85. James, *Pluralistic Universe*, 746.

86. Giles Gunn, *Thinking Across the American Grain: Ideology, Intellect, and the New Pragmatism* (Chicago: University of Chicago Press, 1992), 36.

87. James, *Pragmatism*, 775.

88. Ibid., 766.

89. Ibid., 740.

90. Frank Lentricchia, "The Romanticism of William James," *Salmagundi* 25 (1974): 81–108, at 108.

91. William James, "What Pragmatism Means," in *Writings, 1902–1910*, 509.

92. Gunn, *Thinking Across the American Grain*, 141.

93. William James, "Pragmatism and Humanism," in *Writings, 1902–1910*, 599.

94. Diggins, *Promise of Pragmatism*, 5.

95. Leigh Eric Schmidt, *Hearing Things: Religion, Illusion, and the American Enlightenment* (Cambridge, Mass.: Harvard University Press, 2002), 31.

96. Jacques Barzun, *A Stroll with William James* (Chicago: University of Chicago Press, 2002), 302.

97. James, "Will to Believe," 700.

98. Diggins, *Promise of Pragmatism*, 116.

99. Frank Lentricchia, *Modernist Quartet* (Cambridge: Cambridge University Press, 1994), 31.

100. James, "Will to Believe," 461.

101. James, "What Pragmatism Means," 510.

102. David Wills, *Prosthesis* (Stanford, Calif.: Stanford University Press, 1995), 33.

103. Charles S. Peirce, *Pragmatism as a Principle and Method of Right Thinking* (Albany: State University of New York Press, 1997), 110.

104. Charles S. Peirce to William James, November 25, 1902, in *The Collected Papers of Charles Sanders Peirce*, vol. 8, *Reviews, Correspondence, and Bibliography*, ed. Arthur W. Burks (Cambridge, Mass.: Belknap Press of Harvard University Press, 1958), 189.

105. Ralph Waldo Emerson, "Fate," in *Essays and Lectures* (New York: Library of America, 1983), 955.

106. Charles S. Peirce, "Some Consequences of Four Incapacities," in *Essential Peirce*, 1:54.

107. Niklas Luhmann, *Observations on Modernity*, trans. William Whobrey (Stanford, Calif.: Stanford University Press, 1998), 28–29.

108. Rorty, *Consequences of Pragmatism*, xix.

109. Richard Rorty, *Objectivity, Relativism, and Truth: Philosophical Papers* (Cambridge: Cambridge University Press, 1990), 13.

110. Rorty, *Consequences of Pragmatism*, 174.

111. Rorty, *Objectivity, Relativism, and Truth*, 29.

112. Cohen, *Anti-Mimesis*, 90.

113. Theodor Adorno, *Negative Dialectics* (New York: Continuum, 1981), 189.

114. Cohen, *Anti-Mimesis*, 93.

115. Ibid., 90.

116. Rorty, *Objectivity, Relativism, and Truth*, 24.

117. Cohen, *Anti-Mimesis*, 98.

118. Rorty, *Objectivity, Relativism, and Truth*, 11.

119. Cary Wolfe, "Making Contingency Safe for Liberalism: The Pragmatics of Epistemology in Rorty and Luhmann," in *Observing Complexity: Systems Theory and Postmodernity*, ed. William Rasch and Cary Wolfe (Minneapolis: University of Minnesota Press, 2000), 251.

120. Richard Rorty, "Justice as a Larger Loyalty," *Ethical Perspectives* 4, no. 2 (1997): 139–151, at 147.

121. Reinhart Koselleck, *Critique and Crisis: Enlightenment and the Pathogenesis of Modern Society* (Cambridge, Mass.: MIT Press, 1988).

122. Ibid., 159.

123. Wolfe, "Making Contingency Safe for Liberalism," 252.

124. Diggins, *Promise of Pragmatism*, 457.

125. Cohen, *Anti-Mimesis*, 103.

126. Charles. S. Peirce, "The Doctrine of Chances," in *Essential Peirce*, 1:149.

127. Peirce, "What Pragmatism Is," 345.

128. Ibid., 407.

129. Ibid., 410.

130. Floyd Merrell, *Peirce, Signs, and Meaning* (Toronto: University of Toronto Press, 1997), xi.

131. Peirce, *Pragmatism as a Principle and Method of Right Thinking*, 193.

132. Glanville and Varela, "Your Inside Is Out and Your Outside Is In (Beatles, [1968])," 640.

133. Charles S. Peirce, "Pragmatism," in *Essential Peirce*, 2:402.

134. Peirce, "Some Consequences of Four Incapacities," 52.

135. Peirce, "What Pragmatism Is," 342–43.

136. Susan Haack, "Philosophy/Philosophy, an Untenable Dualism," *Transactions of the Charles S. Peirce Society* 29, no. 3 (1993): 425.

137. Michael Williams, "Coherence, Justification, and Truth," *Review of Metaphysics* 34 (1980): 243–272.

138. Charles S. Peirce, "How to Make Our Ideas Clear," in *The Collected Papers of Charles Sanders Peirce*, vol. 5, *Pragmatism and Pragmaticism*, ed. Charles Hartshorne and Paul Weiss (Cambridge, Mass.: Belknap Press of Harvard University Press, 1935), 402n.2.

139. Peirce, "What Pragmatism Is," 340.

140. Adorno, *Negative Dialectics*, 26.

141. Ibid., 31.

142. Ibid., 53.

143. Roberto Esposito, *Communitas: The Origin and Destiny of Community* (Stanford, Calif.: Stanford University Press, 2009), 138.

144. Peirce, "Some Consequences of Four Incapacities," 55.

145. Esposito, *Communitas*, 16.

146. Jacques Derrida, "Typewriter Ribbon: Limited Inc. (2)," in *Without Alibi*, ed. and trans. Peggy Kamuf (Stanford, Calif.: Stanford University Press, 2002), 73.

147. Merrell, *Peirce, Signs, and Meaning*, vii.

148. Jacques Derrida, *Specters of Marx: The State of the Debt, the Work of Mourning, and the New International*, trans. Peggy Kamuf (New York: Routledge, 2006), 112.

149. Derrida, "Typewriter Ribbon," 74.

150. Esposito, *Communitas*, 54.

151. Peirce, "How to Make Our Ideas Clear," 402n.2.

152. Ralph Waldo Emerson, "Experience," in *Emerson's Prose and Poetry*, ed. Joel Porte and Saundra Morris (New York: Norton, 2001), 207–208.

153. Charles S. Peirce, "Grounds of Validity of the Laws of Logic," in *Essential Peirce*, 1:82.

3. On True Virtue

1. Perry Miller, *Jonathan Edwards* (New York: Sloane, 1949), 46.

2. Perry Miller, "The Marrow of Puritan Divinity," in *Errand into the Wilderness* (Cambridge, Mass.: Belknap Press of Harvard University Press, 1984), 51.

3. Perry Miller, "The Augustinian Strain of Piety," in *The New England Mind: The Seventeenth Century* (Cambridge, Mass.: Belknap Press of Harvard University Press, 1983), 33.

4. Miller, "Marrow of Puritan Divinity," 51.

5. Michael Clark, " 'The Crucified Phrase': Sign and Desire in Puritan Semiology," *Early American Literature* 13 (1978): 278–293, at 282.

6. Ibid., 280.

7. Miller, "Marrow of Puritan Divinity," 97.

8. Clark, "Crucified Phrase," 291.

9. Joan Richardson, *A Natural History of Pragmatism: The Fact of Feeling from Jonathan Edwards to Gertrude Stein* (Cambridge: Cambridge University Press, 2007), 49.

10. Ibid., 50.

11. Ibid., 12.

12. San Hyun Lee, *The Philosophical Theology of Jonathan Edwards* (Princeton, N.J.: Princeton University Press, 1988).

13. Ibid., 14.

14. Ibid., 8.

15. Ibid., 6.

16. Ibid., 9.

17. Ibid.

18. Ibid.

19. R. C. De Prospo, *Theism in the Discourse of Jonathan Edwards* (Newark: University of Delaware Press, 1985), 67.

20. Ibid., 187.

21. Ibid., 175.

22. Stephen H. Daniel. *The Philosophy of Jonathan Edwards: A Study in Divine Semiotics* (Bloomington: Indiana University Press, 1994), 22.

23. Ibid., 127.

24. Ibid., 134.

25. Gregory Bateson, "Form, Substance, and Difference," in *Steps to an Ecology of Mind: Collected Essays in Anthropology, Psychiatry, Evolution, and Epistemology* (Chicago: University of Chicago Press, 2000), 467.

26. Niklas Luhmann, *Observations on Modernity*, trans. William Whobrey (Stanford, Calif.: Stanford University Press, 1998), 109.

27. Daniel, *Philosophy of Jonathan Edwards*, 110.

28. Niklas Luhmann, "Cognition as Construction," appendix to *Luhmann Explained: From Souls to Systems*, by Hans-Georg Moeller (Chicago: Open Court, 2006), 250.

29. Niklas Luhmann, *Theories of Distinction: Redescribing the Descriptions of Modernity*, ed. William Rasch (Stanford, Calif.: Stanford University Press, 2002), 145.

30. Stefan Rossbach, "Gnosis, Science, and Mysticism: A History of Self-Referential Theory Designs," *Social Science Information* 35 (1996): 251.

31. Perry Miller, "From Edwards to Emerson," in *Errand into the Wilderness*, 195.

32. Rossbach, "Gnosis, Science, and Mysticism," 251.

33. Niklas Luhmann, "A Redescription of Romantic Art," *Modern Language Notes* 111, no. 3 (1996): 506–522, at 514.

34. De Prospo, *Theism in the Discourse of Jonathan Edwards*, 78.

35. Miller, "From Edwards to Emerson," 194.

36. Jonathan Edwards, "Of Being," in *The Works of Jonathan Edwards*, vol. 6, *Scientific and Philosophical Writings*, ed. Wallace E. Anderson (New Haven, Conn.: Yale University Press, 1980), 204.

37. Ibid.

38. Heinz von Foerster, *Understanding Understanding: Essays on Cybernetics and Cognition* (New York: Springer, 2010), 214.

39. Ibid., 212.

40. Daniel, *Philosophy of Jonathan Edwards*, 85–86.

41. Ibid., 108.

42. Miller, "Augustinian Strain of Piety," 10.

43. Jacques Derrida, *Acts of Religion*, ed. Gil Anidjar (New York: Routledge, 2001), 293.

44. Miller, *Jonathan Edwards*, 184.

45. Ibid., 298.

46. Ibid., 191.

47. Michael J. McClymond, "Spiritual Perception in Jonathan Edwards," *Journal of Religion* 77, no. 2 (1997): 195–216, at 197.

48. James Hoopes, "Jonathan Edwards's Religious Psychology," *Journal of American History* 69 (1983): 849–865, at 856.

49. McClymond, "Spiritual Perception in Jonathan Edwards," 197.

50. Ibid., 216.

51. Jonathan Edwards, "A Treatise Concerning Religious Affections," in *The Works of Jonathan Edwards*, vol. 2, *Religious Affections*, ed. John E. Smith (New Haven, Conn.: Yale University Press, 2009), 206.

52. Ibid., 99.

53. Ibid., 193.

54. De Prospo, *Theism in the Discourse of Jonathan Edwards*, 91.

55. Jonathan Edwards, *The Philosophy of Jonathan Edwards: From His Private Notebook*, ed. Harvey G. Townsend (Eugene, Ore.: Wipf and Stock, 2009), 23.

56. Jonathan Edwards, "Excellency," in *Works*, 6:336.

57. Ibid., 337.

58. Ibid.

59. Sharon Cameron, "What Counts as Love: Jonathan Edwards's *True Virtue*," in *Impersonality: Seven Essays* (Chicago: University of Chicago Press, 2007), 32. The citations from Edwards in the quotation are from Jonathan Edwards, *The Nature of True Virtue*, in *The Works of Jonathan Edwards*, vol. 8, *Ethical Writings*, ed. Paul Ramsey (New Haven, Conn.: Yale University Press, 1989), 554.

60. Cameron, "What Counts as Love," 28.

61. Ibid., 42.

62. Jonathan Edwards, "The Mind," in *Works*, 6:365.

63. Niklas Luhmann, "Society, Meaning, Religion: Based on Self-Reference," *Sociological Analysis* 46, no. 1 (1985): 7.

64. Ibid., 8.

65. Cary Wolfe, *What Is Posthumanism?* (Minneapolis: University of Minnesota Press, 2010), xxi.

66. Edwards, *Nature of True Virtue*, 540.

67. Ibid.

68. Ibid.

69. Ibid., 541.

70. Ibid.

71. Ibid.

72. Jacques Derrida, *The Gift of Death*, trans. David Wills (Chicago: University of Chicago Press, 1995), 51.

73. Edwards, "Excellency," 364.

4. Neither Here nor There

1. Ralph Waldo Emerson, "Experience," in *Emerson's Prose and Poetry*, ed. Joel Porte and Saundra Morris (New York: Norton, 2001), 200.

2. Ralph Waldo Emerson, *Nature*, in *Emerson's Prose and Poetry*, 35.

3. Quoted in Sacvan Bercovitch, *The Puritan Origins of the American Self* (New Haven, Conn.: Yale University Press, 1975), 21.

4. Emerson, "Experience," 199.

5. Niklas Luhmann, "Speaking and Silence," *New German Critique* 61 (1994): 25–37, at 27.

6. Sharon Cameron, "Representing Grief: Emerson's 'Experience,' " in *Impersonality: Seven Essays* (Chicago: University of Chicago Press, 2007), 57.

7. Emerson, "Experience," 200.

8. Geoffrey Bennington, *Jacques Derrida* (Chicago: University of Chicago Press, 1993), 284.

9. Sharon Cameron, preface to *Impersonality*, xvii.

10. Michel Serres, *The Parasite*, trans. Lawrence R. Schehr (Minneapolis: University of Minnesota Press, 2007), 73.

11. Charles S. Peirce, "What Pragmatism Is," in *The Essential Peirce*, vol. 2, *Selected Philosophical Writings, 1893–1913*, ed. Peirce Edition Project (Bloomington: Indiana University Press, 1997), 340.

12. Floyd Merrell, *Peirce, Signs, and Meaning* (Toronto: University of Toronto Press, 1997), 29.

13. Niklas Luhmann, *Observations on Modernity*, trans. William Whobrey (Stanford, Calif.: Stanford University Press, 1998), 46.

14. Ibid.

15. Quoted in Max H. Fisch, "Peirce's Triadic Logic," in *Peirce, Semeiotic, and Pragmatism*, ed. Kenneth Laine Ketner and Christian J. W. Kloesel (Bloomington: Indiana University Press, 1986), 177.

16. Stanley Cavell, *Emerson's Transcendental Etudes* (Stanford, Calif.: Stanford University Press, 2003), 132.

17. Emerson, "Experience," 198.

18. Ibid.

19. Ibid.

20. Sigmund Freud, "Mourning and Melancholia," in *General Psychological Theory*, ed. Philip Rieff (New York: Vintage, 1994), 165.

21. Ibid.

22. Ibid., 166.

23. Cameron, "Representing Grief," 61.

24. Ibid., 56.

25. Emerson, "Experience," 202.

26. Ibid., 200.

27. Jacques Derrida, *Aporias*, trans. Thomas Dutoit (Stanford, Calif.: Stanford University Press, 1993), 15.

28. Ibid.

29. Ibid., 12.

30. Ibid., 22.

31. Emerson, "Experience," 200.

32. Ibid., 209.

33. Ibid., 212.

34. Perry Miller, "The Marrow of Puritan Divinity," in *Errand into the Wilderness* (Cambridge, Mass.: Belknap Press of Harvard University Press, 1984), 56.

35. Gordon E. Geddes, *Welcome Joy: Death in Puritan New England* (Ann Arbor: UMI Research Press, 1981), 155.

36. Ronald A. Bosco, ed., *The Puritan Sermon in America, 1630–1750*, vol. 4, *New England Funeral Sermons* (Delmar, N.Y.: Scholars' Facsimiles and Reprints, 1978), ix.

37. Geddes, *Welcome Joy*, 165.

38. Bosco, *Puritan Sermon in America*, x.

39. Geddes, *Welcome Joy*, 156.

40. Ibid., 162.

41. Mitchell Robert Breitwieser, *American Puritanism and the Defense of Mourning: Religion, Grief, and Ethnology in Mary White Rolandson's Captivity Narrative* (Madison: University of Wisconsin Press, 1990), 9.

42. Cavell, *Emerson's Transcendental Etudes*, 116.

43. Breitwieser, *American Puritanism and the Defense of Mourning*, 4.

44. Ibid., 132.

45. Ibid., 8.

46. Ibid., 24.

47. Ibid., 22.

48. Alden T. Vaughan and Edward W. Clark, *Puritans Among the Indians: Accounts of Captivity and Redemption, 1676–1724* (Cambridge, Mass.: Belknap Press of Harvard University Press, 1981), 74.

49. Breitwieser, *American Puritanism and the Defense of Mourning*, 117.

50. Ibid., 186.

51. Charles S. Peirce, "On Science and Natural Classes," in *Essential Peirce*, 2:123.

52. Fisch, "Peirce's Triadic Logic," 178.

53. Charles S. Peirce, "The Nature of Meaning," in *Essential Peirce*, 2:225.

54. Emerson, "Experience," 202.

55. Charles S. Peirce, "Pragmatism and Pragmaticism," in *The Collected Papers of Charles Sanders Peirce*, vol. 5, *Pragmatism and Pragmaticism*, ed. Charles Hartshorne and Paul Weiss (Cambridge, Mass.: Belknap Press of Harvard University Press, 1935), 448n.

56. Emerson, "Experience," 200.

57. Ibid., 209.

58. John Deely, *Basics of Semiotics* (South Bend, Ind.: St. Augustine's Press, 2004), 36.

59. Emerson, "Experience," 203.

60. Ibid., 207.

61. Emerson, *Nature*, 29.

62. Ralph Waldo Emerson, "Circles," in *Emerson's Prose and Poetry*, 176.

63. Ibid.

64. Ralph Waldo Emerson, "The Poet," in *Emerson's Prose and Poetry*, 185.

65. Deely, *Basics of Semiotics*, 41.

66. Emerson, "Experience," 208.

67. Ibid., 212.

68. Ibid., 208.

69. Jacques Derrida, *The Margins of Philosophy*, trans. Alan Bass (Chicago: University of Chicago Press, 1982), 27.

70. Emerson, "Experience," 209.

71. Ralph Waldo Emerson, "Love," in *Essays and Lectures* (New York: Library of America, 1983), 328.

72. Emerson, "Experience," 213.

73. Peirce, "On Science and Natural Classes," 123.

5. Every Language Is Foreign

1. Jacques Derrida, *Of Grammatology*, trans. Gayatri Chakravorty Spivak (Baltimore: Johns Hopkins University Press, 1998), 17.

2. Charles S. Peirce, "Some Consequences of Four Incapacities," in *The Essential Peirce*, vol. 1, *Selected Philosophical Writings, 1867–1893*, ed. Nathan Houser and Christian Kloesel (Bloomington: Indiana University Press, 1992), 55.

3. Charles S. Peirce, *Reasoning and the Logic of Things: The Cambridge Conferences Lectures of 1898* (Cambridge, Mass.: Harvard University Press, 1992), 12.

4. Ibid., 26.

5. Quoted in Vincent Colapietro, *Peirce's Approach to the Self: A Semiotic Perspective on Human Subjectivity* (Albany: State University of New York Press, 1989), 63.

6. Charles S. Peirce, "Pearson's Grammar of Science," in *The Collected Papers of Charles Sanders Peirce*, vol. 8, *Reviews, Correspondence, and Bibliography*, ed. Arthur W. Burks (Cambridge, Mass.: Belknap Press of Harvard University Press, 1958), 144.

7. Derrida, *Of Grammatology*, 17.

8. Charles S. Peirce, "How to Make Our Ideas Clear," in *The Collected Papers of Charles Sanders Peirce*, vol. 5, *Pragmatism and Pragmaticism*, ed. Charles Hartshorne and Paul Weiss (Cambridge, Mass.: Belknap Press of Harvard University Press, 1935), 402n.2.

9. Jacques Derrida, *The Animal That Therefore I Am*, ed. Marie-Louise Mallet, trans. David Wills (New York: Fordham University Press, 2008), 132.

10. Ibid., 93.

11. Ibid., 87.

12. Ibid., 112.

13. Jacques Derrida, "Signature Event Context," in *Limited Inc.*, ed. Gerald Graff, trans. Jeffrey Mehlman and Samuel Weber (Evanston, Ill.: Northwestern University Press, 1988), 20.

14. Ibid., 12.

15. Jacques Derrida, "Typewriter Ribbon: Limited Inc. (2)," in *Without Alibi*, ed. and trans. Peggy Kamuf (Stanford, Calif.: Stanford University Press, 2002), 125.

16. David Wills, *Prosthesis* (Stanford, Calif.: Stanford University Press, 1995), 300.

17. Derrida, *Of Grammatology*, 84.

18. Derrida, "Typewriter Ribbon," 136.

19. Cary Wolfe, *What Is Posthumanism?* (Minneapolis: University of Minnesota Press, 2010), 8.

20. Ibid., 20.

21. Niklas Luhmann, *Theories of Distinction: Redescribing the Descriptions of Modernity*, ed. William Rasch (Stanford, Calif.: Stanford University Press, 2002), 169.

22. Charles S. Peirce, "Consciousness and Purpose," in *The Collected Papers of Charles Sanders Peirce*, vol. 7, *Science and Philosophy*, ed. Arthur W. Burks (Cambridge, Mass.: Belknap Press of Harvard University Press, 1958), 366.

23. Charles S. Peirce, "On Science and Natural Classes," in *The Essential Peirce*, vol. 2, *Selected Philosophical Writings, 1893–1913*, ed. Peirce Edition Project (Bloomington: Indiana University Press, 1997), 123.

24. Peter Skagestad, "Peirce's Inkstand as an External Embodiment of Mind," *Transactions of the Charles S. Peirce Society* 35, no. 3 (1999): 551–561, at 553.

25. Ibid., 554.

26. Ibid., 553.

27. Ibid., 559.

28. Wolfe, *What Is Posthumanism?*, 36.

29. Ibid.

30. Charles S. Peirce to William T. Harris, in *Collected Papers*, 8:248 (emphasis added).

31. Colapietro, *Peirce's Approach to the Self*, 42.

32. Ibid., 38.

33. Ibid., 58.

34. Ibid., 96.

35. Ibid., 92.

36. Charles S. Peirce, "Consequences of Common-Sensism," in *Collected Papers*, 5:520.

37. Charles S. Peirce, "The Categories in Detail," in *The Collected Papers of Charles Sanders Peirce*, vol. 1, *Principles of Philosophy*, ed. Charles Hartshorne and Paul Weiss (Cambridge, Mass.: Belknap Press of Harvard University Press, 1932), 324; Colapietro, *Peirce's Approach to the Self*, 93.

38. Jürgen Habermas, "Peirce and Communication," in *Peirce and Contemporary Thought: Philosophical Inquiries*, ed. Kenneth L. Ketner (New York: Fordham University Press, 1994), 243.

39. Charles S. Peirce, "Prolegomena to an Apology for Pragmaticism," in *The Collected Papers of Charles Sanders Peirce*, vol. 4, *The Simplest Mathematics*, ed. Charles Hartshorne and Paul Weiss (Cambridge, Mass.: Belknap Press of Harvard University Press, 1933), 551.

40. Habermas, "Peirce and Communication," 261.

41. Ibid., 264.

42. Ibid., 246. The quotation is from Charles S. Peirce, "The Icon, Index, and Symbol," in *The Collected Papers of Charles Sanders Peirce*, vol. 2, *Elements of Logic*, ed. Charles Hartshorne and Paul Weiss (Cambridge, Mass.: Belknap Press of Harvard University Press, 1932), 303.

43. Habermas, "Peirce and Communication," 263.

44. Ibid., 259.

45. Ibid., 264.

46. Ibid., 262.

47. Ibid., 249.

48. Klaus Oehler, "A Response to Habermas," in *Peirce and Contemporary Thought*, ed. Ketner, 270.

49. Quoted in Colapietro, *Peirce's Approach to the Self*, 89.

50. Ibid., 44.

51. Larry Holmes, "Peirce on Self-Control," *Transactions of the Charles S. Peirce Society* 2, no. 2 (1966): 113–130, at 121.

52. Ibid., 118.

53. Charles S. Peirce, "On the Algebra of Logic," in *Essential Peirce*, 1:201.

54. Holmes, "Peirce on Self-Control," 121.

55. Quoted in ibid., 122.

56. Ibid., 122–123. The material from Peirce in the quotation is from Charles S. Peirce, "Pragmatism and Pragmaticism," in *Collected Papers*, 5:440.

57. Holmes, "Peirce on Self-Control," 118.

58. Don D. Roberts, *The Existential Graphs of Charles S. Peirce* (Berlin: De Gruyter Mouton, 2009), 111.

59. Charles. S. Peirce, *Pragmatism as a Principle and Method of Right Thinking* (Albany: State University of New York Press, 1997), 185.

60. Anne Freadman, *The Machinery of Talk: Charles Peirce and the Sign Hypothesis* (Stanford, Calif.: Stanford University Press, 2004), 134.

61. Louis H. Kauffman, "The Mathematics of Charles Sanders Peirce," in "Peirce and Spencer-Brown: History and Synergies in Cybersemiotics," ed. Søren Brier, special issue, *Cybernetics and Human Knowing* 8, nos. 1–2 (2001): 79–110, at 31.

62. Derrida, "Typewriter Ribbon," 133.

63. See, in particular, Søren Brier, ed., "Peirce and Spencer-Brown: History and Synergies in Cybersemiotics," special issue, *Cybernetics and Human Knowing* 8, nos. 1–2 (2001).

64. Kauffman, "Mathematics of Charles Sanders Peirce," 2.

65. Michael Schiltz and Gert Verschraegen, "Spencer-Brown, Luhmann, and Autology," *Cybernetics and Human Knowing* 9, nos. 3–4 (2002): 55–78, at 11.

66. George Spencer-Brown, *Laws of Form* (Portland, Ore.: Cognizer, 1994), xxix.

67. Schiltz and Verschraegen, "Spencer-Brown, Luhmann, and Autology," 16.

68. Ibid., 13.

69. Niklas Luhmann, "The Paradox of Form," in *Problems of Form*, ed. Dirk Baecker, trans. Michael Irmscher and Leah Edwards (Stanford, Calif.: Stanford University Press, 1999), 17.

70. Schiltz and Verschraegen, "Spencer-Brown, Luhmann, and Autology," 17.

71. Niklas Luhmann, *Art as a Social System*, trans. Eva M. Knodt (Stanford, Calif.: Stanford University Press, 2000), 117.

72. Kauffman, "Mathematics of Charles Sanders Peirce," 56.

73. Derrida, *Of Grammatology*, 9.

74. Quoted in Max H. Fisch, "Peirce's General Theory of Signs," in *Peirce, Semeiotic, and Pragmatism*, ed. Kenneth Laine Ketner and Christian J. W. Kloesel (Bloomington: Indiana University Press, 1986), 343.

75. Ibid.

76. Peirce, "Prolegomena to an Apology for Pragmaticism," 551.

77. Fisch, "Peirce's General Theory of Signs," 343.

78. Derrida, *Of Grammatology*, 40.

79. Ibid.

80. Ibid., 84.

81. Luhmann, *Theories of Distinction*, 169.

82. Niklas Luhmann, *Observations on Modernity*, trans. William Whobrey (Stanford, Calif.: Stanford University Press, 1998), 17.

83. Freadman, *Machinery of Talk*, 189.

84. Ibid., 219.

85. Ibid., 264.

86. Ibid., 273.

87. Luhmann, *Theories of Distinction*, 177.

88. Ibid., 166.

89. Ibid., 177.

90. Charles S. Peirce, "How to Make Our Ideas Clear," in *Essential Peirce*, 1:139.

91. Ibid., 140.

92. Martin Jay, *Marxism and Totality: The Adventures of a Concept from Lukács to Habermas* (Berkeley: University of California Press, 1984), 56.

93. Charles S. Peirce, "On the Logic of Drawing History from Ancient Documents, Especially from Testimonies," in *Essential Peirce*, 2:107.

94. Charles S. Peirce, "What Is Christian Faith?," in *The Collected Papers of Charles Sanders Peirce*, vol. 6, *Scientific Metaphysics*, ed. Charles Hartshorne and Paul Weiss (Cambridge, Mass.: Belknap Press of Harvard University Press, 1935), 443.

95. Charles S. Peirce, "Vitally Important Topics," in *Collected Papers* 1:673.

96. Niklas Luhmann, *Introduction to Systems Theory*, trans. Peter Gilgen (Cambridge: Polity, 2013), 50.

97. Kauffman, "Mathematics of Charles Sanders Peirce," 2.

98. Luhmann, *Theories of Distinction*, 166.

6. The Cybernetic Imaginary

1. Joseph Brent, *Charles Sanders Peirce: A Life* (Bloomington: Indiana University Press, 1998), 209.

2. Quoted in ibid., 210.

3. Ibid., 206.

4. Charles S. Peirce, "The Law of Mind," in *The Essential Peirce*, vol. 1, *Selected Philosophical Writings,1867–1893*, ed. Nathan Houser and Christian Kloesel (Bloomington: Indiana University Press, 1992), 313.

5. Charles S. Peirce, "Evolutionary Love," in *Essential Peirce*, 1:353.

6. For an exemplary overview of this tradition, see Michael A. Sells, *Mystical Languages of Unsaying* (Chicago: University of Chicago Press, 1994).

7. Harold Bloom, *The Anxiety of Influence: A Theory of Poetry* (Oxford: Oxford University Press, 1973).

8. Ralph Waldo Emerson, "Self-Reliance," in *Essays and Lectures* (New York: Library of America, 1983), 269.

9. Charles S. Peirce, *Pragmatism as a Principle and Method of Right Thinking* (Albany: State University of New York Press, 1997), 195.

10. Charles S. Peirce, "A Neglected Argument for the Reality of God," in *The Essential Peirce*, vol. 2, *1893–1913*, ed. Peirce Edition Project (Bloomington: Indiana University Press, 1997), 443.

11. Ibid.

12. Ibid., 441.

13. Michael L. Raposa, *Peirce's Philosophy of Religion* (Bloomington: Indiana University Press, 1989), 3.

14. Peirce, "Neglected Argument for the Reality of God," 434.

15. Ibid., 435.

16. Ibid., 436.

17. Ibid.

18. Floyd Merrell, "Musement, Play, Creativity: Nature's Way," *Cybernetics and Human Knowing* 16, nos. 3–4 (2010): 89–106, at 90.

19. Raposa, *Peirce's Philosophy of Religion*, 150.

20. Quoted in Jacques Derrida, "The Principle of Reason: The University in the Eyes of Its Pupils," *Diacritics* 13, no. 3 (1983): 3–20, at 9.

21. Ibid.

22. Hans Blumenberg, *The Legitimacy of the Modern Age*, trans. Robert M. Wallace (Cambridge, Mass.: MIT Press, 1985), 471.

23. Ibid., 484.

24. Ibid., 489.

25. Ibid., 514.

26. Ibid., 502.

27. Raposa, *Peirce's Philosophy of Religion*, 150.

28. Sells, *Mystical Languages of Unsaying*, 2.

29. Ibid.

30. Ibid.

31. Ibid., 3.

32. Ibid.

33. Ibid., 29.

34. Ibid., 21.

35. Ibid., 28.

36. Ibid., 21.

37. Ibid., 207.

38. Blumenberg, *Legitimacy of the Modern Age*, 491.

39. Nicholas of Cusa, "On Learned Ignorance," in *Nicholas of Cusa: Selected Spiritual Writings*, ed. Lawrence H. Bond (New York: Paulist Press, 1997), 91.

40. Charles S. Peirce, "Issues of Pragmaticism," in *Essential Peirce*, 2:358.

41. Sells, *Mystical Languages of Unsaying*, 32.

42. Peirce, "Neglected Argument for the Reality of God," 437.

43. Sells, *Mystical Languages of Unsaying*, 25.

44. Ibid., 60.

45. Peirce, "Neglected Argument for the Reality of God," 440.

46. Nicholas of Cusa, "On Learned Ignorance," 99.

47. Nicholas of Cusa, "Dialogue on the Hidden God," in *Nicholas of Cusa*, 211.

48. Nicholas of Cusa, "On Learned Ignorance," 91.

49. Gregory Bateson, "Experiments in Thinking About Observed Ethnological Material," in *Steps to an Ecology of Mind: Collected Essays in Anthropology, Psychiatry, Evolution, and Epistemology* (Chicago: University of Chicago Press, 2000), 74.

50. Ibid.

51. Ibid., 75.

52. Ibid.

53. Ibid., 86.

54. Gregory Bateson, "A Theory of Alcoholism," in *Steps to an Ecology of Mind*," 315.

55. Ibid., 317.

56. Steven Best and Douglas Kellner, *The Postmodern Turn* (New York: Guilford Press, 1997), 200.

57. Gregory Bateson, "The Roots of Ecological Crisis," in *Steps to an Ecology of Mind*, 500.

58. Ibid.

59. Niklas Luhmann, *Theories of Distinction: Redescribing the Descriptions of Modernity*, ed. William Rasch (Stanford, Calif.: Stanford University Press, 2002), 68.

60. Charles S. Peirce, "The Basis of Pragmaticism in the Normative Sciences," in *Essential Peirce*, 2:395.

61. Luhmann, *Theories of Distinction*, 62.

62. Ilya Prigogine and Isabelle Stengers, *Order out of Chaos: Man's New Dialogue with Nature* (New York: Bantam, 1984), 213.

63. Ibid., 120.

64. Charles S. Peirce, "Design and Chance," in *Essential Peirce*, 1:221.

65. Prigogine and Stengers, *Order out of Chaos*, xxix.

66. Bruce Clarke, "Heinz von Foerster's Demons," in *Emergence and Embodiment: New Essays on Second-Order Systems Theory*, ed. Bruce Clarke and Mark B. N. Hansen (Durham, N.C.: Duke University Press, 2009), 42.

67. Heinz von Foerster, *Understanding Understanding: Essays on Cybernetics and Cognition* (New York: Springer, 2010), 3.

68. Niklas Luhmann, *Introduction to Systems Theory*, trans. Peter Gilgen (Cambridge: Polity, 2013), 103.

69. Friedrich Heinrich Jacobi, "Jacobi to Fichte," in *The Main Philosophical Writings and the Novel Allwill*, trans. George di Giovanni (Montreal: McGill-Queen's University Press, 1994), 524.

70. Niklas Luhmann, *A Systems Theory of Religion*, trans. David A. Brenner with Adrian Hermann (Stanford, Calif.: Stanford: Stanford University Press, 2012), 111.

71. Ibid., 258.

72. Luhmann, *Theories of Distinction*, 72.

73. Louis H. Kauffman, "Time, Imaginary Value, Paradox, Sign and Space," in *AIP Conference Proceedings* 627 (2002): 146–159.

74. Mitchell Robert Breitwieser, *American Puritanism and the Defense of Mourning: Religion, Grief, and Ethnology in Mary White Rolandson's Captivity Narrative* (Madison: University of Wisconsin Press, 1990), 25.

75. Ibid., 27.

76. Ibid., 26.

77. Ibid., 27.

78. Ibid., 28.

79. Ibid., 12.

80. Perry Miller, "The Marrow of Puritan Divinity," in *Errand into the Wilderness* (Cambridge, Mass.: Belknap Press of Harvard University Press, 1984), 82.

81. Ibid., 56.

82. Ralph Waldo Emerson, "Experience," in *Emerson's Prose and Poetry*, ed. Joel Porte and Saundra Morris (New York: Norton, 2001), 207.

83. Charles S. Peirce, "Grand Logic," in *The Collected Papers of Charles Sanders Peirce*, vol. 4, *The Simplest Mathematics*, ed. Charles Hartshorne and Paul Weiss (Cambridge, Mass.: Belknap Press of Harvard University Press, 1933), 69.

84. Luhmann, *Introduction to Systems Theory*, 253.

85. Ibid., 254.

86. Ibid., 60.

87. Ralph Waldo Emerson, "Method of Nature," in *Essays and Lectures*, 122.

Index

abduction (retroduction), Pierce on: commitment to reason as, 161, 162, 163–164, 170; externalization of, through scientific inquiry, 167

Adorno, Theodor, 81, 89

aesthetic experience, in pragmatism: as binding wholeness, 67; as expression of formerly religious feelings, 65–67

Age of Discovery, and origin of modernity, 2

America: as futurity, in Emerson, 92; meaning of, and pragmatism, 50, 51, 56; Rorty's neopragmatism as evasion of, 81; as *them* of indeterminate future, in Peirce, 91–92

American Evasion of Philosophy, The (West), 51

American philosophy: as attitude of orientation, in James, 71; mystical tradition in, 63–65; and pragmatism's focus on contextual limits of thought in relation to experience, 50–51, 56

antifoundationalism, inevitable circularity in, 80

apophatic (negative) theology: and aporia of transcendence, 172–173, 174, 177; as choice of excluded, transcendent side, 8; influence of, on Miller, 182; and Peirce's logic of vagueness, 172–174; persistence of, and two-sided form created by distinction, 180–181; and refusal of representational adequacy, 173; tradition of, 166

aporia: Derrida on, 121, 125–126; Emerson on experience as traversal of, 121–126, 133–136, 185; Emerson on melancholia of mourning as, 123–124; in Rowlandson's captivity narrative, 130–131; Sells on transcendence as, 172–173, 174

Aquinas, Thomas, 58–59

Arsić, Branka, 30–31

Ashby, W. Ross, 21

Augustine, Saint, and lineage of posthumanist pragmatism, 22

Baker, Herschel, 58–60

Barth, Karl, 182

Barzun, Jacques, 75

Bateson, Gregory: on discontinuity between class and member, 34; ecological critique of science by, 178; on God as immanent Mind, 99; and lineage of posthumanist pragmatism, 21, 39, 178; on loose versus strict thinking in science, 176–178; on metacommunication, 33–34; on schizophrenia, 33–35; on Zen parable of the stick, 33–34

beauty, Edwards on, 111, 114–115

beginnings: modernity as absence of, 7; and re-entry of constitutive distinction, 162; as that which is already lost, 1. *See also* re-entry of constitutive distinction

Being and Time (Heidegger), 125